Abu Salabikh Excavations
Volume 1

THE WEST MOUND
SURFACE CLEARANCE

By J. N. Postgate

with contributions by
E. McAdam, J. Eidem and J. Crowfoot Payne

BRITISH SCHOOL OF ARCHAEOLOGY IN IRAQ
1983

ISBN 0 903472 06 6

Printed in England by
Stephen Austin and Sons Ltd, Hertford

CONTENTS

Preface		v
Note on numbers		vii
Chapter 1	Introduction	
	1.1 The site of Abu Salabikh	1
	1.2 Aspirations and results	3
	1.3 Surface collection on Mesopotamian sites	4
	1.4 Uruk or Jamdat Nasr?	5
Chapter 2	Aims and methods	6
Chapter 3	Archaeological results	
	3.1 General conclusions	11
	3.2 Fire installations	15
	3.3 Drains	17
	3.4 Bricks and brick-laying	18
	3.5 Detailed commentary on the plan	18
Chapter 4	The pottery	
	4.1 Note on the presentation of the pottery	44
	4.2 The mass-produced types and their distribution	44
	4.3 Pottery from the surface of the West Mound (*E. McAdam*)	53
	4.4 Numbered items of pottery	82
Chapter 5	Miscellaneous finds	
	5.1 Baked clay cones (*J. Eidem*)	87
	5.2 Clay sickles (*J. Eidem*)	88
	5.3 Miscellaneous clay items	90
	5.4 Stones	91
	5.5 Stone vessels	92
	5.6 The ground and polished stone industry (*J. Eidem*)	94
	5.7 The flaked stone industry (*J. Crowfoot Payne*)	99
	5.8 Miscellaneous items	103
Bibliography		105
List of AbS and IM numbers		107
Concordance of batch numbers		108
Detailed descriptions of Plates		110
Plates I-XII		

In Memoriam

T. E. Peet (1882–1934)

PREFACE

The investigation of a whole city is unavoidably a long process, and it would not be desirable to await the completion of our excavations before starting to publish a final record of the results. Some excavators in Iraq in recent years have indeed opted for a substantial report on each season's work, but in our case this seems unnecessary because general accounts of the excavations are published in our journal *Iraq,* following a tradition which goes back at least as far as Woolley's annual preliminary reports on Ur. This gives us the freedom to present our results thematically rather than according to the chances of excavation. Hence, we plan to follow the present fascicle with a first volume on the graves, a report on the ash-tip in Area E, and a publication of the seals and sealings from 1975-81.

Although the actual text is the work of those whose names appear on the title page, this fascicle owes much to many others, both in the field and on the drawing-board. In particular, the work on the West Mound was supervised mainly by Robert Killick (1977/78), Ellen McAdam (1978) and Tom Oates (1977), while the registering and drawing of the small finds and pottery was in the hands of Robert Britton, Jane Moon, Roger Moorey and Carolyn Postgate in 1977, and of Siriol Mynors and Frances Wollen in 1978. Our photographers were David Nicolson (1977) and in 1978 R. K. Vincent, Jr., to whom we are also very grateful for printing the photographs for this volume. Valuable help in the preparation of this fascicle was also given by Adrienne Watson in Baghdad and Antony Green and Salvatore and Barbara Garfi in Cambridge.

In 1977 and 1978 our work at Abu Salabikh was generously supported by the British Academy (1977/78), the British Museum (1977/78) and by the National Geographic Society, Washington D.C. (1978). For their continuing support we are most grateful, as we are to the C. H. W. Johns Fund (Cambridge) for a grant towards the cost of preparing material for publication. Sincere thanks are due to the Oriental Institute, University of Chicago (under its Directors R. McC. Adams and J. A. Brinkman) for authorizing, and to Donald Hansen and the late Vaughn Crawford for tolerating good-humouredly our annexation of the site which their discoveries had placed on the map, and I would also like to take this opportunity to record my gratitude to the officers and staff of the British School of Archaeology in Iraq for the moral and material support they have given me during my time in Baghdad and at Abu Salabikh: this includes not only Prof. D. J. Wiseman and J. D. Hawkins, whose generous assistance is sincerely acknowledged, but Prof. David Oates, without whom I should never have been in Iraq in the first place, and Miss G. C. Talbot, Mrs. S. Nan Shaw, Dr. Leri Davies, and the late David Clarke, who looked after our affairs so well and uncomplainingly.

That we could not have done the work without the co-operation of the State Organization for Antiquities and Heritage is self-evident, but it is a real pleasure to be able to acknowledge much friendly assistance freely given. We remember with gratitude not only the ready support of the President of the Organization, Dr. Muayad Sa'id Damerji, but also that of the late Professor Fuad Safar, whose advice and criticism is still sorely missed by us all. Our representatives in 1977 and 1978 were Abdul-Majid Muhammad, Muhammad Yahya, Ali Hashim and Nadhir ar-Rawi, and to them all I would like to extend the thanks and best wishes of the members of the expedition, for having lightened our labours and shared our life style with the greatest good nature.

Lastly, I would like to crave the indulgence of my co-authors, and of the British School of Archaeology in Iraq, to allow me to dedicate this first instalment of the publication of the excavations at a Sumerian city to the memory of my grandfather, T. Eric Peet, who was born 100 years ago this year, and whose publications on the great Egyptian cities of Abydos and El-Amarna are of abiding value to our colleagues working on the other side of the Arab world.

J. N. Postgate
October 1982

NOTE ON NUMBERS

1. *Grid squares:* See Fig. 2 for the 100 m. grid system; the area of the West Mound which we cleared falls within squares 2G and 3G. Within each 100 m. square the 10 m. squares are identified by double figures from 00 to 99, starting from the NW corner (see plan, Fig. 354). Each 10 m. square is therefore designated by a number + letter + two numbers, e.g. as 2G76.

2. *Site datum:* The contour lines in Fig. 3 and occasional spot heights are given above an arbitrary site datum established in 1975 (see *Iraq* 38, 135[7]).

3. *Object numbers:* When excavating normally, all objects (except for potsherds, see note 5 below) recovered from each 10 m. square should be assigned a unique number affixed to the designation of the square in question, e.g. 2G76:83. However, in the case of surface clearance it has proved necessary to adapt this system slightly, and instead all the objects from 2G surface were numbered in a single sequence affixed to 2GS (for "2G Surface"), and similarly to 3GS for items from 3G, e.g. 3GS:18. These numbers are assigned on site, and since many items received no other number by which they can be designated, it is used in this volume as the basic system, the catalogues of different classes (in Chapters 4.4 and 5.1-8) being arranged in numerical order within their sections.

4. *Catalogue and Museum numbers:* Relatively few items were assigned official "catalogue numbers" (e.g. AbS 1484); these were all deposited in the Iraq Museum, and are also assigned IM numbers. A concordance of AbS and IM numbers with their *object numbers* and with the Chapter and section under which each is catalogued in this volume is to be found below (p. 107).

5. *Batch numbers:* Each separately recorded archaeological operation is assigned a 4-figure number known as a "batch number". This is broadly equivalent to "units" or "lots" in other systems of recording, and since it constitutes the basic link between an object and its provenance each object's batch number is stated in Chapter 5. To save space, though, in Chapter 4.3 we have converted the batch numbers to provenances; a cross-index is given below (pp. 108-9). Note that as well as defining the origin of individual numbered items, the batch number is also the only designation of the entire body of sherds from the operation in question.

6. *The § numbers:* Purely to ease reference within this volume, the discussion of the pottery in Chapter 4.3 is divided into sections (§§), and the § numbers in the Figs., in Chapter 3.5 and elsewhere refer to these sections of Chapter 4.3.

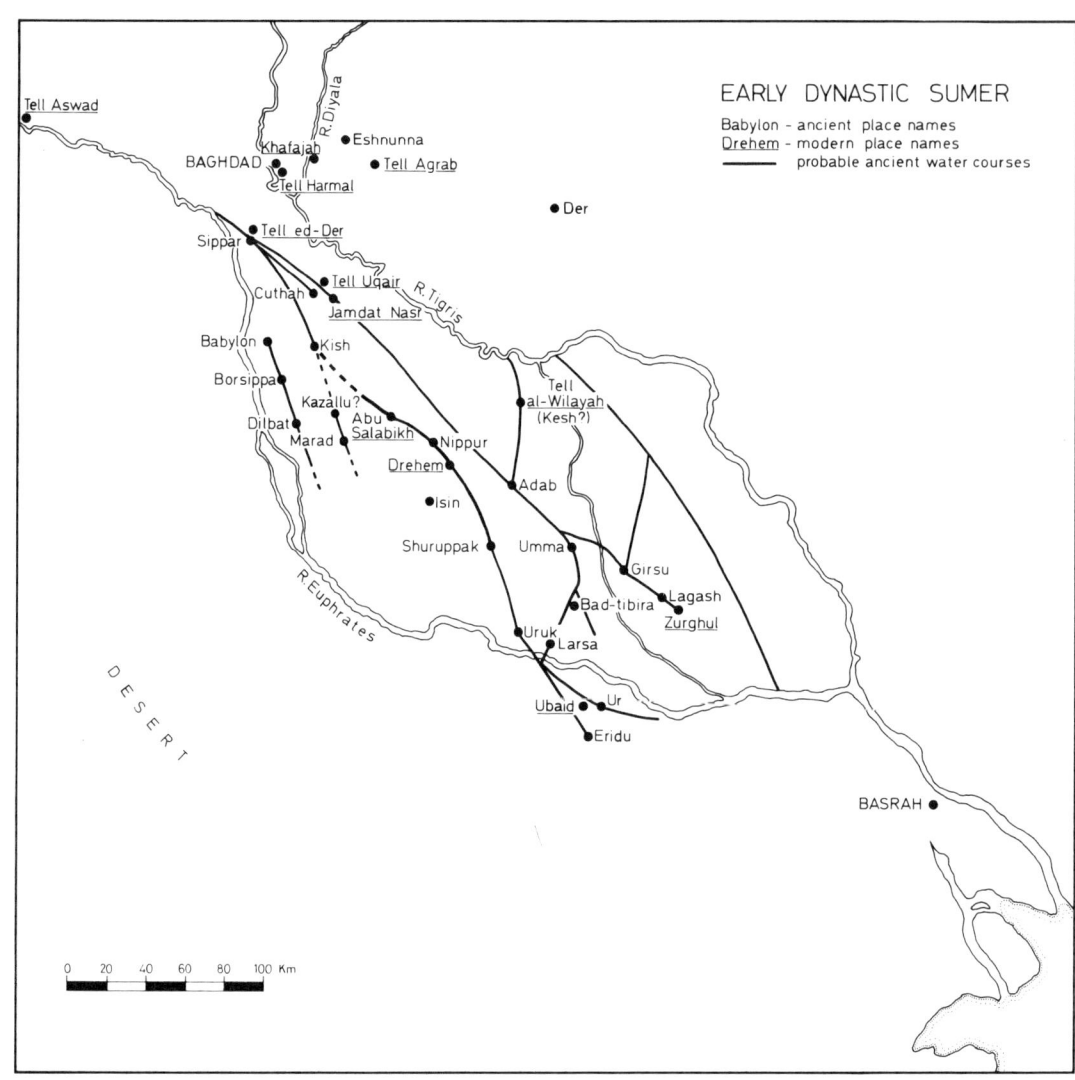

Fig. 1. Map of major ED sites (corrected from Curtis 1982, p. 49 after Adams, 1981).

Chapter 1

INTRODUCTION

1.1 *The site of Abu Salabikh*

Descriptions of the site and of the stages of its investigations are to be found in our preliminary reports, and the threads will be pulled together in some future volume of our final report. Here it is necessary only to say enough to place our work on the West Mound in a rudimentary context. The site of Abu Salabikh, representing the remains of a 4th and 3rd millennium city whose Sumerian name is not yet known for certain, is situated at 45° 3′ 11″ E and 32° 15′ 0″ N, almost at the eastern limits of modern cultivation where it gives way to sandy desert. According to the surveys of R.McC. Adams, the nearest major cities in antiquity must have been Nippur, some 21 km. to the south-east, and Marad, 30 km. away in a south-westerly direction (Adams 1972, No. 282). Northwards the nearest contemporary site recorded of any size is 20 km. upstream (Adams 1972, No. 256 "Mainly Uruk-ED"), although No. 258 (Ishân Abû Jasib), lying only about 10 km. to the north-west, boasts some Uruk occupation. My use of the term "upstream" is deliberate, and reflects our conviction that a site of this size could not have survived long without a fair-sized waterway. As to the nature and precise course of such a river or canal we have no archaeological or textual evidence, but meander patterns, presumably from an early Euphrates branch, are recorded by Adams close to Abu Salabikh on the east, and on this basis he reconstructs a direct link by water from No. 256 through No. 258 and Abu Salabikh, to Nippur (Adams 1972, Maps 2-3; 1981, pp. 64-5, showing meanders [transpose captions!]). This seems inherently probable, and we need only observe that since the ED I land surface round the site is shrouded in more than 2 m. of alluviation, we could not expect any ancient meanders closer to the mounds themselves to be detectable. As we shall see below, occupation of the site seems to have shifted eastwards with time, and it could well be that this was following an eastward movement of the river-bed.

If we turn to look at the individual mounds which compose the site (Fig. 2), it is as well to remember that this same overburden of alluvial soil probably conceals less continuously occupied areas of the site which would none the less link the mounds together were they not under the alluvium. The main mounds, where the major excavations in Areas A and E are, belong to the Early Dynastic period, with ED III levels at the surface. Later (Akkadian/Ur III) occupation is attested exclusively by surface sherds and by others found in use as packing round drains dug from levels now eroded (see *Iraq* 39, 295). In view of the potency of erosion at the site, and the destructive effects of the surface salts, we have no means of knowing how extensive this post-ED occupation may have been. It *may* have been "at most very limited" (Adams 1981, p. 294 on A 275), but it must be faced that a great volume of soil has been eroded over the last 4,000 years, and it seems premature to be confident that a considerable Akkadian and Ur III occupation has not been entirely eroded. A similar consideration does in fact apply to the ED III levels themselves away from Areas A and E: ED I levels lie at the surface of the mound immediately between these two areas, but it is probably reasonable to suppose that later ED III housing has in fact been lost here to the action of the weather, and the same could have been true of the West Mound, despite the absence there of unequivocal ED III sherds.

With these provisos in mind, we may say that as far as our evidence goes the ED I period was the time of the city's greatest spread. On the main mound levels of this date extend beneath Areas A and E, and seem to represent the earliest buildings on this place. This was established by two soundings to (or nearly to) the bottom of the mound: in Area A the 1963 sounding of D. P. Hansen reached virgin soil without finding anything earlier than ED I, and that made by us in 1976 in the courtyard of the Southern Unit (6G54c) penetrated three phases of ED I architecture (Level III) before being halted by water. Although fragments of clay sickles, and clay cones, are not infrequent on the main mound, not to mention the occasional bevelled-rim bowl sherd, there is still no good reason to assume any Uruk Period occupation there. It is true that there was a patch of the mound's surface just to the south-east of Area A, where there was an abnormal concentration of clay cones, but the scraping of this area in 1981 showed beyond question that these were coming out of plano-convex bricks, which had presumably been made from soil taken from an earlier level, quite possibly at some distance.

How big the initial ED I settlement of the main mounds was is of course an open question at present. Other areas of ED I occupation can be briefly summarized: apart from the West Mound, which is dealt with in this fascicle and in our preliminary report on the excavations in 1981 (*Iraq* 44), we only know of the North-East Mound, which appears, from a very small

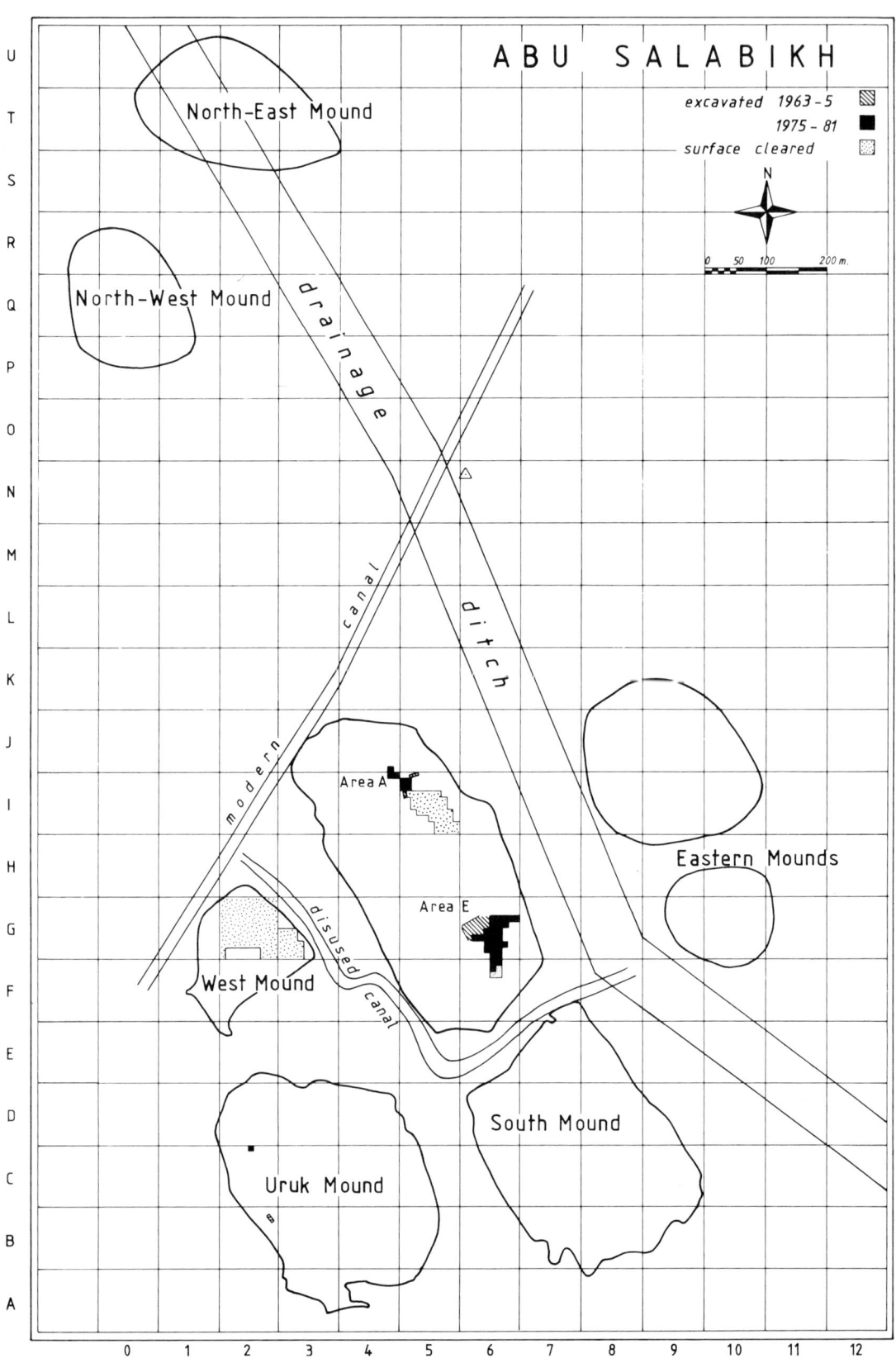

Fig. 2. Site plan, Autumn 1981. Scale 1:10,000.

sounding undertaken in 1978 to have been founded early in the ED I period (see *Iraq* 42, 96-7). The neighbouring North-West Mound yielded exclusively Uruk surface sherds, and the same applies to the main Uruk Mound lying south of the West Mound. Only two further comments seem to be called for here. One is to point out that the trend of settlement at our site looks to have been towards the east, as noted above. The other is a word of caution: work at Al-Hiba in particular has recently underlined the length of the ED I period, and it would be rash to assume that all "ED I" parts of the site were necessarily inhabited at the same time. The material from the West Mound is certainly, and that from the North-East Mound probably, from the first part of the period, but at present we cannot say how much of an overlap—if any—there was between these levels and the bottom of the sequences in Areas A and E.

1.2 Aspirations and results

The foregoing paragraphs are designed to give some context in which to view the area of ED I housing uncovered by the West Mound clearance. Before describing this operation in detail, we feel it desirable to make some comment on its background and its validity. When we began work at Abu Salabikh in 1975 it was with the rather simple expectation of finding ED III levels of an approximately contemporary phase across the extent of the main mounds at least. We knew, of course, of the existence of the Uruk Mound, but the two outlying northern mounds were concealed from us by standing maize crops and also relatively inaccessible, while it was rather indolently assumed that the West Mound was of much the same date as the rest of the site. Closer inspection led to some doubts, though, and in 1976 Robert Biggs and Jonathan Tubb collected the surface sherds in 2G99, which revealed plenty of solid-footed goblets and other indications of an earlier date. The hope of fresh data on the poorly known ED I period was certainly one factor in our selection of the West Mound for the experiment of large-scale surface clearance the next year, in 1977.

Now that the plan of the West Mound has been recovered, it suggests where one should dig for the solution of specific problems, but it would be a mistake to see the operation as primarily, or even equally, as a convenient guide to the position of next season's trenches. The essential reason for the scraping (as described below, in Chapter 2), is to recover usable information about the layout of a much wider area of the city than would be conceivable today by excavation. This is a deliberate component of the expedition's long-term objective, which is to reconstruct in as much breadth as possible the character of a Sumerian city. It is still too early to say whether the presence of different periods on the surface of the different parts of the site will be a help or a hindrance to this objective: while the value of having accessible areas of ED I to compare with ED III housing is evident, it is to some degree offset by the lack of a sample from the entire occupied area at any one date.

Building plans recovered only by surface scraping cannot have the same validity as those properly excavated with regard for their stratified history. Nevertheless, it is not necessary to discount our results as valueless because they are "impure". It must be accepted that we are not attempting, on the basis of these surface indications, to reconstruct anything as precise as the detailed plan of each building: our objective is less ambitious, to recover a general conception of the layout of the town quarter, and on this level the individual uncertainties are greatly compensated for by the area uncovered. Equally, we can make firm statements about wall-thicknesses, room sizes, and sometimes about the quality of the bricks and their laying and bonding. Additional information is supplied by the easily recognized water and fire installations. In detail, it may legitimately be wondered how we can know that certain walls were contemporary. Sometimes it is possible to see detail of the brickwork showing that two walls are structurally bonded, and more often one may see that the plastered wall-face is continuous round a corner. Even without such structural indications, a continuous identical soil deposit can often be seen lying against the faces of two different walls, and showing that they were both standing simultaneously at least once, while a genuine break in the stratification will generally show clearly as such, with discontinuities in both architecture and soil deposits. As for dating the walls we are fortunate in that the plano-convex brick is both very distinctive and an accepted indicator of Early Dynastic date; our rough attributions to more precise periods, based on surface sherds, have tended to be confirmed by a small sounding made in the West Mound in 1981, and we should turn now to consider this ceramic evidence briefly.

Apart from the architectural plan, the other body of primary data from the West Mound is of course provided by the artefacts recovered from on, and immediately below, the surface. These are mostly potsherds, and the publication of potsherds in bulk is never a very satisfying undertaking for writer and reader alike; it might well be argued that since their provenance is unstratified, these particular sherds could beneficially have been consigned to oblivion. We have however presented them below, because they can act as a case-study (see below), and because of the intrinsic interest of the ceramic corpus itself, which covers the transition from Late Uruk into ED I, still very poorly documented in South Iraq. Obviously future excavation will enable us to be more precise, but the size of the sample and the occasional confirmation from our 1981 sounding suggest that our separation of the sherds into two broad divisions—Uruk and Early Dynastic—is essentially correct (see Chapter 4.1). In making this division we have in effect, although unconsciously, followed the maxims enunciated by Nissen (Adams & Nissen 1972, 99 f.): "From the observation that a number of sites produced sherds of only a single mass-produced pottery type, the possibility emerged that they were occupied only during . . . a single period. Furthermore, starting from the known sequence of mass-produced types, wider pottery assemblages could be worked out . . .". In our case the assemblage in 3G, which was characterized by many bevelled-rim bowls, was called "Uruk" and kept separate from that in the ED squares associated with solid-footed goblets. As was to be hoped, there emerged distinct differences between these two assemblages, which generally coincide comfortably with results from other sites, especially Nippur. More interestingly, we have been able to isolate some features which have not so far received much attention. One of these is the very distinctive combed grey ware—which has, indeed, been recorded sporadically but never recognized as the useful chronological indicator it probably should be—, and another is the "cut-rim conical bowl" which can fairly confidently be described as a transitional type between the bevelled-rim bowl and the typical Early Dynastic conical bowl.

There are two main reasons for presenting the West Mound surface material in print at this stage, rather than waiting until we have some excavated data with which to amplify and perhaps supersede our results. One is the wish to present all our Abu Salabikh results in a final form as soon as possible, to avoid the build up of an alluvium of publication backlog which tends to surround most Mesopotamian sites. The second reason is to keep separated our conclusions as based on the surface clearance from the subsequent results of excavation. Chapters 2 to 5 were substantially written before our 1981 excavation season; since then words or phrases may have been altered, but the sentiments remain the same. Where hindsight has proved irresistible, dated additional comments have been added in square brackets: these additions are not a substitute for a report on the excavation work itself, which will be briefly described in *Iraq* 44, but are intended to show where the later evidence seems to contradict our earlier opinion, or confirms a point which was speculative and in need of confirmation. Our underlying objective—to present a series of deductions based exclusively on the surface clearance—should not thereby have been vitiated.

1.3 *Surface collection on Mesopotamian sites*
In this way, we hope to have made a small contribution to the technique of surface survey in Mesopotamia. Much theorizing has been based on the presumed date and size of archaeological sites in Southern Iraq and Susiana in recent years, and little has been done to check the degree of correlation that actually exists between surface indications and the interior of the *tell* in question. Sherds and other artefacts have usually suffered various changes of fortune before they are collected by the 20th century archaeologist, eager to fit them to his theories and usually with an eye attuned to some kinds of object more than to others. A typical example of the risks of self-deception can be quoted in the words of one of the most thoughtful of the current practitioners of the art of surface survey: "Our team examined the site in the autumn of 1970, and was impressed by the quantities of Uruk sherds on the surface. Had we undertaken a systematic surface study at that time we would have established that, in most areas of the site, Uruk sherds were mixed with later Elamite and earlier Susiana sherds, and we would have realized that most of the site had been disturbed. For better or worse, this was not done until we were committed to excavation" (Wright 1980, 268). This can hardly be a rare occurrence, although it may rarely be admitted. In our case, we only became aware of the existence of relatively "early" and "late" sectors of the West Mound during our second season of clearance, although the change, plotted square by square (cf. Figs. 22-9) looks very hard to miss.

The study of surface evidence has been used in the past in two main contexts: to answer specific questions about the site itself, and in the context of a regional survey. Evidently the second application is dependent on the first, and both implicitly entail the assumption that material found on the surface has a direct relationship with what lies beneath (or lay above—although this is not often recognized). The validity of this assumption, which thankfully seems to be supported by our work on the West Mound, was tested in south-east Turkey on two prehistoric sites of about the same size as our West Mound. The issues involved are well summarized by the authors of a report on this work: "If there is a coherent relationship between the surface and subsurface of a site—and our data support this—then sampling the site surface will provide data for determining in general outline what is underground. Areas to be excavated can then be chosen more precisely according to one's own research problems and hypotheses, in the context of the entire site, with the expenditure of less time and money excavating, than other methods of choice entail" (Redman & Watson 1970, 279). If the quality of the information recovered by *systematic* surface collection is so much superior, and experience begins to suggest that it is, then clearly some form of systematic collection is needed to enhance the results of those moving from site to site as part of a regional survey, as Redman and Watson go on to point out. This is acknowledged also by Adams in his most recent work in south Iraq (Adams 1981, 45).

Only rarely will an excavator or surveyor be able to collect the entire surface material as we have done on the West Mound. Usually some form of sampling is required, and Redman and Watson suggest that a "stratified unaligned systematic sample" such as they used on Girik-i-Haciyan is well suited to the task, because it "eliminates the main disadvantages of a simple random sample, but retains its unbiased nature" (pp. 281-2). This same method was adopted by the Italian Mission to the Hamrin basin at Tell Yelkhi (and Abu Husaini), although they used squares of 2.50 x 2.50 m. rather than 5 x 5 m. (Invernizzi 1980, 25-8). Here, although the comparison of the detailed results from surface collection with the excavated data awaits the computer processing, the director comments that the sherds on the surface "were in a distribution pattern that had no substantial concentrations useful for working out the position of a sounding trench" (ibid., 28). A further refinement of the technique was initiated at Girik-i-Haciyan and Çayönü, where the results were analysed using contoured distribution maps, and it was considered "whether the relative proportions of artefact categories covary in a meaningful manner" (Redman & Watson 1970, 287). In theory these procedures could be applied to some of our Abu Salabikh data too, but enough is enough, and the additional information it might yield is more than compensated for by the building plans revealed by the topsoil clearance. Nevertheless, it has seemed worth while to present some of the surface distributions in visual form (see Figs. 20-30), and any who wish to draw contours on this basis are very welcome to do so.

Surface collection is a blunt instrument, to whatever use it is put; some may think too blunt to be worth using at all. But consciously or unconsciously no archaeologist could refrain from basing assumptions on what can be seen lying on the top of the site which is about to be dug, and there can be no harm in getting the facts right before assumptions are founded on them.

1.4 *Uruk or Jamdat Nasr*
The sherds published by E. McAdam in Chapter 4.3 have been described in two groups called "Uruk" and "Early Dynastic". We have used the term Uruk here to mean nothing more precise than "Pre-Early-Dynastic", and there are two reasons why we have avoided the term "Jamdat Nasr". In the first place, we are very short of type-fossils which would prove that this period (generally equated with Eanna III) is actually represented in our sherd material. Secondly, we consider that, even if it is, "Jamdat Nasr" is a misleading term which would be better restricted to a polychrome pottery style. Some explanation follows.

The absence of "Jamdat Nasr" type-fossils has caused severe headaches for Adams and Nissen in their regional surveys (cf. for example Adams 1981, 81). According to Nissen, during this period no entirely distinctive mass-produced type was in production, so that on the Warka Survey it was necessary to identify sites falling between Late Uruk (=Eanna IV) and Early Dynastic I by a negative criterion, viz, the absence of both bevelled-rim bowls *and* solid-footed goblets. By these criteria, the overlapping of the distributions of these two types on the West Mound would make it impossible to identify a "Jamdat Nasr" occupation there, whether or not it existed. Excavation in 1981 found no level without either bevelled-rim bowls or solid-footed goblets, which could thereby be hailed as Jamdat Nasr, although it is true that there *is* a break in the architectural as well as the ceramic sequence, at the beginning of the ED I levels. This could correspond to an absent Jamdat Nasr phase, but in fact our suspicion is that at Abu Salabikh at least the posited "bevelled-rim bowl vacuum" between Eanna IV and the first ED I level simply did not exist, and that certain types, especially perhaps the "cut-rim conical bowl" are genuinely transitional in time as well as in form, and should be accepted as markers of the Eanna III period. However, these are problems which can only be discussed with reference to our excavated evidence from the West Mound, and our sole purpose here is to explain that "Uruk" is used to refer to everything before the earliest ED I level, which *may* correspond in time to Eanna III just as much as Eanna IV (see *Iraq* 44, 120-3).

Chapter 2

AIMS AND METHODS

It has already been explained in the Introduction that one of the chief objectives of our work at Abu Salabikh has been from the beginning to recover a picture of a Sumerian city *as a whole*—not just its public buildings. Working in the 1970s we could not expect to excavate wide expanses of the site, constrained as we are by rising costs and the increasingly demanding standards of archaeological technique. Thus it rapidly became apparent that, in view of the small area we could even partially excavate in a three-month season, we should have to lay plans for several generations ahead if we hoped by this means to recover an idea of the city which was at all comprehensive.

Only one way to escape this dilemma seemed satisfactory, the clearance of wide areas of the surface. Even had we the funds to dig for a longer period or to increase substantially the scale of the operation, the corresponding increase in artefacts and excavation records to be processed would swamp us with an unmanageable backlog of publication. This would not only be irresponsible in itself, but it would prevent us from isolating those points of enquiry from which our tactics for future seasons should be formulated, so negating the purpose of a research excavation. Another possibility would have been to place our soul in the hands of the statisticians, and hope that by siting trenches at random we could recover a sample from which the intervening portions could be reconstructed by some statistical process. Regardless of the very real question of the predictability of the data, there was a problem here, in that to recover a genuinely adequate sample would land us back in the same shortage of time—for it is clear that given the scale of the rooms and of other architectural features no square of less than 10 x 10 m. would yield data significant enough to be used in this way: we should be asking the statistician to predict not merely walls or even rooms, but entire houses, streets, etc., so that his basic samples would need to become miniature excavations in their own right. There is certainly a good case for making such soundings in different parts of the site, but it would not solve this particular problem for us.

We therefore felt convinced that the best solution was to recover the plan of the largest possible area with the least possible excavation. Something of the kind had already been achieved by J. E. Reade at Tell Taya, where it was made possible by the extensive stone foundations visible above the surface. Some walls at Abu Salabikh do show on the surface of the mound, especially when the soil is drying after rain, but they only form rough bands, and if planned would yield merely disconnected lengths of doubtful meaning. We did of course consider the possibility of aerial photography, but apart from the difficulty of arranging this, we suspected that it would not yield improved accuracy, although more features would probably be detected. We also obtained permission to test a resistivity meter on the site. The problems inherent were discussed with Dr. Martin Aitken, of the Research Laboratory in Oxford, and it became clear that it would be difficult because the mud-brick of the walls is so similar in composition to the rest of the soil. It seemed that the best hopes of recovering information by this means would rest in the differing water-content of the walls and the rest of the earth, which would be most acute after rain; so here again for the best results we should be reduced to waiting for the whim of Adad—or should I say Iškur?—and no regular programme could be planned. In the event, we never received the machine from the manufacturer, and we have not felt any need to test the method since then.

Our preferred solution then was to scrape the surface of the mound, and record the details so exposed. From opening new squares (e.g. 4J98 in 1976) we knew that under favourable conditions it is possible to plan with accuracy the walls and features which emerge directly below the surface, and it seemed logical to apply this technique methodically. For the experiment we selected the West Mound. It had the advantage of being undisturbed by the modern excavator, and it was also small enough for us to clear a significant proportion of its surface. We were also attracted to it by the surface sherds, which were predominantly ED I, a period which is buried inconveniently deep on the main mound.

For ease of recording, the surface was scraped in the 10 m. squares prescribed by the overall site grid. Some such arbitrary divisions were essential, and the use of these squares means that surface finds are provenanced to within 10 m., and that our attention was directed regularly to each area cleared in turn. During 1977 we found that a skilled Sherqati workman with three locals could easily process a square in a working day, although one would usually need to return subsequently to scrape particular areas for added detail. To begin with we cleared in long strips, from south to north (2G90-2G80-2G70 etc.), but since we were clearing only two squares daily, this had the disadvantage that the squares to east or west were cleared at an interval of at least 5 days, during which the features of the first had long since dried out and become hard to detect. Later therefore we preferred to clear rather in blocks of four, although inevitably of course the same problem arises at some stage.

The procedure for clearing a square ran as follows: first, all objects lying on the surface were picked up—potsherds, cones, stones, flints, etc. Occasionally some shells or bone were also found, but these survived much less often. The loose soil was then removed with shovels and wheel-barrows, and in theory any objects from this soil were also collected, being placed in a "sub-surface" batch. After removal of the top-soil the Sherqati workmen began their search for features, scraping the ground as clean as possible; before the wall lines emerged they sometimes needed a further layer removed, and of course in some squares there were no features recognizable. Only in a few cases did we make small soundings to check points of stratigraphy, and the only actual "digging" was really the excavation of three large jars from Room 8 and the exposure of the south-east end of the drain in 2G12. Both for practical and for methodological reasons we were not anxious to remove the deep layers of fill or eroded wash which clearly shrouded some of the architecture (especially at the centre of the mound), although it was occasionally difficult to restrain the predatory instincts of the Sherqati wall-hunters.

Once the surface was clean and the features revealed to the best of our ability, we planned and photographed the square. The process of planning needs no comment, but a few words may be said about the photography. In 1977 general pictures were taken from our photographic tower in colour of most squares, from a height of about 4 m., at an angle. These give a good impression of the overall appearance, but do not help with any points of detail. Also, we took vertical black and white photographs of the cleared surface, square by square. This was done with a wooden "bipod", which raised the camera to a height of about 8 m. The basic design was borrowed from Messrs. Helms and Fleming (see *Levant* 8 [1976] 30-1), and has the virtue of great simplicity, with the camera being raised and lowered by a simple pulley. Since that time an improved version has been described by David Fleming which raises the camera to a height of 10 m. (see *Bulletin of the Institute of Archaeology* 15 [1978] 131-48). To photograph each 10 m. square three separate pictures were required—or more exactly, six pictures for two squares. Although the process of moving the bipod from point to point is rather cumbersome, requiring a minimum of 5 people for safety, the operation was in general successful. However, after studying the printed photographs, it became clear that they do not supply any more detail than we had been able to observe, and often did not show at all features which had been clear to us on the ground. As we commented at the time, "no doubt the main reason for this is that a single photograph cannot show us the ground under different light and humidity conditions, whereas the process of locating the walls and other features carries on throughout several days if necessary" (*Iraq* 40, 81). Hence we did not feel any need to repeat the vertical photography process by bipod in 1978.

As far as the detection of features was concerned, the procedure did not differ from the normal process of observation when preparing to excavate a square. Some soil changes and their stratigraphic significance were immediately apparent, others more elusive. Any fire installation was, as usual, easily seen, and some pits were also perfectly clear. Our problems naturally centred round the correct identification of mud-brick: generally this would show by its colour, although texture also played a part in its recognition. At some levels the ED I walls were well preserved with their plastered faces clear, but elsewhere they had suffered damage and so lost clarity before being buried. Since plano-convex bricks are not rectangular, and can be laid in a variety of ways with varying amounts of mortar, it is often impossible to be sure if nondescript lumps are part of a wall or not. Our success in recognizing the less clear brickwork depended greatly on the light and the weather. From about 10.00 a.m. to 4.00 p.m. the almost vertical sunlight banishes all but the most extreme colour differences; moonlight was not unsatisfactory—but could not of course be relied on throughout the month. As for the weather, the precondition of success is that it should have rained, but not too hard. Our attempts to detect features in autumn 1978 were futile until after the first rainstorm had restored some dampness and consequently colour-differential to the soil. When working on the surface clearance of 5I in 1981 we found an agricultural spray very useful for dampening specific areas where the details were unclear, but this is no substitute for rain over the whole area, and it is desirable to fix our season of work with this in mind.

The walls we have identified by these methods do in fact come together into a surprisingly coherent plan, especially in the north-west part of the mound. Even where there could be doubt as to whether we are not looking at more than one phase it was usually clear from the deposits associated with the walls if a break in the stratigraphy had occurred or not. In contrast to the ED I buildings, we had little success in recovering a plan of those on the Uruk part of the mound: the existence of the occasional plano-convex brick wall here may hint that the erosion of the surface has reached an intermediate point between the bottom of the ED I walls and the tops of the surviving Uruk walls, which would explain the absence of a coherent plan comparable to that further north-west.

The surface collection As already mentioned, the collection of surface and sub-surface sherds and other objects was in the hands of the workmen, and it would be idle to pretend that there was a 100% recovery. This applies especially to the sub-surface batches, where the sherds could more easily be missed in the heaping of the soil; fortunately this irregularity is less important because the varying depths of soil removed make the statistical value of the sub-surface weights more dubious in any case. It must be admitted, however, that the completeness of collection probably tailed off as each season advanced, and certainly varied in response to who was overseeing the operation and how officiously. Another variable is that it was much easier to see and in particular to pick up the sherds after heavy rain had softened the salt crust which forms on the surface, encasing them in rigid lumps. In spite of all these reservations, we are confident that the quantitative variation in the sherd weights from the different squares is wide enough to be significant.

The provenance and significance of surface sherds We have discussed the procedure of surface clearance at some length so as to make it entirely explicit how we obtained the results presented here. Only so can we hope to win any recognition of their validity, and justify our intention of continuing with similar clearance on other parts of the site. For much the same reason we must also consider what interpretation we are justified in placing on the material recovered, since in future, as in the past, surface collections will be used to draw conclusions about the date and extent of settlement on different sites. The clearance of the West Mound was probably the most intensive work of this kind yet done in Mesopotamia, and although its final test can only be excavation, we have taken the risk of suggesting conclusions to be drawn in advance, so that they will not be tinged with hindsight.

In the case of the West Mound we are of course at a half-way stage: the results of clearing the topsoil have given us much more evidence about the character of the underlying mound than could a simple examination of the surface. On the whole, these results seem rather encouraging for the surface collector: in that part of the mound occupied predominantly by ED I sherds we have conclusive proofs of the existence directly beneath the surface of ED I buildings, and in that part of the mound with a preponderance of Uruk pottery there are at least some walls of rectangular bricks to support an attribution to that period. However, we may of course be dealing with a mound of unusual simplicity, and the apparent simplicity may be dispersed in some degree by a more detailed look at the evidence.

The first question to be asked is the provenance, or past history, of the sherds we pick up today on the surface: a sherd can be in an "authentic" context—e.g. on the floor where it was first dropped—or entirely accidental—e.g. thrown at a dog a week ago. It could have been dug up relatively recently from below ground—e.g. by a fox—, or have reached its resting place by having the soil eroded gradually from beneath it. Clearly these vicissitudes could be combined in a variety of ways, and different fates could have befallen the object at different dates, but these are the initial options with which we have to contend. Archaeologists working in more temperate areas may not be prepared for the scale of the erosion perpetrated by the combination of wind and sand in south Iraq, but it is certain that most sherds on the surface are there because their original matrix of soil has been whisked away from under them. It was for this reason that we took care to keep the sherds found *on* the surface separate from those *just below* it. For it is clear that the surface-sherds proper should reflect only what is *not* present—i.e. what is on the point of being, or has already been, eroded—whereas the sub-surface sherds should give a more reliable idea of the date of the levels now lying immediately under the surface of the tell. In practice, of course, the distinction need not matter too much, since the chances that a major change of level will occur at the mound's surface across even as little as a 10 m. square are fairly remote, but the surface sherds could still be misleading: we have encountered "late" incised ware (Ur III ?) sherds in various places on the main mound, and without excavation it would be rash to assume that buildings of that period actually survive there; the only excavated sherds of this type come in fact from the packing of two vertical drains (in 6G65 and 76), and are probably well below the floors of the buildings to which they belonged.

On the other hand, it must be borne in mind that sherds are not indestructible, and the most effective means of destruction seems to be to leave them on the surface of a mound like Abu Salabikh, where they suffer from the heavy concentrations of salt which are dissolved into them by the rain and drawn out of them by the sun. One consequence of this was vividly illustrated by the comparison of contemporary ED I sherds from our sounding in Area E Level III with some from the West Mound surface: those which had been buried deep were predominantly of a buff or reddish colour, while those from the surface had a distinct olive-green tinge, resulting from the higher temperature of firing which has made them much tougher and so more resistant to the salts. It is virtually only the highly fired, or indeed over-fired, sherds that survive for any length of time on the surface, which accounts for the excellent survival rate of clay sickles, which were deliberately hardened in this way (even though the occasional example with reddish fabric turns up, as below the surface in 2G45). The different survival rates of differently fired wares has been commented on by Matson: "It is a good idea to observe the sherd detritus on the surface of a site and on the dumps from the excavations to judge whether the sample one collects for colour distribution studies truly reflects the range of products coming from the kilns. Figure 4.2 shows such a sherd strewn surface . . . at Tell 'Uqair. Much high-fired 'Ubaid pottery had been obtained at this excavation, but it was amazing to see the large number of chips of low-fired ware intermingled with the white sherds" (Matson 1966, 74-5). The consequence of this is that in theory one should note carefully which sherds in a surface collection are over-fired, that is, of olive-greenish colour, and which normal, because if seeking an indication of the date of the walls and floor now at the surface, only the normal sherds with a shorter life-span should be used. However, this might prove to be a rather small percentage, and in the case of the West Mound a corrective was provided by the sub-surface batches, which are not so seriously affected by the problem of destruction by salt, and we did not make the distinction suggested. On balance, perhaps, the effects of the salt cancel out for the surface-collector, in that sherds from long since eroded levels are less likely to have survived and to mislead us as to the date of the deposits, but their loss also means that the evidence for the former presence of those levels is lost, affecting estimates of settlement area where these are attempted.

Although paramount, the question of date is not the only one which can be reflected in the sherd coverage. One factor is the sheer quantity, which varies considerably across the West Mound as shown by our charts. The fact of relatively dense sherd cover will prove nothing by itself, but we should at least ask ourselves what may have caused it. Mud-brick and brick debris will obviously not contain many sherds, while the other extreme is represented by rubbish tips. The relatively small volume of potsherds recovered from the surface in the 2G03, 04 and 14 area reflects the fact that we were in a building with its walls standing and filled with cleanish soil; below the surface there was much more pottery, because we were close to the floors, as the jars in 2G03 showed. Very heavy concentrations of potsherds were found in 2G51, clearly from a large rubbish pit, and in the Uruk squares (3G70-72, 80-82, 90-92), where there was evidently a wide stratum of soil containing much broken pottery and overlying some of the walls. It is interesting that this concentration, which has been exposed by erosion, is not matched by the quantity of sherds from the sub-surface batches in these squares: presumably the sherd-bearing stratum had already nearly given out, in particular towards the east. A similar situation is probably to be seen in the uninformative area 2G62-67 and 72-77, squares which consistently have more pottery on, than below, the surface (although it is true that the amount of sub-surface soil cleared here may have been less than usual).

Turning now to the reliability of surface collection as an indicator of date, let us consider Figs. 22 and 23, in which we have plotted the incidence of the classic Uruk type fossil, the bevelled-rim bowl, across the mound, and also Figs. 24 and 25, where this same distribution is plotted against the total weight of sherds. Two points are clear: there is a significant concentration of Uruk sherds in the 3G area (including 2G97 and 98), and a significant absence of Uruk sherds in two areas: 2G68-69, 78-79, 88-89, and 2G03-04, 13-14. A similar pattern emerges for the clay sickles (see Figs. 303-4). If we look then at Figs. 22-3 and 26-7 we will see that the bevelled-rim bowl distribution is complementary to that of the solid-footed goblets, accepted indicators of ED I date, and this can adequately be accounted for (despite the fact that we are dealing as much with surface as with sub-surface sherds) by the existence *under* the surface of an undisturbed ED I building in the 2G03-04 area, and of a large ED I pit surrounded by Uruk deposits in the south-eastern part of the mound.

These observations have the advantage of numerical preponderance. What of the rather general scatter of Uruk type fossils over the rest of the mound, where we know for stratigraphic reasons that there are no pure Uruk deposits directly below? Being hard-fired, these pieces—bevelled-rim bowl sherds, cones, and clay sickles—have survived better than the more evanescent pottery, and they are also very easily recognized, which would exaggerate their apparent frequency. Nevertheless, they are more or less absent in some "pure" ED I areas, and some explanation for their presence should be attempted. My guess would be that, both in the centre of the mound and in the large area of fill to the south of the double wall, we have earth taken from other parts of the site which consisted of, or at least included, Uruk deposits. We can be certain that these areas are not themselves of Uruk origin, and yet from the surface of 2G64-66 and 74-76 we recovered more sickle fragments than from "genuine" Uruk squares like 3G81-83 and 91-93. We deduce that a large mass of artificial fill has eroded away, leaving sickles (and a few cones) on the surface as evidence of its ultimate origin.

Chapter 3

ARCHAEOLOGICAL RESULTS

3.1 General conclusions

It will be easier and sufficient for most readers if we begin with a summary of what we seem to have learned about the character of the West Mound. Since a square-by-square description of our results is given later, perhaps in greater detail than necessary, we can afford here to push our deductions beyond the strict limits of the evidence into conjecture, and we do so quite deliberately, so as to have formed these conjectures before actual excavation enables us to confirm or reject them with hindsight. Thus we should have an interesting control of the validity of hypotheses based on surface clearance, a useful yardstick for the future.

First we must mention the late intrusions. Down the west side of the mound there runs a double line formed by the banks of a small ditch, with sandy fill in between. Also in this area (and surprisingly rarely elsewhere) there are many small and a few large oval sand-filled pits, some of them with the remnants of linings formed of reed-stems planted upright. A few surface finds of glazed sherds, glass fragments, and perhaps even the copper bowl in 2G34, confirm the transitory presence of "Islamic" man or woman, but there is no sign of actual occupation. One other feature of late origin must be mentioned, though only because it is referred to in our preliminary report (*Iraq* 40, 82). This is the pair of parallel ridges which much puzzled us in 1977. On reflection, we have reverted to an explanation which we rejected earlier, that the ridges were made by the tyres of a recent visitor to the site, perhaps in 1973 when the contour survey was in progress. They are separated by about 1.50 m., close enough to the width of a Land-Rover, and those who have witnessed the persistent effects on the soil of a path trodden across the site would be willing to accept that even the pressure of a car's tyres would in fact, by

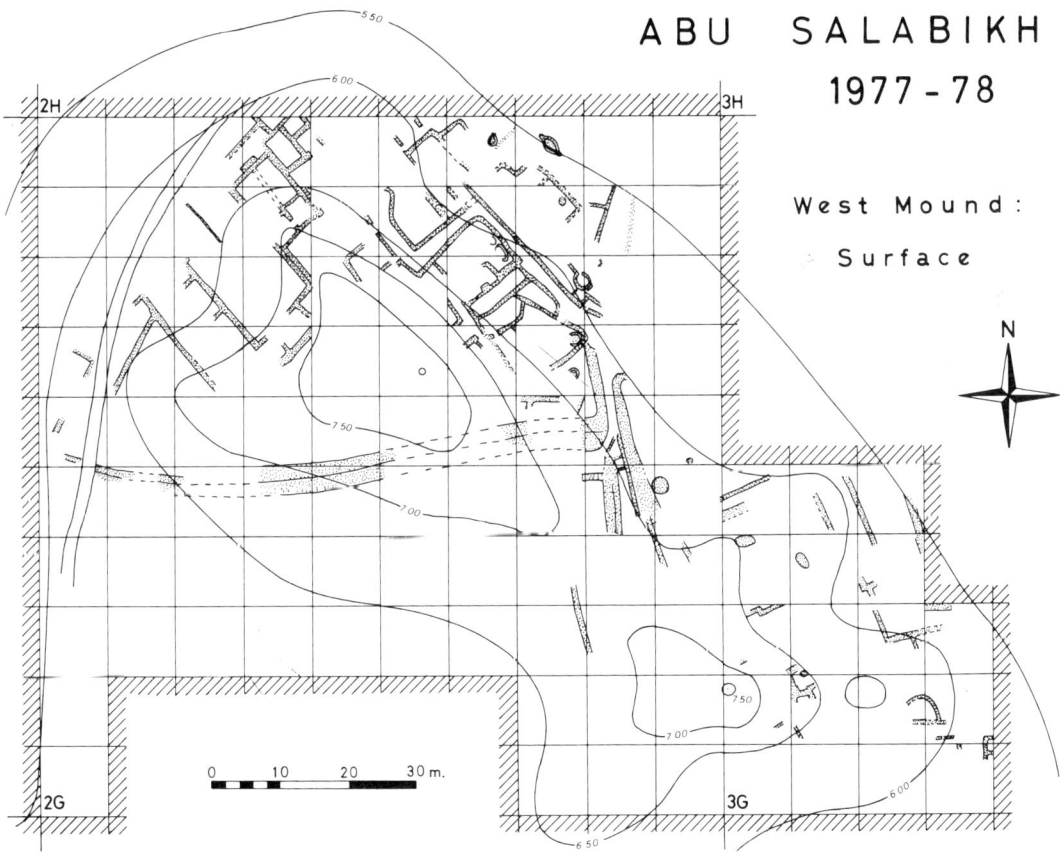

Fig. 3. Plan to show contours of West Mound before surface clearance.

11

compressing the soil beneath, create ridges rather than furrows several centimetres below the surface. These parallel lines therefore no longer feature on our plan of the site.

A negative point worth recording is that although pits and cuts were quite often observed, we found nothing resembling a grave—a very marked contrast to the result we should have had if an equal area had been cleared on the Main Mound. We can only speculate why this is so, since we do not yet know enough about the ED I burial practices at the site. On the North-East Mound one grave (Gr. 160) containing solid-footed goblets certainly had a grave-shaft; on the other hand, three or four burials close by on the same mound seemed to be very shallow (ca. 30 cm.). So we may either choose to suppose that graves were not dug within the houses of the West Mound, or guess that they were dug shallow, without grave-shafts, so that they would be encountered less often and be more difficult to recognize.

Returning now to the positive results of the clearance, we will begin at the top. The highest point of the mound, albeit not very high (some 3 m. above the surrounding plain), is in 2G35, and is roughly the centre of an oval lump of featureless fill overlying the architectural features which emerge from beneath it each side. We did not observe anything in the surface collections from here which distinguished these squares from the other ED I pottery, and if we were pushed to suggest a date for this deposit we should have to offer "late ED I", but without much conviction. Still, this does agree with the situation further to the south-east, discussed below. As to what this mass of soil represents, we have no clues: we found no brickwork in it, but since it forms the centre and main backbone of the mound it must be the remains of something relatively substantial—perhaps the foundation fill for a large building now completely eroded.

Logically the south-eastern summit of the mound in 3G80 may also date to the same period, and here again there is no sign of anything later than ED I. Here in fact an ED I date is virtually certain: overlying the enclosure walls of Blocks C and D there is more featureless fill, but dug into this fill is a large pit, containing many solid-footed goblet sherds. Again, we do not have any clue to the function of this "fill", but the large pit suggests that during a later ED I phase this part of the site was not built over, but used as a rubbish dump, and perhaps as a source of soil for building purposes. Naturally this does not necessarily imply that it was not within an enclosure wall.

Were we to excavate the mound, these two cappings of featureless soil would obviously

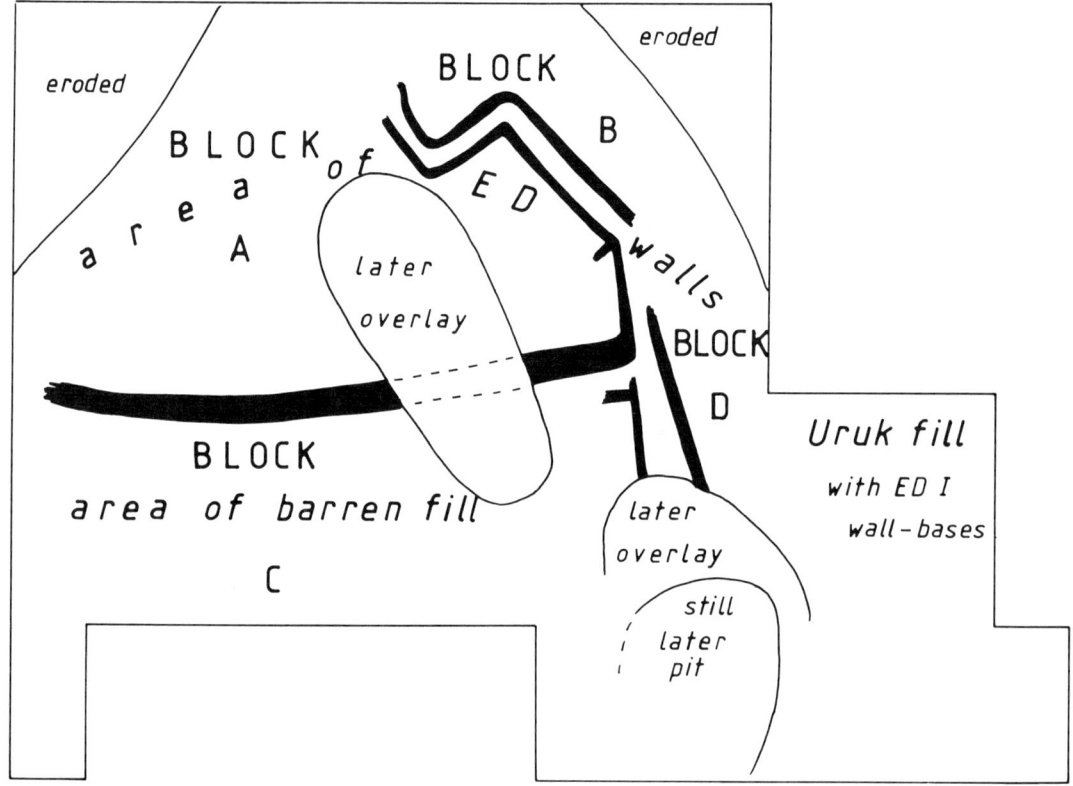

Fig. 4. Sketch to show Blocks A to D.

constitute our "Level I", and in that case "Level II" would be the most extensive and important on the mound. It is represented by plano-convex brick architecture which can be divided into four groups of rooms, here called "Blocks", which because of their connections with one another must all or nearly all be at least partially contemporary. In the south-west is Block C, whose existence as a separate unit is deduced solely from its supposed eastern enclosure wall, which borders the lane in 2G58; it is also possible that the existence of Block C explains why the long east-west south wall of Block A is built double, but this is uncertain, because other such walls seem to have been double (e.g. in 2G58, and the treble wall of the ED Bagara at Al-Hiba). By analogy with other blocks, we would suggest that all we now see of Block C is a large area of deliberate fill intended to raise its buildings on a terrace above the level of the other blocks; for this reason, we have lost through erosion all trace of those buildings. This suggestion is made with greater confidence because after the 1977 season, when we had no idea we were dealing with more than one enclosure (Block A), we wrote that this "area of clean but mixed lumpy soil looks like a wide deposit of building rubble or perhaps deliberate fill" (*Iraq* 40, 82).

Most of the clear architectural detail on the West Mound belongs to Block A, with its southern limit formed by a double enclosure wall stretching at least 80 m. from the western edge of the mound and obviously originally longer still. Its walls extend northwards into square 2H, giving a north-south dimension of at least 60 m. Within this space we can distinguish two groups of rooms, the connection between them being broken by erosion and overlay. On the west we can with fair confidence reconstruct a courtyard layout, with Rooms 7, 10 and 12 forming the east, 13 to 15 the south, and 16 to 18 the west sides of the court, which will thus have measured about 15 x 11 m. The northern side of the court is lost to erosion, but that we are right to restore a range of rooms here too is shown by the sectional pottery drain, which must have passed beneath the room walls to flow out into the court, carrying water from at least 7.50 m. further north. Beyond the courtyard house to the south-west, there are at least two walls on a different alignment, which seem to be designed to run at right-angles to the enclosure wall; but these are unfortunately badly preserved.

Further to the north-east the rooms straggle on; the walls are here close to the floors, and so very clear, but we had difficulty locating the doorways with any certainty (perhaps because of pits), and so cannot be sure whether Rooms 2, 3, 4, 6 and 9 belonged with the courtyard unit or have a separate focus of their own, perhaps in 2H to the north. Any doubts as to the date of these rooms, and, by consequence, of Block A and the other Blocks as a whole, are dispelled by the three large and typical ED I jars found in situ on the floor of Room 8.

Moving eastwards, we found clear walls emerging again beyond the late overburden, and our initial assumption that they were contemporary seems to be confirmed by their connection with the double wall, provided by the short east wall of the Block. Nevertheless, it would be rash to assume that the two parts of the complex are rigidly contemporary: in 2G25, 35 and 36 we also find traces of a later phase, intermediate between "Level I" and the main phase of the Block A building. This subsidiary phase certainly does not deserve a "Level" of its own, but at least it tempers the suspicious simplicity of the apparent stratification. In the rooms of the main phase we are again very close to the floors, and one reason why we were able to plan them so confidently is the contrast between the clean yellow bricks of the walls and the more or less ashy deposits covering the floors. This part of the complex, with its many hearths and ovens, gives the impression of a working area, and although it seems to have belonged within the same enclosure, it may well have been structurally independent.

The division between Blocks A and B is not marked by the usual thick wall, but by a narrow lane or passage, which continues towards the north-west the lane in 2G48, turning twice before we lose it in 2G04. Although we did not identify any doorway giving access to the lane, the complementary plans of Blocks A and B might be taken to reflect a closer association between them than between the other blocks, or even to show that they are two halves of a single even bigger enclosure, penetrated at this point by an entrance. What remains of Block B is also of a rather domestic character, with black courtyard deposits and several recognizable fire installations. As with Block A, it is obvious that the walls continued northwards into 2H, though we are so close here to the limits of the mound that it is doubtful whether scraping would have allowed us to trace them much further.

On the south-east we finally come to Block D. Its existence is certain from the heavy wall making the eastern side of the lane in 2G48 and 58, even if the wall itself seems to have suffered a variety of alterations and building repairs. Of the structures inside the presumed enclosure

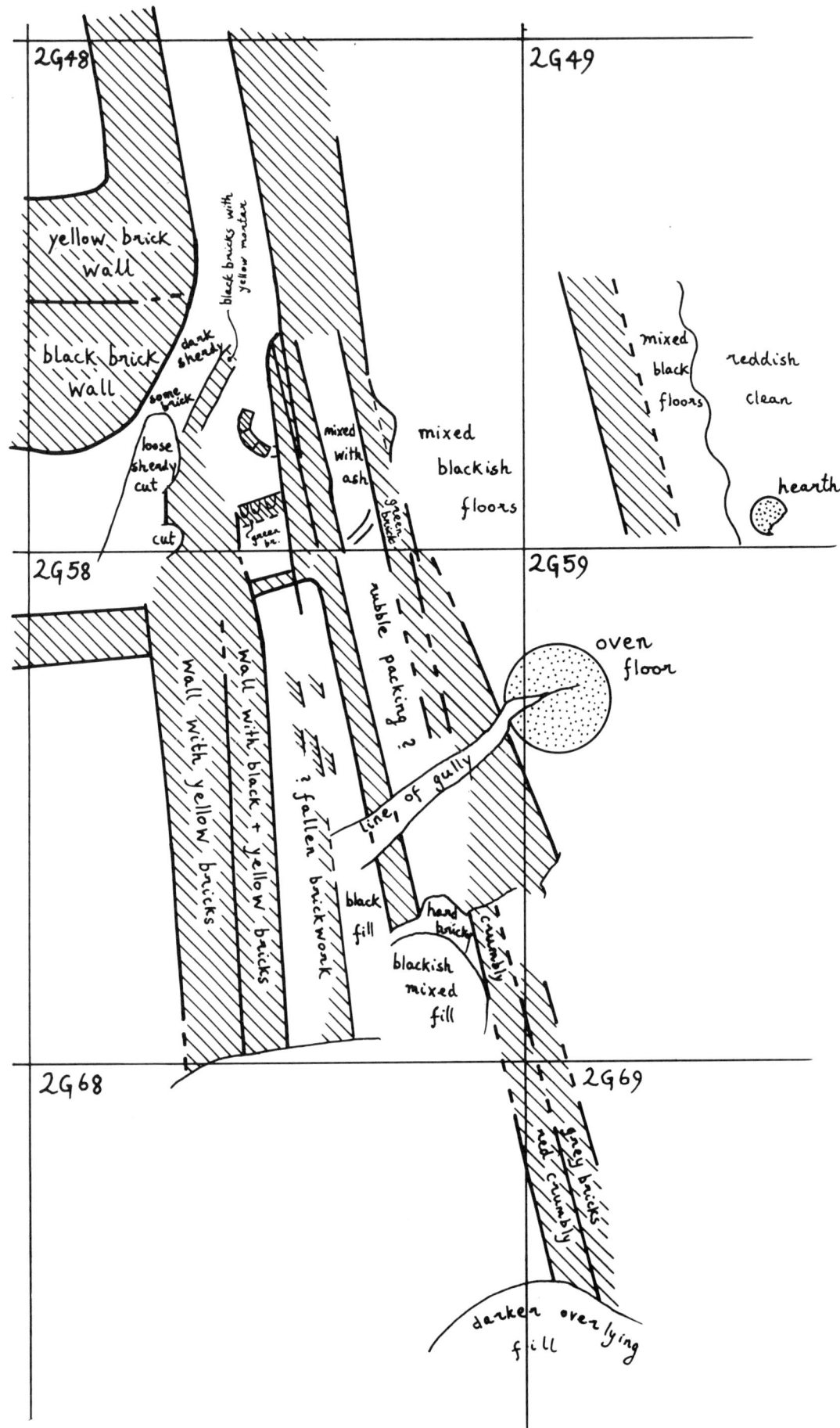

Fig. 5. Sketch to show details in 2G48-49, 58-59.

virtually nothing remains except a large oven-base, a fragment of wall, and in 2G49 the base of a jar and a small hearth, which were probably sunk below floor level. While once more the date of the enclosure may reasonably be assumed by analogy with Block A, it is worth noting that in 2G49-59 there is a concentration of bevelled-rim bowls, suggesting that the ground immediately beneath the now-eroded walls was full of Uruk potsherds. Taking account of this, and of their alignment, we must therefore raise the possibility that the walls whose foundations are laid in Uruk fill in 3G50-52 are also in fact the remnants of buildings belonging to Block D. Unfortunately, so little of them remains that it is unlikely that this will ever be proved or disproved.

A similar problem exists further south, in 3G70-71 and 80-81 in particular. Where discernible, the walls seemed to be in plano-convex brick, and the stone bowls and pottery from 3G81, which presumably came off a floor-level, do not contradict such a date. On the other hand, the surface sherds here were predominantly of Uruk date. A solution to this would presumably be given by a careful observation of the stratigraphy when excavation takes place [November 1981: the plano-convex wall proves to be only one brick deep, laid in Uruk deposits].

This exhausts the evidence for the ED I settlement. Whether there was earlier occupation of the site in the northern and western areas is not known, although it seems likely. In the south-eastern part, however, as we have just seen, the ED I walls were built on earlier levels, and that these levels do indeed belong before the Early Dynastic period is confirmed by the existence of three small patches of rectangular bricks towards the eastern edge of the area cleared. The concentration of Uruk pottery extended also as far west as 2G97-99 (and, as mentioned above, 2G49-59), and it is likely that the south-eastern part of the mound was already higher than the rest of the immediate site during the Uruk period. Blocks A and B would have been built on lower, flatter areas to the north, while the extra height we have assumed for the Block C enclosure could be the result of its relationship to the earlier high point of the mound.

Finally a few words about the extension of the mound beyond the limits of our clearance. Obviously the ED I occupation stretched well past these limits in places, although there is good reason to think that more architectural detail would be forthcoming only in small areas of 2H, and towards the south and east in 3G and 3F. It is clear, however, that much must lie hidden beneath the barren soil lapping round the edges of the mound and resulting from alluviation or from the erosion of the *tell* itself. Virgin soil on the Main Mound lies at about +2.10 m., and there is no reason to suppose it would be higher here. The walls of Block A are founded at a level of ca. +6.00 m., and we should not therefore be surprised to find archaeological deposits continuing downwards for almost another 4 m. Judging from the contours of the visible mound (which may of course not be a valid procedure), this could mean that the *tell* extends beyond our clearance at least 70 m. further to the north and 90 m. to the east, where it would merge with the western outskirts of the Main Mound. To the south and west the low flat area, although apparently barren within our clearance, presumably also consists of archaeological deposits, but without excavation it is impossible to predict whether these are a continuation of the Uruk deposits on the same level, or ED I buildings beyond the southern limit of the earlier Uruk settlement; in view of the existence to the south of the substantial Uruk Mound itself, the former possibility might be preferred.

3.2 *Fire installations*

The various hearths, ovens and kilns are of course among the most conspicuous features in any archaeological operation, with their violent colours, and are often clear to see when nothing else can be made out. We have collected below a list of those noted during the West Mound clearance; it does not include areas described as "patches of ash" or "burnt area, perhaps hearth". We have distinguished between *hearths,* thought to be small circular open fire-places, *ovens,* larger structures thought to have been covered over with an opening at one side, and *kilns,* seeming similar to the ovens but distinguished by the presence of clinker. Since we have only a single horizontal cross-section of each installation, this is not the occasion to embark on a serious attempt at categorizing them further, but a few comments on the three types are needed.

The hearths are usually without any clear edge, but FI 77/1 seemed to have a baked clay lining such as we normally find round the *tannours* of the ED III period on the Main Mound; there was a brick edging to the very small fireplace FI 77/14, and FI 77/7 had a very clear hard-baked black floor but no surviving trace of a wall. A special category is formed by two jar-tops which had been inverted and used as a hearth or for some other purpose associated with ashes, FI 77/11 and 12. With just these two examples we might have been tempted to attribute this to chance, but clearance of ED I levels in square 5I in 1981 uncovered more than five further instances of the same thing, obviously a regular ED I practice. One of these was in close association with a large oven, and it may not therefore be coincidental that FI 77/11 was so close to the hearth FI 77/10. Similar inverted jar-top hearths were frequent in the ED levels of Tell Razuk in the Hamrin basin (Gibson 1981, pp. 40, 43; Plate 24:2; etc. My thanks to Prof. Gibson for this reference).

Most of the larger fire installations, which we have called ovens, have a clear "wall" around them, and we presume that this was usually brought up to a domed roof, with an opening at one side (not, as with modern Iraqi *tannours,* at the top). We have no examples on the West Mound of the large oval ovens, with internal partitions, so familiar from ED III levels at Abu Salabikh itself, Khafajah and elsewhere; this is a little surprising, since several of them were found in the surface clearance of slightly later ED I levels in 5I in 1981. The only oven of comparable size is FI 77/2 (see Fig. 6), but this is exceptional, consisting of two ovens placed back to back.

Finally, there are the two oval kilns on the Uruk part of the mound, in and around which we observed a large amount of over-fired clay, presumably either from brick or from pottery production. These we excavated in 1981, and they will be published in greater detail later. Here it need only be said that they consist of simple oval pits in the ground, probably lined with bricks, but with the interior surfaces baked so hard that there is a very distinct inner rim of olive-green, in places vitrified, clay, quite different from any of the other fire installations on this mound. The contents of the pits confirmed our suspicions that they were used for firing pottery, or perhaps, in the case of FI 78/7, baked bricks.

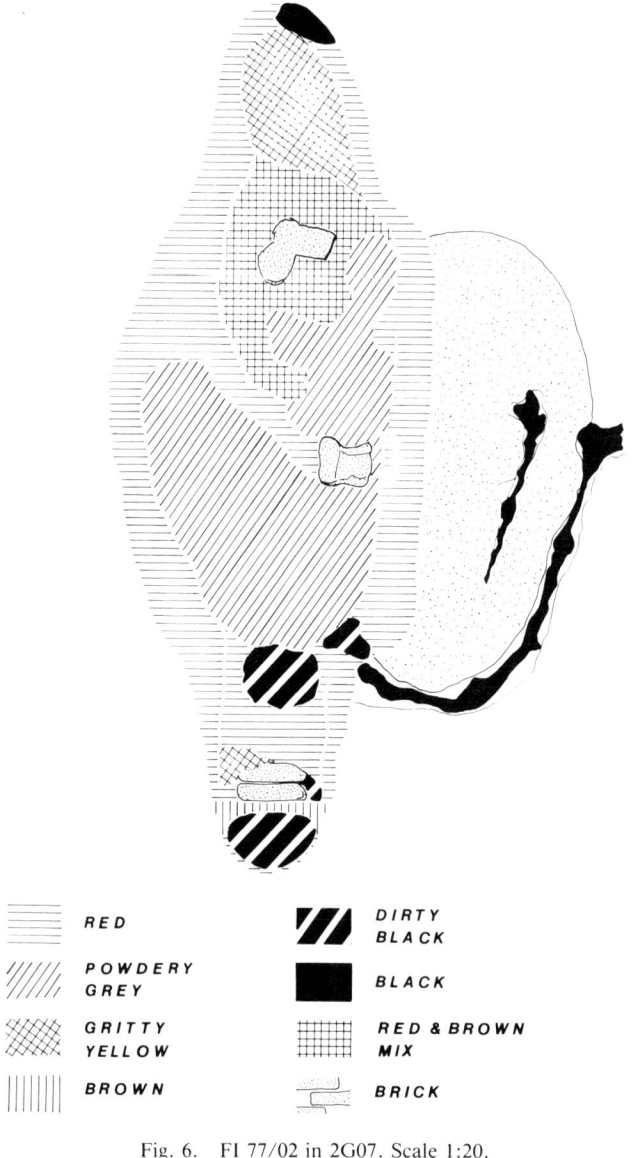

Fig. 6. FI 77/02 in 2G07. Scale 1:20.

77/1	2G06	1.63 N-S; 1.60 E-W	circular oven; baked clay lining in SW
77/2	2G07	L. 4.49; W. 1.50 m.	double walled oven; entrances to NW and SE; see Fig. 6
77/3	2G07	Di. 0.30 m. or less	circular hearth
77/4	2G12	Di. 0.55-0.60 m.	circular hearth
77/5	2G16(N)	2.00(+) x 1.30(+) m.	walled oval(?) oven; wall th. ca. 0.35 m.; entrance to W(?)
77/6	2G16(S)	1.35 x 2.25 m.	walled oval(?) oven; wall th. ca. 0.20 m.; entrance to W(?)
77/7	2G17(NE)	Int. di. 1.12 m. (NW-SE)	circular oven or hearth
77/8	2G17(SW)	Di. ca. 0.60 m.	circular hearth
77/9	2G27-28	Di. 1.35 m.	circular oven; wall th. 0.30 m.; entrance to N
77/10	2G31	Di. not measured	small hearth
77/11	2G31	Di. ca. 0.30 m.	jar-top inverted [2GS:99]; Plate IIIc
77/12	2G33	Di. ca. 0.30 m.	jar-top inverted [2GS:189, q.v.]; Plate IIId
77/13	2G37(NE)	Int. di. 1.80 m.	circular oven; wall th. ca. 0.30 m.; entrance to W(?)
77/14	2G37(W)	Ext. di. 0.65 m.	small hearth, ringed with bricks
77/15	2G37(SE)	Int. di. 1.10 m. (NW-SE)	circular oven; wall th. ca. 0.20 m.; entrance W or SW
78/7	3G60	2.00 x 1.40 m.	oval kiln; wasters [excavated as FI 81/25]
78/8	3G61	2.30 x 1.50 m.	oval kiln; wasters [excavated as FI 81/26]
78/9	3G71-72	0.90 x 0.75 m.	circular hearth
78/10	3G71-81	Di. ca. 1.40 m.	circular hearth
78/11	2G49	Int. di. 0.80 m.	circular hearth(?)
78/16	2G59	Int. di. 2.00 m.	circular oven; wall eroded except on W

3.3 Drains

In 2G12 a drain was found composed of at least 11 tubular segments and a rectangular end piece (see Chapter 3.5 under 2G12 and Fig. 7). Drains of this sort are frequent in the Uruk levels at Warka and elsewhere, and indeed are already attested in 'Ubaid times. The point of special interest about our example is that it demonstrates the purpose of the rectangular outflow piece for the first time (2GS:219, see Chapter 4.4). Such outflow pieces are already recognized as typical of ED I settlements (Adams & Nissen 1972, 214; found at WS 262, 230, 288, 372 and

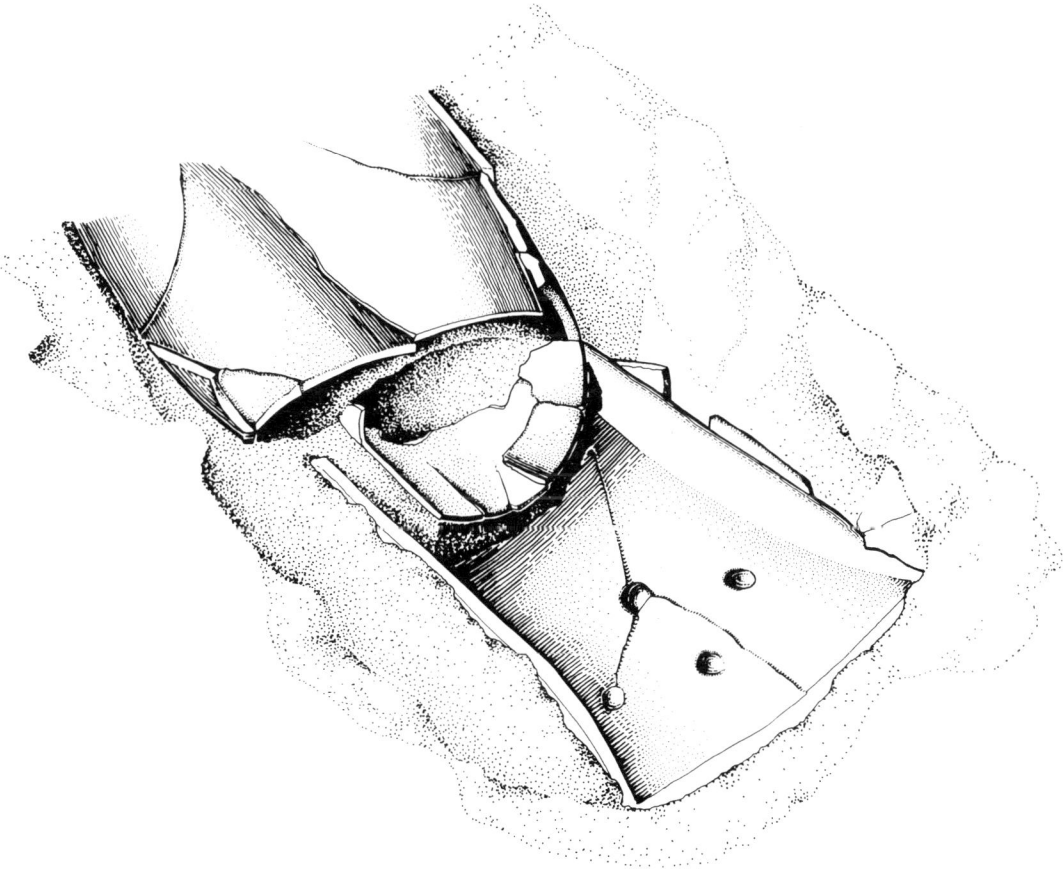

Fig. 7. View of drain end in 2G12, from SE.

387; also on Bismaya, see under 2GS:219); a very similar piece from Habuba Kabira has no holes in the base (Ludwig, apud Margueron n.d., p. 73). These outflow pieces should probably not be confused with more usual U-shaped drains or gutters (cf. 2GS:155; Ch. 4.3 §161; and of Uruk date(?) §78).

Pieces of tubular drain segments will have been harder to spot and may well have been missed among the conical bowl and solid-footed goblet sherds. Some were noted: in 2G07 and 2G38 (see Ch. 4.3 §161). In 2G13 a single cylindrical pipe was inserted in the base(?) of the SE wall of Room 10; this was at least 60 cm. in length, but may have been incomplete; it was left in situ. A similar application was observed in 1975 in an ED III context in Area E, the pipe leading through the foot of a IB wall separating the Corridor (Room 49) from the courtyard to its S (now Room 58); it is marked as a broken pair of lines in the SW corner of 6G65 in the plan in *Iraq* 38, 144.

3.4 *Bricks and brick-laying*

Rectangular ("Uruk") bricks were identified in 3G52, 3G73 and 3G83. In 3G52 these bricks were recorded as being 0.40 x 0.19 cm., and so were clearly laid flat, as would be expected; obviously when scraping it is not possible to determine the thickness of bricks unless some were laid on edge. The Uruk date of these bricks was subsequently confirmed by the sounding dug in 1981 in 2G46, where rectangular bricks were used in all walls prior to the first construction of the enclosure wall(s).

With plano-convex bricks it is also difficult to determine their thickness, because although they are frequently laid on edge, their apparent thickness will depend on whether the cross-section passes through the middle of the brick, and at what angle the bricks were laid. In general, the bricks measured approximately 0.30 x 0.15 m., but this varied considerably; they were about 0.08 m. in thickness, as far as we could tell, but in places looked thinner. Most ED walls on the West Mound were about 0.70 m. in width, corresponding to about two brick lengths; there was usually a liberal application of mortar on the faces of the wall and between rows. We did not note any cases where the bricks were laid flat, although this kind of laying, mixed with herring-bone masonry, is well known later in the Early Dynastic period (e.g. in Area E, Room 39, or at Khafajah—see Delougaz 1933, p. 21 Fig. 19e). The "normal" bricklaying is probably represented by the main wall in Fig. 10; in this case we assume that the bricks were laid herring-bone fashion, but this could hardly be proven during surface clearance. Where a wider wall was needed various solutions were adopted, involving laying one or two extra rows of bricks on their sides, parallel to the length of the wall (cf. Figs. 8, 10 and 11). A narrower wall could also be achieved by a single row of bricks on their sides flanked one side or the other by a row of bricks laid lengthwise (as in the slight partition wall between Rooms 8 and 11, see Fig. 8).

In Fig. 9 it is possible that the thick NE end of the wall between Rooms 38 and 39 was of two phases; certainly the NW part of the wall was made of irregular lumps, more roughly laid than the two rows the other side of the lengthwise bricks. However, the nature of the plano-convex bricks militates against tidy laying, and in the case of the enclosure walls it seemed clear that although sometimes we could clearly detect 8 or 9 rows of laid bricks (cf. 2G54), in other cases a thin, two-row wall was built each side and the intervening space filled with little more than rubble (cf. on 2G58). This must have been a regular practice at this date for at Khafajah also there were instances of "two rows of regularly laid bricks on each side, with irregularly laid bricks between them" (Delougaz 1933, p. 26 with Fig. 25).

3.5 *Detailed commentary on the plan*

This section describes the surface features square by square. By giving a commentary on the detailed plan (Fig. 354), it is intended to provide justification for the "reconstruction" already attempted in Chapter 3.1, explaining the reason for some of the assumptions made there and supplying information which is better conveyed verbally. This information is taken from the 1:100 plans made in the site notebooks at the time, on which the detailed plan is based, and from the notes which accompany those plans. Quotations in inverted commas are taken verbatim from the notebooks.

Under each square the objects found there are listed according to their "batch numbers" (see above, p. vii), and the following information is given about each batch:
1. the batch number and sherd weight;
2. the §§ of Chapter 4.3 under which sherds from this batch are mentioned;
3. the individual items from the batch, quoted by their "object numbers" with a cross-reference to the section of Chapter 4 or 5 in which they are more fully described.

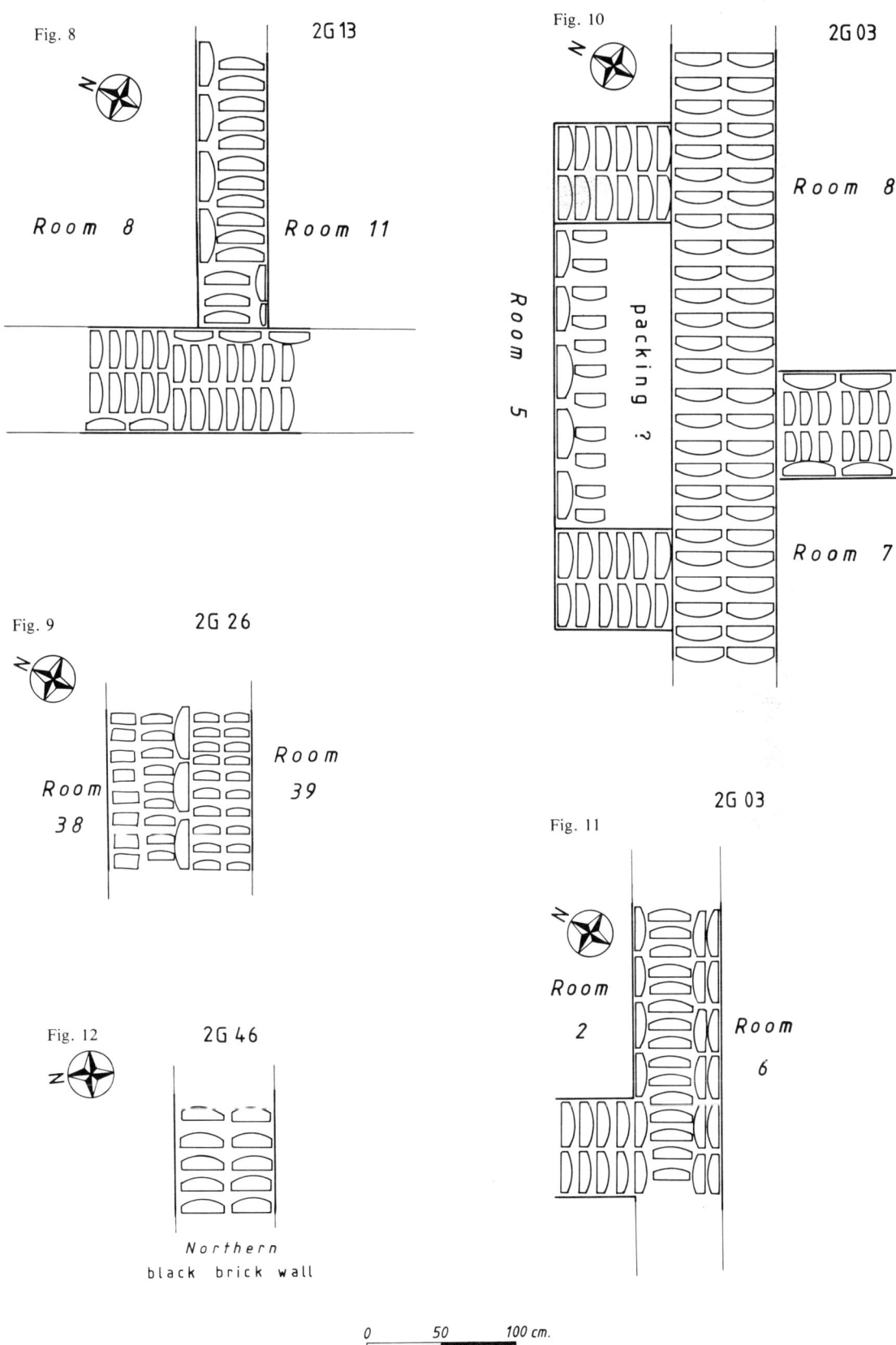

Figs. 8-12. Sketches of brick-laying in plan.

Note however: cones and sickles are only listed here if individually mentioned in Chapter 5.1 or 5.2 respectively, all other pieces being incorporated into the quantitative data presented in Figs. 295-6 and 303-4. Further, some other items are listed in Chapter 3.4 which are not separately described in Chapter 4 or 5: in this case any details we have are included here (this applies especially to a few stone tools from 1978 which were not seen by Jesper Eidem, being in Baghdad at the time).

2G00

Close to NW edge of visible mound, lying beyond the line of the modern ditch, and sloping slightly down to the NW. There are no traces of walls, with the possible exception of the patch of "red and yellow bricky" soil near the centre. The only other features are small pits, of a type common along the western side of the mound, and surely recent.

Surface: 5019   2 kg.
Sub-surface: 5020   15.5 kg.
            §§86; 91; 110; 120; 142; 149; 159
            2GS:51   sickle fragment
            2GS:45   clay wheel (Ch. 5.3)

2G01

Close to N limit of visible mound, sloping slightly down to NW. Soil of same consistency over whole square, except for pits, and for the W edge of the modern ditch (in SE corner). The pits probably all recent; the large one at S side extending into 2G11 is lined with reed-stems. No architectural features were observed in this square.

Surface: 5032   0.5 kg.
            §§105; 119
Sub-surface: 5035   [not recorded]

2G02

In the NW part of the square is the continuation of the homogeneous soil in 2G01, delimited by the line of the modern ditch which runs through the square from NE to SW. This ditch presumably cut into the W side of an ashy area, which also included "bands of yellow and reddish-brown soil", suggesting that erosion has here cut through sloping layers of debris such as one would find outside houses. On the E side of the square there are the broken ends of walls coming from 2G03; the northern wall had a distinct NW face, though its SE face was less clear, but to the S the individual bricks of both the "bench" and the wall itself were quite distinct, lying apparently on their ends, and therefore presumably laid herring-bone fashion (see on 2G03).

Surface: 5050   1 kg.
            §§149; 151; 160
Sub-surface: 5052   3.75 kg.
            §§137; 146

2G03

Virtually the entire surface of this square belongs to the main architectural level identified on the mound, and we recovered more detailed brickwork here than in any other square. The walls were sufficiently coherent for us to assign room-numbers, and the description here is therefore arranged room by room.

Room 1 The fill of this room, which extends to the W and N, is recorded as "dirty black". The line of the NE wall, separating Rooms 1 and 2, is clear, but the SE wall shared with Room 5 dies out before a return was noted, although the wall-face was clear. This room was presumably therefore a long room (min. 6.50 m. long), or else the corner of a courtyard.

Room 2 Only the S corner of this room is within the area cleared, filled at this level with mixed dirty soil with black. The laying of the bricks in the wall was clear enough to record in detail, and is represented schematically in Fig. 11. Note that the W wall between Rooms 2 and 5 was not as wide as the SE wall (0.50 m. as opposed to 0.65 m.) and they are not technically bonded.

Room 3 A small room (ca. 2.10 x 2.50 m.). At the SE side the soil is black, but this is overlain towards the NW by cleaner reddish soil. The NW wall is the continuation of that between Rooms 2 and 6, with the same pattern of brick-laying; the SW wall was also 0.65 m. thick, but here the bricks were in three rows on edge, at least in the W part. Close to the E corner of the room the SE wall was broken by a cut about 1 m. wide: to begin with we supposed this was a doorway, and it may have been, but it could as well have been a subsequent cut extending into the room itself. We could not make a final decision without excavation. The NE wall of the room was quite clear, but we could not locate its further edge with any confidence, nor could it be traced towards the SE into 2G04.

Room 4 Only the W end of this room was noted, there being a big gap in the remains of this level in 2G04 and eastwards. For the NW wall see on Room 3 above. The SW wall is relatively thin, although the individual bricks could not be recorded, and of the SE wall only a short stub (ca. 0.40 m.) survived; however, this was traced with some care, and probably represents one jamb of a doorway, with a shallow reveal on the SE face giving on to Room 9. The room-fill at this level was mixed with sherds and much black; the room's dimensions were probably 2.40 x 2.50 m., but the relevance of the fragment of wall shown in 2G04 is doubtful.

Room 5 The status of this room is quite unclear, partly because the bricky soil which filled it could not be distinguished from the actual walls in places. Thus the exact line of the NW wall is uncertain, and the outer angle of Room 6, which protrudes into the SE corner of Room 5, could not be precisely defined. On the other hand, many of the bricks in the SE wall of the room were entirely distinct, as shown in Fig. 10: the main wall is composed of two rows of vertically placed bricks giving a width of 0.65-0.75 m.; against its NW side there is a very clear feature in brick, looking like a "bench" and measuring some 3.30 x 0.70 m. The maximum dimensions of the room are ca. 3 x 8.50 m.

Room 6 This room has all four walls, and measures 3.00 x 4.80 m. In the NW the bricks of the walls are clear, but beyond the line of the NW wall of Room 8 the SW wall shows no brick-joints, only clean reddish clay. We presume this is a mortar course between bricks. The fill of the room is blackish, except for a large cut extending from the SE wall into the middle of the room, which has much cleaner, clayey soil. Although this is later than the darker fill, its conformity with the wall-lines shows, I think, that it was contemporary with the room's use. Close to the SW corner were the eroded remains of a jar (not further recorded). Unfortunately, it was not clear where the doorways had been.

Room 7 Only the N corner of this room falls within 2G03, the W corner being in 2G02 and 2G12. It was some 3.40 m. in width, and, if the broken stub in 2G13 is its S wall, then 7.40 m. in length. In the N corner the original fill of the wall was recorded as being brown soil; but this was cut away by one large and one or two smaller pits occupying the NW corner of 2G13. In one of these smaller pits which cuts the NE wall of the room was a heavy concentration of potsherds, including large pieces of conical bowls.

Room 8 The walls of this room were clear, except for the SW wall which has been cut by the pit mentioned above under Room 7. The room measured 6.80 x ca. 2.50 m., although the thin SE wall may be a subsequent addition, in which case the combined lengths of Rooms 8 and 11 would have been 10.40 m. For the NW wall see Room 5, and for the NE wall, the bricks of which only become clear 1 m. N of 2G13, see on Room 6. The fill of the room, where undisturbed, was of brown soil. After the first clearance of the surface, fragments of a jar, including a spool-lug, were collected. Subsequently it became clear that these belonged to a large jar, which was lying next to two other jars in the W corner of the room. These were excavated, and we presume that they were lying together on the latest occupation floor of the room, although we did not trace this level beyond their immediate vicinity (see Ch. 4.4, 2GS:93, 101 and 104). [Excavation here in 1981 recovered further sherds from one of these jars, and suggests that all three were sunk below an upper floor-line with their bases resting approximately on a lower one].

Room 9 Only the NW and SW walls of this rooms were noted, the E side of the room, in 2G04 and 14 not having walls preserved at this level. The fill was relatively clean, brown soil, like that in Rooms 7 and 8. Given the position of the doorway leading through to Room 4, it seems probable that the long axis of the room, which must have exceeded 5 m., ran from SW to NE.

Rooms 10-12 See on 2G13.

 Surface: 5053   1.5 kg.
      §§109; 114; 115
 Sub-surface: 5055 11.5 kg.
      §§87; 112; 113; 135; 149
      2GS:93 Red-ware jar (Ch. 4.4)
      2GS:101 Large jar with applied decoration (Ch. 4.4)
      2GS:104 Large jar with excised decoration (Ch. 4.4)
 Sub-surface: 5075 3 kg. Batch reserved to group of pottery in small pit at border with 2G13.

2G04

Lying at the N end of the mound, and sloping gently down towards the N, this square is mostly rather featureless with clean brown fill. Towards the centre is a small fragment of wall, aligning with the NE wall of Room 3, but not certainly associated with it; if it does belong to the building in 2G03, this piece of wall would no doubt form the NE wall of Room 4, but this cannot be considered certain. To its SE was a patch of bricky soil, perhaps more decayed wall, and two pottery vessels. To their NE, an area of "dark, gritty textured mixed fill", which extends into 2G05, might suggest a courtyard. The only other features are a black patch in the SW corner, extending into 2G14, and just to its E an area of whitish soil (?decayed brick).

The almost complete absence of architectural detail recovered in this square is curious, by comparison with the squares each side to E and W. The most likely explanation is that erosion here has not removed quite so much of the overlying soil as either side, so that the walls of the same level are not yet exposed; but it is also possible that the walls have been destroyed, and what we see is fill in their place.

 Surface: 5086 1 kg.
 Sub-surface: 5087 8 kg.
      §§82; 127; 161
      2GS:155 Pottery gutter out-flow (Ch. 4.4)

2G05

This square lies on the NE edge of the mound, and hence has a slope down towards the NE, of more than half a metre. In the NW there is the continuation of the area of mixed fill from 2G04, here described as "very black", while to its south the clean brown fill of 2G04 also occupies the W side of the square. To the E however wall lines emerged clearly, forming the northernmost elements traced in the complex of rooms along the eastern flank of the mound. On the N is Room 22, of which the SW and NE walls were clear, with clean brownish soil between them; although this fill was delimited to the NW by a clear change in the soil, we could not in all honesty claim to see bricks there, while a similar soil-change along the SE side marked a clear division between the fill of the room and that of the corridor, which runs along the NW wall of Room 23. We do not pretend to understand what caused these clear distinctions in the fill, but the cause was certainly integral to the architecture. At the SW end of the corridor there was almost certainly a door, or at least a doorway of some kind, suggested by the projection at the corner of the NW and SW walls of Room 23. Unfortunately the plan is so disjoint to E and W that we cannot guess whether this doorway led into another room or a courtyard. The width of Room 23 is about 4.10 m., but the loss of the further continuation of the walls towards the SE prevents us from knowing its length or whether these walls belong with those in 2G14 and 15, which are obviously not on the right line to join with Room 23. The fill of the room is described as very clean brown; this gives way to a hard, whitish patch, which may be lying over the continuation of the wall-lines.

 Surface: 5102 4 kg.
      2GS:180 fragmentary stone tool (7.8 x 5.5 x 3.3 cm.)
 Sub-surface: 5103 3.5 kg.
      §§139; 161
      2GS:185 small fragment close-grained dark grey stone; used as rubber? (6.1 x 3.1 x 1.5 cm.)

2G06

The square lies close to the NE limit of the visible mound and was deeply furrowed by a meandering "wadi" passing roughly from SW to NE. In the SW corner of the square we had the continuation of the clean brown fill of Room 23 (see 2G05), and the fill of the N end of Room 24 was similar; this room was 3.30 m. wide at the NW end, but either because of overlying soil, or in this case more probably through the action of the wadi, the SE continuation of the walls is lost. There is little reason to doubt that the wall-line in the SW part of the square represents the continuation of the SW wall of the room, but the position with regard to the NE wall is much less certain. To the E of Room 24, at the N side of the square, the soil was conspicuously colourful, greenish-black and ashy, which points to a courtyard area, probably contemporary with the room, and agrees with the evidence of the oven, which formed a very black patch within this area. The oven was roughly circular, measuring 1.63 m. from N to S and 1.60 m. from E to W; at the SW side—presumably less eroded to judge from the slope of the mound—there were the remains of its baked clay lining.

This courtyard area was bounded on the S by a line of brick running SW to NE; it was cut near the centre of the square by a roughly rectangular pit filled with soft whitish soil, and we were not able to discern its line to the SW of the pit. Nor were we able to identify the SE face of the brickwork, since it gave way to patches of bricky fill, or, towards the centre of the square, to "pinkish mud-brick". Some of this was probably building debris, and it is impossible to say whether the zig-zag wall separating Rooms 28 and 29 was of the same phase as the other walls in this square.

 Surface: 5120 5 kg.
      §130
      2GS:200 stone grinder (Ch. 5.6)
      2GS:208 stone pounder (Ch. 5.6)
 Sub-surface: 5121 9.5 kg.
      §130

2G07

Lying on the NE side of the mound, part of this square is already beyond the limits of profitable clearance. What walls could be detected do not fit together to form any very coherent plan, and it must remain uncertain whether the walls in 2G07 belong with those in 2G05 and 06 on the one hand, or with 2G18 on the other, although the fact that they lie at approximately the same level makes it likelier than not. The most conspicuous feature in the square is the oven at its centre. This was very easily seen, and the photograph (Plate IIIb) gives some idea of it, although it would be much clearer in colour. Although apparently of rather irregular outline, it does seem that a reconstruction can be attempted from this horizontal cross-section from near the bottom of the oven: on the E (right) there is a crescent-shaped cleaner patch of soil outlined by black ash, which indicates that it was a free-standing block (see Fig. 6). Built against its straighter west side there must have been two circular ovens, back to back: their entrances show clearly at each end as a narrow whiter patch, and their W sides form a double bulge along the whole feature's western edge. Without sectioning the feature vertically we cannot say more: obviously the floor of the two ovens was either higher or lower than that of the entrances where the white ash is visible, accounting for the cleaner soil within, but it is impossible to say which at present (FI 77/2; see Ch. 3.2).

Beyond the kiln to the NE was an area of brown soil mixed with burnt red bricky material, possibly from its destruction, and beyond this again, in the extreme NE, was another patch of heavy black burning, perhaps from a hearth or another oven. To judge from the size of the main kiln, it must have been out-doors; Room 31 was therefore probably a courtyard, and there is an area of dirty deposits on the S side of the square, leading towards Room 32. Immediately W of the kiln is a strip of clean brownish soil, hardly a wall or brick, and W of this again is an area of blackish fill delimited by the walls of Rooms 28 and 29. The wall-faces of Room 29 were very uncertain, and we are not sure whether there was a doorway connecting it with Room 31. Against the NW wall there was a small hearth (FI 77/3; Ch. 3.2).

 Surface: 5130 5.5 kg.
      2GS:230 stone grinder fragment (Ch. 5.6)
      2GS:233 stone grinder fragment (Ch. 5.6)
 Sub-surface: 5131 15.5 kg.
      §161
      2GS:237 stone pounder (Ch. 5.6)

2G08

This square was plainly beyond the limits of profitable clearance, and no recordable features were observed. It should however be noted that the patch of blackish soil in the NE corner of 2G07 would surely have come through into 2G08 a little, and that we did not observe this is probably because this square was among the first to be cleared in 1978 (on 12th October), when there was no dampness in the surface and the colour differentiation was much poorer.

 Surface: 5146 2.75 kg.
 Sub-surface: 5147 2 kg.

2G09

The NE part of this square is indeed off the mound altogether, lacking on its surface the dark damp appearance of the archaeological deposits, and being instead of whiter soil (alluvial from the canal or the mound), in which camel thorn grows with vigour. No features were recorded after clearance.

Surface: 5132   2.5 kg.
Sub-surface: 5133   2 kg.

2G10

There are no features of interest in this square. As in 2G00 there are several small and probably recent pits, with a couple of ashy patches on the N and S sides of the square.

Surface: 5017   2 kg.
               §135
Sub-surface: 5018   10.5 kg.
               §§103; 104; 118

2G11

The SE part of this square is occupied by the modern irrigation ditch and its spoil, which here spreads wider than usual. Apart from the usual pits, the other features are a patch of "bricky soil" at the centre of the square, a bricky and ashy area to its N, and some ashy soil close to the W side of the ditch in the very N, quite likely a continuation of the ashy area cut by the ditch in 2G02. Given the overall plan of the building to the E, it seems quite likely that both the bricky and the ashy deposits have their origin in its NW wing, but in view of the absolute level of the square we could not expect any coherent wall plans here.

Surface: 5031   2 kg.
               §§86; 105; 115
Sub-surface: 5034   5 kg.
               §§84; 115
               2GS:66   clay weight(?) (Ch. 5.3)

2G12

In the NE of the square is the NW corner of Room 7 (see on 2G03 and 13). At 1.60 m. to its W is a small circular hearth (Fl 77/4; di. ca. 0.55-0.60 m.); this may have belonged with the building, since it is clear from the drain that we are at an approximate floor-level. This drain was the most conspicuous feature of the square, running across it from NW to SE. There survived 11 cylindrical pottery segments laid end to end; at the SE end was a straight-sided open outflow piece, with holes in the base to assist the water to escape. This suggested that the water was meant to flow down from NW to SE, which was confirmed by its absolute heights (as marked on the plan): NW end +6.12, centre +6.11, SE end (base of outflow piece) +6.02. This corrected our initial impression, resulting from the slope of the mound in the other direction, that the drain had flowed from SE to NW, and if we consider the plan as a whole it is evident that the drain must have channelled water from a washing-room in the NW—now completely eroded—beneath the house walls and into the courtyard. Since the drain will have passed under the floors, and we found it at the mound's surface, it is not surprising that no sign of the walls forming the NW wing was detected. It should be noted that the NW end of the drain was already lost through erosion: as can be seen in the photograph (Plate IIIa), only the base of the cylindrical segments was preserved at this end. See also below.

At the SW corner of the square was a "confusion of mud-brick"; one clear line (i.e. wall-face ?) was made out against the W side of the square, but our notes do not make it clear if this was connected to the bricky area further S. However, it is a possibility worth mentioning, since it is well aligned with the rest of the building.

Surface: 5049   3 kg.
               §§114; 118; 142; 149
               2GS:88   clay wall-cone (Ch. 5.1; Fig. 300)
Sub-surface: 5051   16.5 kg.
               §§94; 98; 103; 105; 113; 119; 134; 142; 143; 144; 146; 149; 159
               2GS:89   stone bowl sherds (Ch. 5.5; Fig. 328)
Drain etc.:   5070   pottery from clearance of drain; not weighed.
               5104   further clearance of drain; not weighed.
               2GS:219 pottery gutter outflow (described below, Ch 4.4); details of the pottery cylindrical segments, which were left in situ: they are from 60 to 70 cm. long, and each segment has a flange at one end into which the next was fitted. As can be seen in Plate IIc, the wider end was to the NW, which entirely agrees with the direction in which we presume the water to have flowed. Excluding the outflow, the length of the eleven segments was 7 m. In detail, they measured in situ, from SE to NW, (1) 65 cm. (2) 65.6 cm. (3) 64.7 cm. (4) 69.5 cm. (5) 63 cm.(?) (6) ca. 64 cm. (7) 61 cm. (8) 61.2 cm. (9) 61.2 cm. (10) 65.2 cm. (11) 60 cm. Their approx. max. di. is 27 cm., but this may be deceptively wide because some of the segments were much squashed outwards.
               2GS:218 conical bowl found in mouth of last segment (Ch. 4.4; see Plate IIc).

2G13

The walls in the NW quarter of the square are cut by a large pit with blackish fill (cf. 2G03 on Room 7). Within this pit was another, which was full of sherds, and overlaps into 2G03. There was also another, still smaller pit, and the rim of a jar found in it (2GS:92).

Room 7   Both E and W walls are largely destroyed by the pit; see 2G03.
Room 8   See 2G03.

Room 10 measures ca. 2.40 x 3.50 m. Although outside the pit, the W part of the cross-wall between Rooms 7 and 10 is missing, and the W wall of Room 10 was presumably removed in the same way. This means that we cannot say anything definite about access to Rooms 7 and 10 from the courtyard. In the NE wall a clear doorway gave access to Room 11; and in the middle of the SE wall the brickwork is broken by a pottery drainpipe, suggesting that either Room 10 or Room 12 was an outside area. At the SW corner of the room the SE wall is not bonded in to the W wall of the courtyard, but turns to form a double wall, along the W side of Room 12.

Room 11 measures 2.80 (SW-NE) by 3.30 m. (NW-SE). Its E and W walls are clearly continuations of those of Room 8 (see on 2G03), but the cross-wall between the two rooms is perhaps a later addition, being unusually thin, composed of only one brick length plus one thickness (i.e. brick on its side); see Fig. 8 for the laying of these bricks. The fill of both Room 10 and Room 11 is recorded as "mixed". A thin secondary skin of darker-coloured brick is built against the outside of the E corner of this room; it may have been no more than a reinforcing.

Room 12 For the NW wall see above on Room 10. Unfortunately the other limits of the room are not clear, although it is obviously possible that it extended in the SE as far as the wall of Room 36. In this case it would have had to be an unroofed space, and the drain-pipe in the NW wall and dark ashy patch in 2G14 to the E could be taken as support for such a reconstruction. The only obvious explanation for the double wall on the west is that each belongs to a different unit, but this cannot be demonstrated in the present condition of the plan (see also on 2G23).

Surface: 5054 3.5 kg.
Sub-surface: 5056 23.75 kg.
  §§83; 94; 97; 99; 111; 119; 125; 141; 149; 152; 157; 158; 161
  2GS:85 globular pottery object (Ch. 4.4) "in room fill"
  2GS:86 tall cup (Ch. 4.4)
  2GS:92 jar rim in situ in NW; rim di. 13.5 cm. (Fig. 194)
  2GS:90 stone pounder (Ch. 5.6)

2G14

There is little to be said about this square. The walls appeared as decayed, fairly hard, whitish lumps, and individual bricks could not be distinguished. It is therefore uncertain whether the eroded wall-lines visible belonged with the building to the west, or with that to the east, or to both, or neither. The only probable association is between the fragments of wall on the east side of the square and the line of the west wall of the main corridor. West of them the soil is described as relatively clean brown fill, while to their east there is darker mixed soil, with some greenish components. For the large ashy patch in the NE part of Room 12 see already on 2G13.

Surface: 5084 3.5 kg.
  2GS:138 grindstone fragment (Ch. 5.6)
Sub-surface: 5085 8.5 kg.
  §§130; 150

2G15

Most of this square is occupied by Room 25, which was filled with fairly clean but mixed brownish soil. In the very NE corner is part of Room 26, overlapping with 2G16. The corridor or street, numbered Room 46, runs along the SE and SW exterior walls of Room 26, and at the western edge of the square it turns to run due N, and then again to the NW. The brickwork shown at this point was quite distinct, but in view of its irregular shape and the way it blocks the passage, we suspect that it is no more than a fallen lump. Against its E side, in the bend of the corridor, the soil is particularly ashy; otherwise it was noted that the passage in this square "had a distinctive mixed brownish fill which persisted throughout its entire length", constituting important evidence that the walls in 2G15-17 and 25-27 do all belong to a single phase. One problem is posed by the W wall of the corridor: the curves in the E wall would lead one to expect a corresponding curve in its western wall, which is certainly not provided by the apparent W wall of Room 12. On the other hand, the lump of brickwork we have planned is no solution either.

Room 25 Measures 5.50 m. from SW to NE; the length from SE to NW must have been more than 5 m., but to the N the walls are lost. Given the shape of the room, it seems likely that it was an open, unroofed space.

Surface: 5100 6.5 kg.
Sub-surface: 5101 2 kg.
  2GS:181 grinding slab (Ch. 5.6)

2G16

For Rooms 26 and 46 see on 2G15. The status of Room 27 is uncertain, since the bricks dividing it from Room 26 were clear, but did not extend for more than 2 m. Since the E wall of the passage (Room 46) continues, to become the E wall of Room 27, one might suppose that the break in the SE wall of Room 27 is not accidental, and that Room 27 is so only a branch of the same passage; however, the passage fill was very distinctive (see on 2G15), and it was clear at the time that it did not extend NW beyond this point. The NE corner of the square beyond the E wall of the passage contained no significant features, only "red bricky fill". This area may then have been a courtyard or other open space.

Room 38 This was separated from the passage by an unusually thin wall (only 0.50 m. in places). In the N part of the room the soil was black, obviously as a result of the two fire installations against the NE wall. Since we have only a horizontal cross-section of these, and an incomplete one at that, there is a limit to what can be said about them. The wall of that to the N (FI 77/5) was only preserved on its eastern side, and is about 30 cm. thick; it is built right up against the wall face, and seems indeed to be let into it. The southern one (FI 77/6) is slightly more complete: from E to W its internal diameter is 1.35 m. (min.), but from N to S about 2.25 m., with a clay wall of about 17 cm. thickness. It too was built close against the wall-face, although it does not touch the SE wall of the room, and unfortunately in neither case was the oven sufficiently preserved to show where the entrance had been. For the remainder of Room 38, see on 2G26.

Surface: 5118   4.5 kg.
                 §§127; 150
Sub-surface: 5119   4 kg.

2G17

The extreme SW corner of the square is cut by the NE wall of the passage, and as in 2G16 the soil to its NE contains few significant features and was described as "fill" of various colours. Towards the SW corner there is a small circular patch of burning, perhaps a hearth (FI 77/8). In the NE corner of the square there are walls associated with those in 2G07 and 06; what we see is the NE side of a small room, some 6 m. in length NW-SE, and filled with very dirty blackish soil. Close to the NE wall was a hearth, or more likely the floor of a clay-walled oven, slightly oval in shape and measuring 1.12 m. internally, NW to SE. The NE face of the NE wall was not clear, the brick giving way to clean soil in which details could not be distinguished.

The interpretation of this square is not easy. One would tend to assume, looking at the slope of the mound, that the cleaner fill to the W overlies the walls and dirty room fill in the NE corner, and this may indeed prove correct. But if this is so, and if the fill on the W is contemporary with the E wall of the passage, it would imply that Room 30, and with it Rooms 29 and 28 at least, belong to an earlier phase than the passage walls, or an earlier phase *of* them. Thus we could envisage an earlier phase, in which the building now represented by Rooms 28-31 occupied the space east of the passageway, and a later phase, in which the passageway wall still stood, but the building had been replaced by an open area filled with cleaner debris, very likely resulting from the collapse of that building. These possibilities could only be settled by observation of the stratigraphy during excavation.

Surface: 5129   5 kg.
                 2GS:224   flint (Ch. 5.7)
Sub-surface: 5128   5 kg.
                 §147
                 2GS:235   stone grinding slab (Ch. 5.6; perhaps the item marked on the plan in the SE corner of the square)
                 2GS:236   cube-shaped stone (Ch. 5.6)

2G18

A "wadi" nearly 2 m. wide runs through this square from N to S, carrying much water from the NE side of the mound. As shown in the plan, there seemed to be brickwork along its E side, and it is likely that the course of the wadi was here defined by a wall-line. This was probably on the same alignment as a long narrow wall some 3 to 3.50 m. to the W, with a cross-wall taking off from it towards the W, separating Rooms 32 and 33. Since the E side of the walls in 2G17 was not clear to us, it is impossible to say whether they are in any way connected with these walls in 2G18, which could easily belong to an earlier phase.

It seems worth mentioning that the walls planned in 2G18 were quite invisible to us in October, 1978, when the square was first stripped; but after it had lain exposed for a while the wall lines showed up fairly conspicuously because the soil surrounding the brick, unlike the brick itself, had risen several centimetres in a loose crumbly formation, caused presumably by the salts. The accuracy of the brick line could be confirmed by scraping along the edges, although nowhere could we discern the individual bricks.

Surface: 5144   1.25 kg.
Sub-surface: 5145   4.25 kg.
                 §124
                 2GS:244   flints (Ch. 5.7)
                 2GS:246   2 natural shells: half bivalves (2.5 x 5.2 cm.)

2G19

No discernible features in this square, which was effectively off the mound, although there were a fair number of potsherds.

Surface: 5134   2.75 kg.
Sub-surface: 5135   5 kg.
                 2GS:245   2 wall-cone fragments (Ch. 5.1)

2G20

Most of the features in this square are small pits resulting from recent occupation; near the centre, is a larger sandy pit with reed-stems round the edge. Possibly more ancient are patches of mixed bricky and ashy soil on the N side, but there is nothing to which any meaning can be attached.

Surface: 5015   (weight not recorded; nil or lost)
Sub-surface: 5016   7 kg.
                 §§108; 115
                 2GS:26   clay sickle (Ch. 5.2; Fig. 305)
                 2GS:27   grindstone fragment (Ch. 5.6)
                 2GS:28   stone pounder (Ch. 5.6)
                 2GS:31   stone cube (Ch. 5.6)

2G21

The unproductive area extends from 2G20 up to the line of the modern ditch; it is interesting that a couple of modern pits are dug into the ditch fill, proving that it is not the most recent feature on the mound. In the S of the square we have walls belonging to the main building of Block A: the position and alignment of the NE wall of Rooms 19 and 20 show that it belongs with the W wing of the building, and patches of ash and brick debris in the soil suggest an association with approximately this phase of occupation. However, the plan here is too fragmentary to allow us much basis for speculation, and we cannot propose with any confidence the role of Rooms 18 and 19 in the building. For Room 17 see on 2G22 and for Room 20 2G31. The NW wall of Room 19 was of greenish bricks, unlike the others which were of yellowish sandy brick, and it seems to have cut into the line of the NE wall of the room, suggesting that it is structurally a later addition. In the S side of the square, in the area which would form the W side of Room 19 if the walls projected that far, there was a concentration of potsherds sufficient to provoke special comment.

Surface: 5033 1.75 kg.
§116
2GS:64 seal impression (Ch. 5.3)
Sub-surface: 5030 8 kg.
§§96; 99; 103; 106; 135; 149; 159; 161
2GS:105 dish with internal channel (Ch. 4.4)
2GS:60 perforated stone (Ch. 5.6)
2GS:61 flint (Ch. 5.7)

2G22

The dominant feature of this square is the wall which runs from its NW to its SE corner and on into 2G33, forming the W side of the area we suppose to have been a large open courtyard. The brick itself is not well preserved, consisting of hard whitish lumps, and indeed on the first clearance the wall was not identified as such. It was only in the light of the evidence of the drain in 2G12 that we re-examined the area and found this wall and the two cross walls abutting on its western face, and delimiting Rooms 16, 17 and 18. In Room 18 the surviving corner in the SE has black ashy room fill, but this extends no further than the cross wall itself, both presumably being obscured or destroyed for the same reason. There is also a roughly circular pit filled with soft grey soil, very nearly in the extreme NW corner of the square. The wall presumably extended northwards into the confused area of mud-brick in the SW corner of 2G12, but there does not seem to have been the beginning of the NW wall of the courtyard, returning from the E face of the long wall; this is however mostly eroded.

There is nothing significant to say of Room 17, unless the extensive patch of ashy soil in the SW corner belongs with the room, and still less to say of Room 16. It is regrettable that the loss of detail as one moves westwards makes it impossible to reconstruct the plan of the rooms along this side of the courtyard; it is not evident whether a third wall running NW-SE should be reconstructed between the two already planned, or whether rather the rooms were abnormally wide. In the presumed courtyard there is only another pit filled with soft grey soil to mention, the fill being otherwise unremarkable. A relatively large amount of potsherds was noted in the NW corner.

Surface: 5045 2 kg.
Sub-surface: 5048 12.5 kg.
§§85; 105; 112; 113; 114; 135; 143; 147; 150; 152; 161
2GS:70 sieve-based bowl (Ch. 4.4)
2GS:84 conical bowl (Ch. 4.4)
2GS:217 conical bowl (Ch. 4.4)
2GS:71 grindstone (Ch. 5.6)

2G23

The W half of the square, presumably representing the courtyard, was described as relatively clean brown fill, with little pottery. The walls, on the E side, are not well preserved, and leave a number of uncertainties. In particular, it is not certain whether the breaks in the double wall on the NE were once doorways, or a single doorway blocked by the subsequent building of the eastern, thinner wall, or simply later cuts. Our opinion at the time was that there had been a doorway in the wider wall, but that the eastern wall ran continuously, blocking it; there could however be other explanations which allowed for the doorway to penetrate both. Whether cut or doorway, it is worth mentioning that a nearly complete solid-footed goblet was found in the break in the western wall (2GS:157).

The wider wall has a clear return to the W, forming the SE limit of the courtyard. It runs for some 5 m. before disappearing, apparently cut—which throws some doubt on the contemporaneity of the courtyard fill. Just beyond the surviving stub of the wall was found the cylinder seal 2GS:94; its position is very close to the line of the NW face of the wall, indeed probably within that line, so that it belongs stratigraphically with the later fill, not with the building whose walls we planned. Coming off the wall to the SE, and separating Rooms 13 and 14, is a wall with its NE face clear but the SW face less so. There is nothing to report of Room 13, but the fill of Room 14, as far as the walls were traced, was dirty and contained much pottery including parts of more than one hollow stand.

Surface: 5057 6.5 kg.
§115
Sub-surface: 5060 23 kg.
§§79; 83; 99; 146; 149; 150; 153; 158
2GS:157 solid-footed goblet (Ch. 4.4)
2GS:291 hollow stand (Ch. 4.4)
2GS:98 stone pounder (fragment; 8.2 x 7.2 x 5.0 cm.)
2GS:94 cylinder seal (Ch. 5.8)

2G24

With the rise in the contours in this square the walls of Block A which were traceable further to the W and N are no longer appearing, presumably being buried beneath a later overlay. Only in the N of the square is there a line of decayed brick associated with a return in 2G14, but here again it is impossible to suggest a certain connection with the walls surviving at a slightly lower level to either side. The soil in 2G24 is in general clean and brown, with some flecks of ash towards the SE corner, and a rather more mixed patch within the angle of the walls in the NE.

In 1977 parallel humps or "tramlines" were noted beneath the surface in this square, running from the SE down the slope of the mound into 2G12, and these are planned on the preliminary plan of the West Mound published in *Iraq* 40, 83. As mentioned above (Ch. 3.1), we now think that these were only tyre marks, but in order to investigate the mystery a small stratigraphic cut was made on the western edge of 2G24, to a depth of 0.35 m. (batch 5105); much pottery came from this cut, which was stopped when we reached a floor.

Surface: 5082 3.5 kg.
§127
Sub-surface: 5083 9.5 kg.
§157
Stratigraphic cut: 5105 31.5 kg.
2GS:156 clay sealing (Ch. 5.3)
2GS:165 white limestone fragment; one surface worked (4.0 x 3.1 x 2.8 cm.)
2GS:160 flint (Ch. 5.7; Fig. 350)
2GS:166 3 lumps of bitumen with rope and reed impressions (Ch. 5.8)
2GS:167 a bone

2G25

This square occupies the NE side of the mound, where it achieves its nearest approach to a steep slope. Here, and in 2G35 and 36, there was visible on the uncleared surface after rain a distinct straight line running parallel with the contours, which we guessed must represent the line of a wall. In fact we were wrong, since it proved to be only the transition from the rather clean fill in the SW corner of the square, continuous with that in 2G24, and the much dirtier "dark greenish-black" soil which is associated with the walls in the NE corner of the square. These walls clearly belong with the main phase of the Block A rooms, and the clean fill higher up the slope is obviously obscuring the continuation of this phase to the W.

On the N side of the square we have the angle of the passage which separates Block A from Block B; the walls abutting on it each side are less clear, but it seemed likely to us at the time that on the E we have the W corner of Room 38, with the beginning of its western wall, though its continuation could not be traced. No trace was recorded in 2G25 of the other wall running parallel in 2G26, but this need not in fact mean that it is not there. Once again, there is too much later overlay in this square to enable us to recover the plan without excavation.

Surface: 5096 26.5 kg.
§151
2GS:126 stone vessel sherd (Ch. 5.5)
2GS:125 grind-stone fragment (Ch. 5.6)
2GS:124 flint (Ch. 5.7)
Sub-surface: 5099 [no weight recorded, as this is one of the batches which unaccountably "vanished"]

2G26

The walls in this square, being close to their floors and contrasting, with their yellowish bricks against the black room fill, were beautifully clear, and form the eastern wing of the building in Block A. The N half of Room 38 is already described under 2G16; in 2G26 we have a small pottery drain (internal di. ca. 0.45 m.) close to the W wall, while the line of the SE wall is broken by a buttress-like projection towards the middle and by a small partition wall which turns back westwards after projecting about 2 m. into the room. The room fill to the W of this partition was much less burnt than next to the oven on the other side, but against its western face, as shown, there were a few bricks placed on end, baked red (and so clearly visible). They need not, of course, have been in their original place. Given the size of the room (about 8 x 9 m.), and the variety of domestic installations, it was almost certainly in fact an open courtyard. Although we have tentatively restored a western wall, it is also possible that the space lay open to the corridor which runs northwestwards from the S side of the square, at least during part of its history. A sketch of the brick-laying in the SE wall of Room 38 is given above (Ch. 3.4; Fig. 9).

Room 39 This lies along the SE wall of Room 38, and would appear, from the junction of their NE walls, to have been a later addition. No doorway was identified, although the brick walls were clear along all four sides, and therefore we are unable to say how the room was entered, or whether there was direct access from Room 38 or the corridor. The fill of this room was relatively clean, brown soil, distinguishing it from Room 40, the fill of which was much blacker. Room 39 measures only 2 m. across, but is 9 m. long, and could hardly have been other than a storeroom.

Room 40 This room certainly belongs to the same building as Room 39, but its exact status remains rather uncertain because of the problems in 2G36. With its peculiar shape it can hardly have formed part of any original architectural design, and if there is a doorway into Room 41 it may have been a small room attached to yet another open court. The fill is blackish, as observed above, and therefore similar to the fill of Room 42.

In the SW corner of the square the W wall of the passage forms the E wall of Room 37, which has the same dirty room fill as 2G25. If we have not missed a wall in 2G16, it seems most likely that Room 37 is yet another open court, judging from its size and the character of its fill.

Surface: 5116 13.5 kg.
Sub-surface: 5117 19 kg.
§§115; 136; 159
2GS:184 unworked piece of stone

2G27

The square is divided from NW to SE by the passage separating Blocks A and B. In the SW is the NE wall of Room 42, which runs from half-way along Room 39 to the eastern extremity of Block A where Room 42 meets the eastern enclosure wall. The irregular triangular space NE of this wall is enclosed by a flimsy line of brick—in places no wider than 0.30 m.—which looks very much like an afterthought, and forms the southward extension of the W wall of the passage. Unfortunately its junction with the NE wall of Room 42 is obscured by a pit filled with sandy soil. Just S of this point there is a break in the wall of Room 42, but we were not able to decide for sure whether this was a doorway or not. Within Room 43 the soil was dirty black.

The eastern wall of the passage was straight and clear, and there was a distinct angle at its SE end, with no obvious brickwork immediately continuing the line (despite the piece of wall in 2G28). In Room 34 the soil was clean, brown and red, though with plenty of sherds included; a line of bricks perhaps only one course wide formed what may have been a sill leading into Room 35. To the E again is an oven (FI 77/9), overlapping into 2G28, with the usual heavily blackened baked clay floor and a wall round it about 0.30 m. thick, on the E and N; the walls of the building themselves seem to have formed its S and W limits, and the entrance to the oven was probably at the N. It measures some 1.35 m. in diameter.

Surface: 5126 7 kg.
2GS:228 small fragment of pinkish stone
2GS:232 small fragment of stone, probably grindstone
Sub-surface: 5127 4 kg.
§99
2GS:214 flint (Ch. 5.7)
2GS:231 stone grinder (Ch. 5.6)

2G28

As with 2G18 little detail survived in this square. On the W side we have the features already described under 2G27, and there is little to add to this. In the NW part of the square is a small burnt patch, enclosed to its E and S by clean bricky material, but it lies disjointed from any architectural context. Otherwise one must suppose that any buildings on the E side of the square have been eroded away below their foundations, or are concealed by overlying fill.

Surface: 5142 3 kg.
Sub-surface: 5143 3.5 kg.

2G29

Apart from a small, roughly rectangular, pit filled with sand in the NW corner, there were no features recorded in this square of which we could be certain. Lightly indicated, however, there is the position of a linear feature which seemed to be a northward extension of the W wall of Block D, the remains of a wide enclosure wall. No bricks could be distinguished although there was a definite change in the soil, so perhaps this was mud packing beneath the wall proper, or simply a difference caused by the depression of the underlying earth by the weight of the wall.

Surface: 5136 3.5 kg.
Sub-surface: 5137 1 kg.

2G30

Like others along the western edge this square is riddled with recent pits. There are however traces of walls which, taken in conjunction with those observed in 2G31 and 2G40, are likely to have belonged to buildings in Block A. The only other ancient features noted were a patch of mixed ash and brick towards the S side, and a small hearth and a pottery vessel in situ N of the N wall of Room 21; unfortunately neither of these was separately recorded and we have no further details of them. Down the E side of the square runs the recent ditch, removing any direct association there may once have been with the long wall in 2G31.

Surface: 5013 1.75 kg.
§114
Sub-surface: 5014 7 kg.
§§92; 105
2GS:29 stone pounder fragment (Ch. 5.6)
2GS:30 stone smoother fragment (Ch. 5.6)

2G31

E of the modern ditch we have a wall running the whole length of the square at a curious angle to the wall it joins in the N in 2G21. That wall, to judge from the overall plan, is correctly aligned with the main Block A courtyard, while our wall running from its W side takes off at an acute angle so as to meet the curving line of the double enclosure wall more nearly at right-angles, and so as to align itself more closely with whatever construction the fragments of wall in 2G30 represent. This reconstruction, combined with the length of the stretch of wall in which no cross-walls were noted, suggests that it delimits an open area on one side, if not on both. Unfortunately its southward continuation, if there was one, is now disturbed by the modern ditch. The soil to the E of the wall line is described as being mixed with much pottery (note the weight of the sub-surface sherds). In the extreme NE corner against the SW face of the other wall were

a small hearth (FI 77/10) and just to its north an inverted jar top (FI 77/11; 2GS:99, see Plate IIIc).
Surface: 5036   2.75 kg.
                2GS:67   stone bowl sherds (Ch. 5.5; Fig. 325)
Sub-surface: 5029   20.5 kg.
                §§85; 86; 96; 99; 130; 145
                2GS:99   jar top (Ch. 4.4)
                2GS:242   hollow stand fragments (Ch. 4.4)
                2GS:55   flint (Ch. 5.7)

2G32

The only feature of interest here is the long NW-SE wall which we guess to have been the W edge of the courtyard-building of Block A. At its SE end it is interrupted by a large pit, filled with soft grey soil. Otherwise the wall separates the fill on the W, continuing from 2G31, from fairly clean featureless brown soil, which may well belong to the general later overlay at the centre of the mound. Against the E face of the wall was part of a large spouted jar (2GS:100), with the spout emplacement but no rim or base; not separately recorded.

Surface: 5046   7.5 kg.
                §§103; 159
                2GS:77   stone bowl sherd (Ch. 5.5; Fig. 326)
Sub-surface: 5047   19 kg.
                §§92; 96; 106; 107; 109; 112; 119; 136; 149; 150; 152

2G33

The W wall of the courtyard enters this square from the NW, and turns eastwards before being broken or obscured by soil which may be the same as in 2G23, but is here described as dirty brown fill, with an admixture of black. The cross-wall, forming the W wall of Room 14, is also lost except for a stretch of 1.50 m. against the rather irregular S wall of this room. This wall was over 1 m. in width, and may therefore reasonably be assumed to have been the outer wall of the building, although it too is broken to both E and W, and, like most walls recognized at this height, was badly eroded, appearing as hard whitish lumps. In Room 15 the fill was described as "very dirty", but to its S and W it gives way to cleaner brown fill identical with that in 2G32. In the SW corner is the continuation of the large pit already referred to under 2G32, and on the E side of the square is a patch of dirtier fill mixed with pottery, which may well be associated with the exterior wall. The pottery from this square, of which there was a great quantity in the sub-surface soil, was described as "sewage-stained" and probably mostly comes from this SE area. On the plan is marked the position of 2GS:189, an inverted jar top which can be identified as a fire installation by analogy with that in 2G31 and several on the main mound in square 51 (FI 77/12).

In Room 14 there was another concentration of pottery which extended into 2G23 and was excavated separately (batch 5067).

Surface: 5058   12 kg.
                §§94; 98; 109; 114; 119; 125
Sub-surface: 5059   45 kg.
                §§95; 99; 113; 117; 119; 142; 146; 149; 150; 158; 159; 161
                2GS:189   inverted jar rim (Ch. 4.4; FI 77/12)
                2GS:96   stone bowl sherd (Ch. 5.5; Fig. 329)
                2GS:97   flint nodule used as pestle; one flake struck from one end, other end snapped off (L. 8.0; Di. 3.6 cm.)
                2GS:95   grindstone fragment (Ch. 5.6)
                2GS:220   flints (Ch. 5.7)
Pottery group in Room 14:   5067   7 kg.
                §§149; 159

2G34

We are here close to the summit of the mound, and in levels which overlie the main ED I buildings. Virtually the whole square consisted of "relatively clean compact brown fill". Only on the E side is a patch (or pit?) of softer soils with mixed colours. At the S side the fill is continuous with 2G44, and here a bronze bowl, probably of Islamic date, was found inverted (2GS:102).

Surface: 5080   9 kg.
Sub-surface: 5081   11 kg.
                §159
                2GS:150   bevelled-rim bowl (Ch. 4.4)
                2GS:215   bevelled-rim bowl (Ch. 4.4)
                2GS:102   bronze or copper bowl (Ch. 5.8)

2G35

The mound here begins to slope down towards the E, and in the NE corner there is the line forming the limit of the dirty room fill coming through from 2G25. The layer above this (and to the W) is not entirely homogeneous: in the S and W of the square it is still the relatively clean fill of 2G34, but as indicated on the plan there is a transitional level of "darker mixed brown fill, quite dirty in places" before reaching the room fill in the extreme NE corner. There was a great deal of pottery in this dirtier northern part, as there was in 2G33, on the western side of the overlay.

Surface: 5097 14.5 kg.
§§81; 100
2GS:128 stone grinding slab (Ch. 5.6)
Sub-surface: 5098 47 kg.
§§107; 145
2GS:143 bevelled-rim bowl (Ch. 4.4)
2GS:147 conical bowl (Ch. 4.4)
2GS:145 stone bowl sherd (Ch. 5.5)
2GS:144 stone grinder fragment (Ch. 5.6)

2G36

The SW part of this square is still occupied by the relatively clean later overlay. The walls which do appear in the NE part are rather hard to interpret. There is probably a doorway leading through from Room 40 into Room 41, which contains "dirty black fill"; but the W jamb of this doorway gives way to fill before it meets the W wall of the room, and it is not clear whether the line of brick to its S, the W side of which is also obscured by the fill, belongs with the same phase of Room 41 or not. In any case, it seems certain that the western walls belong to a later phase than both, which could well be represented also by the intermediate layer of fill mentioned above under 2G35.

[The E side of this square was excavated in 1981, but the description offered above has not been changed in the light of these results. In fact, we were right to suppose there were two phases of architecture present, but the wall on the W side is unexpectedly earlier than the eastern wall, which belongs with a level now almost entirely eroded. It seems probable also that a mistake was made in the extreme NE corner of the square: the brick of the wall is to the SW of the wall-edge shown, and not to its NE. See *Iraq* 44 (1982), 107, Fig. 2.]

Surface: 5114 17 kg.
§146
2GS:192 flint (Ch. 5.7)
Sub-surface: 5115 8 kg.
§130
2GS:170 clay cone fragment (Ch. 5.1; Fig. 302)
2GS:169 stone bowl sherd (Ch. 5.5; Fig. 336)
2GS:183 stone bowl sherd (Ch. 5.5)
2GS:168 perforated stone (Ch. 5.6)
2GS:186 stone pounder (Ch. 5.6)

2G37

The main feature of this square is Room 42, probably in fact an open court. In its eastern angle stands an oven (FI 77/13); the remains of its walls are visible except on the SW, where the entrance probably was, and the internal diameter from NW to SE is 1.80 m. The floor debris associated with this oven spreads out westwards for some 7 m. from the corner of the room, where it gives way to cleaner brown fill (overlying?). Just beyond the limit of the dirty floor deposit is a small hearth made with a semicircle of three or four bricks; it is possibly not complete, and measured externally only some 0.65 m. in diameter (FI 77/14). As already mentioned under 2G27, we are uncertain whether there was a doorway in the NE wall of the room, but the SE wall is preserved unbroken for a stretch of 8 m. before giving way to the brown fill in the W. To its S there is probably yet another open space with an oven: Room 44, which is bounded on the E by the main enclosure wall. The fill of this space was blackish, and it too gives way to browner fill towards the W. Close to the centre of the space is another oven, with a clear wall, measuring internally 1.10 m. from NW to SE (FI 77/15). According to the field notes, there may have been yet another fire installation further south, but unfortunately we have no plan or other record of this one.

Surface: 5124 15 kg.
§§132; 147
2GS:223 stone vessel sherd (Ch. 5.5)
Sub-surface: 5125 12 kg.
§§130; 159
2GS:222 stone pounder fragment (Ch. 5.6)
2GS:225 grindstone fragment (Ch. 5.6)

2G38

Rooms 42 and 44 have already been described under 2G37. In 2G38 the eastern enclosure wall, some 1.40-1.50 m. in width, runs N to abut against the outer corner of Room 42, to meet which it curves slightly westwards in the last 1.50 m. of its course. Although the outer face is slightly broken at this point, there is no question of any opening, as the inner face on the W is continous right up to the other wall.

To the E of this enclosure wall the ground was almost flat, and the soil very homogeneous, details being hard to make out. We have indicated as in 2G29 the rough outline which at times could be discerned of a possible northward extension of the enclosure wall delimiting the W side of Block D. Certainly some sort of soil change was present, and that no bricks could be made out does not necessarily disqualify this line from indicating a wall (see on 2G29).

Surface: 5140 5 kg.
Sub-surface: 5141 1.25 kg.
§§146; 161

2G39

This square is virtually off the edge of the mound, and except for a fragment of a hearth(?) on the W side, and a sandy pit to the N, there are no features recorded. If there were once walls in the square belonging to the buildings in Block D, they were founded above the present surface of the mound, i.e. above 6.00 m. The soil is not however likely to be virgin soil at this level, and we are uncertain whether it consists of an "archaeologically" deposited layer earlier than the walls of Block D, or eroded soil from higher up the mound, which could have been deposited here naturally much later, after those walls and their foundations had already been eroded themselves.

Surface: 5138   3.75 kg.
                §10
Sub-surface: 5139   2 kg.

2G40

Apart from 2G30 this is the only square in which the Sumerian remains appeared to the W of the recent ditch. The ditch itself runs along the E side of the square, and we dug a small sondage (1.00 x 0.50 m.) across its W edge to check its stratigraphic status. This showed the sloping cut made by the ditch-diggers into the deposits to its W, and, clearly distinguished from these deposits, the yellow sandy fill which must have accumulated once the ditch fell into disuse.

At the centre of the square is a stretch of plano-convex brick wall running for some 2.50 m. from SW to NE, and accurately aligned with a wall traced in 2G30. Towards the N this brick is lost, and presumably cut; the soil is "mixed brownish with sherds". At about the place where the wall is broken, there is a small hearth close to its E edge, not separately numbered. We also lost the continuation of this wall to the S, no doubt because of the cluster of modern pits, one of which, crossing the W side of the square, had been reed-lined. In among these pits there were signs of brick, but only towards the S side could we define a good edge. Although we were not aware of it at the time, this edge was almost certainly the S face of the yellow-brick enclosure wall, where it gave way to the southern black-brick wall; its connection with these walls further to the E was of course disrupted by the modern ditch.

Surface: 5008   0.75 kg.
                2GS:18 two grindstone fragments (Ch. 5.6)
                2GS:20 flint (Ch. 5.7)
                2GS:17 copper fragment (Ch. 5.8)
Sub-surface: 5011   10 kg.
                §§96; 99; 103; 114; 115; 132; 148; 159
                2GS:22 copper bead(?) (Ch. 5.8)

2G41

In the NW the clean brown soil continues from the N part of 2G40. This gives way to two large patches of debris including bricks and ash, which may be roughly contemporary with the main ED I phase. There is one small pit in the S, but no traces of walls were noted.

Surface: 5025   4 kg.
Sub-surface: 5028   11.25 kg.
                §§80; 96; 113; 118; 119; 149; 150; 159

2G42

A westward arm of the later overlay seems to project over this square, and so except for the SW corner of the large pit already mentioned under 2G32 there is nothing to record; the soil was described as "brown fill".

Surface: 5042   6 kg.
                §§80; 87; 100; 116
Sub-surface: 5043   12 kg.
                §§92; 95; 109; 111; 119; 125; 127; 130; 143; 148; 149
                2GS:75 flint (Ch. 5.7)

2G43

Most of this square also is taken up with brown fill. There is one small patch of brickwork, to which we could give no real shape, but which is in line with the E wall of Room 20, maybe not accidentally. Otherwise there was only a patch of greenish fill which also extends into 2G44. For the enclosure wall on the S, see under 2G53.

Surface: 5061   4 kg.
                2GS:114 3 clay sickles fused together (see Ch. 5.2)
Sub-surface: 5062   3.5 kg.
                2GS:87 stone bowl sherd (Ch. 5.5; Fig. 327)
                2GS:119 stone bowl sherd (Ch. 5.5; Fig. 330)

2G44

The great majority of this square is occupied by the later overlay, described as noticeably clean, light brown fill. Only in the W do we have a slight intrusion of greenish fill from 2G43, and in the S the northern face of the enclosure wall, described under 2G54. Note there also the mention of black bricks against the N face.

Surface: 5076   14 kg.
                2GS:139 clay sickle fragments (Ch. 5.2; Fig. 306)
                2GS:142 flint (Ch. 5.7)
Sub-surface: 5077   14 kg.
                §159
                2GS:153 conical bowl (not separately recorded)
                2GS:132 two grindstone fragments (Ch. 5.6)
                2GS:133 flint (Ch. 5.7)

2G45

The mound here begins to descend again towards the E, but the overlay obscures all details except in the SW of the square, where the yellow-brick northern enclosure wall could be traced for another 3 m. before succumbing to the later overlying level. This is unfortunate, because it is at precisely this point that it seems to lose its general W-E alignment, and turn sharply northwards. Probably the brick indicated N of the line of the rest of the wall is something different: a third parallel wall, as in 2G44/54 and 2G46, or an abutting wall on a quite different line. The soil of the overlay is described as "soft brown fill, quite clean, mixed with some red and greenish lumps", a type of deposit also noted in 2G53 and so on.

Surface: 5094   12 kg.
                §89
Sub-surface: 5095   9.5 kg.
                2GS:199   grindstone fragment (Ch. 5.6)
                2GS:204   perforated stone (Ch. 5.6)
                2GS:203   flint (Ch. 5.7)
                2GS:122   copper waste (Ch. 5.8)
                2GS:198   bone

2G46

Most of this square was covered in the later overlay; only on the E side does the enclosure wall emerge from beneath it. At this point the yellow-brick northern wall is 1.40 m. in width, but running along its N face is a third wall of two rows of black plano-convex bricks, here laid on edge or herring-bone, making in all another 0.70 m. in width (see Fig. 12). The southern edge of the black-brick, southern enclosure wall is here not defined, but just to the E in 2G47 it was 1.30 m. wide; the bricks in this wall too are laid either on edge or sloping, not flat.

A surprising cluster of things, including large pieces of three stone vessels, was found just N of these walls, as shown on the plan. Indeed, as 2GS:164 was actually found at a spot which should lie within the brickwork of the northernmost black-brick wall, it is likely that it and the other items belonged to a phase when this wall at least was disused and almost or entirely buried. The soil covering the wall, however, was probably not the same as the main later overlay: here as in 2G35 there was probably an intermediate layer which we did not distinguish clearly. A pointer in this direction is that we noted that the three walls here are not simply overlaid by the soil to the west, but also cut, the cut being filled with dirty black soil.

[The E side of this square was excavated in 1981, but as with 2G36 the above description has not been changed materially since it was written in 1980. Mercifully it corresponds well with the results of excavation].

Surface: 5112   11.5 kg.
                2GS:195   flint (Ch. 5.7)
Sub-surface: 5113   20.5 kg.
                2GS:172   conical bowl (Ch. 4.4; see plan for position)
                2GS:162   stone bowl (Ch. 5.5; Fig. 333; see plan)
                2GS:163   stone bowl (Ch. 5.5; Fig. 334; see plan)
                2GS:164   stone funnel (Ch. 5.5; Fig. 335; see plan)
                2GS:171   stone pounder (Ch. 5.6; see plan)
                2GS:191   flint (Ch. 5.7)

2G47

On the W side of the square the three parallel enclosure walls extend for about 1.30 m. before breaking off, probably cut. Against the W edge of this square we made a shallow cut across the walls, to see how they were related to one another stratigraphically. This cut, 1 m. in width, went down only 0.30 m., since we were not engaged in a proper excavation, but to that depth at least each wall continued down side by side with its neighbour, and we concluded that they were in simultaneous use for at least some of the time.

Most of the rest of the square is taken up by clean brown fill. Only in the N have we further remains of walls, here rather hard to interpret. It is impossible to guess whether the N wall of Room 45 is contemporary with either the enclosure wall—which seems quite plausible—or the building to the N. In the angle of the wall in the NW corner of the square was a large jar left in situ (2GS:294).

Surface: 5122   15.5 kg.
                2GS:221   two fragments of stone (not separately listed: one small white, unworked; other bluish stone, one face rubbed smooth, 8.5 x (5.4) x 3.6 cm.)
Sub-surface: 5123   13.5 kg.
                §151
                2GS:294   large jar in situ (Ch. 4.4; see plan for position)
                2GS:226   model boat (Ch. 5.3)
                2GS:241   clay sickle fragment; red fabric; from sounding (Ch. 5.2; Fig. 307)
                2GS:240   stone bowl sherd (Ch. 5.5)
                2GS:229   stone bowl sherd (Ch. 5.5; Fig. 337)
                2GS:238   stone pounder (Ch. 5.6)
                2GS:239   flint (Ch. 5.7)

2G48

This square, together with 2G49 and 58-59, forms perhaps the most complex area we encountered during the clearance operation (see Fig. 5). Not only does it witness the unexpected northward turn of the enclosure wall, proving that these heavy parallel walls belong to the same architectural period as the units to their north, but the close proximity of the W wall of Block D and the E wall of Block C brings with it problems of interpretation rivalled only by the intractability of these same walls further S in 2G58. The double enclosure wall re-emerges at almost exactly the dividing line between squares 2G47 and 2G48; in the 8.50 m. since it was last sighted further W the thin northern black-brick wall has vanished, but perhaps in compensation the yellow-brick wall is 1.90 m. in width. Various explanations could be put forward for this. Constant on the S side is the black-brick wall, but here it is swollen to a width of 2.90 m., perhaps more convincingly to be explained as a corner tower or buttress. As far as we could tell, the E wall of Block A, which runs N into 2G38, is of the same construction as the yellow-brick wall, although only about 1.50 m. in width. Before leaving Block A, it only remains to draw attention to another stone bowl sherd (2GS:248; cf. on 2G47).

Across a passageway only 1.40 m. in width is the W wall of Block D. This may have extended as shown as far N as 2G29, but it was only clearly discernible here and a little way into 2G38. Here it is about 1.60 m. in width, and predominantly of yellowish brick. To its E the soil is mixed blackish occupation debris.

On the S side of the square we have the meeting of three enclosure walls, and the juxtaposition of associated brick features is better shown in the sketch (Fig. 5) than described verbally. Here we will only observe that although it seems very likely that the passageway extended northwards from 2G58 into 2G38, it was blocked by at least one row of bricks; of course, this need have been no more than a temporary sill. To the SW it is possible that another branch of the lane turned westwards along the outside of the double enclosure wall. If so, the entire wall served as the southern boundary of Block A. On the other hand, if instead we see this point as a possible entrance to Block C from its NE corner, then the black-brick wall may have been Block D's northern boundary. Unfortunately, any detail which might have solved these doubts is destroyed by a cut at this point. As for the smaller architectural features we present them as shown on the plan without further comment.

Surface: 5148 4.5 kg.
Sub-surface: 5149 3.5 kg.
   2GS:248 stone bowl sherd (Ch. 5.5; Fig. 339)
Sub-surface: (a second scrape in squares 2G48-49 and 58-59) 5182 unweighed
   §§129; 149
   2GS:289 clay cone (Ch. 5.1; Fig. 298)

2G49

Most of the NE part of this square is beyond the limits of profitable surface clearance (cf. 2G39). Only as the ground rises slightly towards the SE are some details recoverable. Close to the centre of the square is the base of a large jar (almost a pithos), which although broken may have served some secondary purpose as it lay, for it looked very much in situ: perhaps it lined the bottom of a hole (2GS:250, see plan). At the S edge of the square was a small patch of soil burnt red, which marked the base of a hearth or other fire installation (FI 78/11): it was only some 0.80 m. across, with no clear trace of oven walls, and on its E side it was cut by a gully. Finally, on the W there is the clear line of a wall, which delimits the blackish soil lying against the E face of the enclosure wall in 2G48. The E face of the short stretch of wall in 2G49 was not clear enough to plan, but it gives way to more floors with blackish occupation debris; and E of this again, before reaching the pot and hearth, the slope of the ground exposes a reddish layer which probably underlay these floors. We must therefore be very close to the base of the ED I walls at this point, and all other walls have entirely vanished. No doubt this explains the high proportion of bevelled-rim bowl sherds from this square, which has led us to classify it as "Uruk" along with those in 3G.

Surface: 5150 5.25 kg.
Sub-surface: 5151 17 kg.
   2GS:250 base of pithos (see above)
   2GS:249 clay bead (Ch. 5.3)
   2GS:247 stone bowl sherd (Ch. 5.5; Fig. 338; see plan)
   2GS:251 perforated stone (Ch. 5.6)

2G50

Apart from recent pits and the continuation of the ditch, there were few features worthy of comment. In the NE corner there is a stretch of the yellow-brick enclosure wall, but we did not observe the black-brick one to its S, although it may well have been there. If so, it was probably cut by the ash-filled pit which lies on the dividing line between 2G50 and 2G51. On the surface, in the NE and perhaps from the bank of the ditch, came a complete plano-convex brick (22 x 14 x 7.5 cm.).

Surface: 5007 1.5 kg.
   §§118; 120; 147
   2GS:32 flint (Ch. 5.7)
Sub-surface: 5010 8 kg.
   §§90; 100; 111; 116
   2GS:21 copper fragment (Ch. 5.8)

2G51

The double enclosure wall runs across the N side of the square. The yellow-brick wall was here about 1.10 m. in width, and what we could see of the black-brick wall only 0.90 m. wide. N of the yellow-brick wall there was a cut or pit, with many potsherds in it, on the W side, and on the E, overlapping into 2G41, a hearth about 1 m. in diameter (no FI number assigned). E of this hearth we noted the presence of brick, and it is possible that the second, northern, black-brick wall (observed in 2G44 and 46) was here too.

Occupying all the centre of the square, and cutting through the double (or treble) wall, is a large pit filled with a variety of occupational debris ranging from black to yellowish, and mixed with sherds. S of this there is soft brown fill to the W, and harder, light sandy fill on the E side of the square. The great majority of the sherds in this square came from the large pit, and they include more than 300 conical bowl sherds; this pit was probably also the origin of the stone bowl sherds from this square.

Surface: 5026 4.5 kg.
    2GS:47 stone pounder (Ch. 5.6)
Sub-surface: 5027 44.25 kg.
    §§83; 85; 93; 94; 97; 103; 104; 105; 109; 112; 116; 117; 118; 120; 121; 134; 135; 149; 158; 159
    2GS:56 stone bowl sherd (Ch. 5.5; Fig. 323)
    2GS:57 stone bowl sherd (Ch. 5.5; Fig. 324)
    2GS:58 stone bowl sherd (Ch. 5.5)
    2GS:290 stone bowl sherd (Ch. 5.5; Fig. 341)
    2GS:40 grindstone fragment (Ch. 5.6)
    2GS:42 perforated stone (Ch. 5.6)
    2GS:43 bitumen fragments (Ch. 5.8)

2G52

Except for the stub of the yellow-brick enclosure wall which intrudes on the NW corner, this entire square is occupied by brown fill similar to that in 2G42. We do not know if this is lying over the walls, or is the fill of a cut which destroyed them; it could of course be a combination of the two.

It was noted in this square that the yellow-brick wall consists of a row of bricks along each face, with a filling of brick rubble between, not laid so neatly. However, this was not always the case (see 2G54).

Surface: 5041 9.75 kg.
    §114
Sub-surface: 5044 6.25 kg.
    §§83; 132; 144
    2GS:72 two clay sickle fragments (Ch. 5.2; Fig. 308)
    2GS:69 copper pin head (Ch. 5.8)

2G53

In the N, the double enclosure wall reappears, both walls here being about 2 m. in width. S of these is brownish fill, possibly identical with that in 2G52, but towards the S edge of the square this gives way on the surface to a more hard-packed whitish fill with red and green lumps (already mentioned under 2G45). Close to the SE corner of the square we made a small sounding to determine the relationship between these two types of fill, and it was established that the whitish fill runs under the brownish, and may therefore also abut against the S face of the double wall at a lower level.

Surface: 5063 14 kg.
    §§106; 150
    2GS:109 seven clay sickle fragments (cf. Ch. 5.2; Fig. 313)
    2GS:108 flint (Ch. 5.7)
Sub-surface: 5064 1 kg.

2G54

After running eastwards for another 3 m. or so, the double wall takes a perceptible turn towards the N. S of the wall the brownish fill continues, and to its S the whitish fill which lies beneath it (cf. under 2G53). The black-brick wall was at its clearest in this square: on the E side it could be seen to have 8 (or possibly 9) rows of black plano-convex bricks, 22 x 9 cm., laid on their sides and possibly in herring-bone fashion. The combined width of these rows comes to 2.27 m., which includes generous applications of yellow mortar.

In 2G44 our field notes observed that "there seem to be fragments of black brick in yellow mortar reminiscent of" the southern enclosure wall, against the N face of the yellow-brick wall. Since at this stage we had not yet cleared 2G46 or 47, where the third brick wall was plainly distinguishable, it is obvious that although we did not plan any of the bricks observed this same third wall was present here too.

Surface: 5078 12 kg.
    2GS:131 three sickle fragments (Ch. 5.2; Fig. 309)
Sub-surface: 5079 5 kg.
    2GS:149 stone bowl sherd (Ch. 5.5)
    2GS:135 stone pounder fragment (Ch. 5.6)
    2GS:151 flint (Ch. 5.7)

2G55

Although the yellow-brick wall could be followed a little further to the E in 2G45, here there was no sign of the black-brick wall, presumably obscured by later overlay. In fact, further W as well we had to scrape deeper to recover the line of the black-brick wall than for the yellow-brick wall. The brown soil which occupies the N half of the square looks to be continuous with that in 2G54, and there is the same transition to a harder whitish soil with red and greenish lumps as we saw already further W.

Surface: 5092 11 kg.
    §83
Sub-surface: 5093 14 kg.
    §§127; 138; 140; 141; 146
    2GS:152 flint (Ch. 5.7)

2G56

No features of any sort were recorded in this square, save for the parallel humps which have been finally diagnosed as wheel tracks (see under 2G24). The distinction noted in 2G53-55 between clean brown fill to the N and the whitish fill to its S was not recorded here, although this does not necessarily mean it was absent.

Surface: 5110   12.5 kg.
                2GS:182   stone pounder (Ch. 5.6)
                2GS:176   fragment of coarse flint with cortex
Sub-surface: 5111   11 kg.

2G57

The mound here begins to slope off towards the E, but the surface still shows nothing but apparently homogeneous fill constituting the later overlay.

Surface: 5156   1.75 kg.
                2GS:259   flint (Ch. 5.7)
Sub-surface: 5157   0.5 kg.

2G58

Like 2G48 to the N, this square was exceedingly complex, and we had to return to it several times before we thought we had extracted most of the "scrapable" information. The broad lines are clear: down the W side of the square runs the eastern enclosure wall of Block C, which is here built of two lines of brick, the western in yellow brick and 1.20-1.30 m. wide, the eastern in black and yellow bricks and only 0.90 m. wide. This wall comes to an uncertain end at the N, but a solid wall was found taking off it to the W, about 0.90 m. wide; it disappears below the fill in 2G57. At the S side of the square the double eastern enclosure wall is also lost, as it too is shrouded by the later fill in 2G68.

Beyond the wall of Block C there was certainly a passage filled with occupation debris, but there is first a line of much cleaner soil, and we could not decide if this was a third component of the same wall, or simply an accident, such as a lump of fallen masonry. On the other side of the corridor is the western enclosure wall of Block D. This too was a complex feature, and some of our uncertainty will be obvious in Fig. 5, where the wall-lines are shown stopping and starting in a way which suggests that we have to do with various phases of reconstruction, perhaps combined with a practice of building two relatively narrow brick walls and filling the space between with rubble to make a solid enclosure wall. This wall also disappears below later fill at its S end, but its nature as an enclosure wall is evident both from its thickness and from its length—at least 28 m., and more than 40 m. if one includes the doubtful stretch in 2G38 and 29.

Surface: 5152   14.25 kg.
Sub-surface: 5153   3.5 kg.
Sub-surface: (second scrape)   5183   unweighed
[For 5182 see under 2G48]

2G59

As a result of the slope of the mound virtually no features survive in this square except for part of the western enclosure wall of Block D and the floor of a large oven backing on to its E face (Fl 78/16). The floor of this oven was easily discerned, being burnt to a brick-red, and it measures internally almost exactly 2 m. in diameter. Traces of the walls of the oven and of patches of associated burning were also visible, but nothing that could be satisfactorily planned. As with 2G49, it is clear that this feature belongs with the ED I occupation of the space delimited by the enclosure wall, but all the associated walls and other features are now lost to erosion.

Surface: 5154   22 kg.
Sub-surface: 5155   20.25 kg.
                2GS:256   pebble; not listed separately
                2GS:262   fragment of flint; not listed separately

2G60

Beyond the limits of profitable surface clearance. Some recent pits, and the line of the recent canal are the only features recorded. If the ashy patch at the N really overlapped the eastern edge of the canal then it too must be recent, but the canal's edge was not clear at this point.

Surface: No pottery or other artefacts recovered
Sub-surface: 5006   3.75 kg.
                §132
                2GS:33   grindstone fragment (Ch. 5.6)
                2GS:16   glass sherd (Ch. 5.8)
                2GS:9, 10, 13   shells (Ch. 5.8)

2G61

Still in a very flat, barren, part of the mound, with only a couple of very small pits to relieve the monotony. In the SE corner the soil gives way to a hard, crusty white soil which is also present on the S side of 2G62.

Surface: 5021   5.25 kg.
                §91
                2GS:15   animal figurine (Ch. 5.3; Fig. 314)
                2GS:52   flint (Ch. 5.7)
Sub-surface: 5023   3.5 kg.
                §§109; 121
                2GS:54   stone bowl sherd (Ch. 5.5; Fig. 322)

2G62

Except for the distinction already noted under 2G61 between brown mixed fill in the N and white crusty soil further S, no features were recorded here. It should be pointed out that this transition from one sort of fill to another is reminiscent of the situation in 2G53-55, and it is not inconceivable that the one is a continuation of the other. In that case, we should have been unlikely to notice it because at this stage we were clearing the mound in long N-S strips, one row of 10 m. squares at a time, so that the transition, if it was indeed continuous, would have run along the edge of our clearance up the E side of 2G62.

Note that in this square, as in others to the E, there was much more surface than sub-surface pottery recovered.

Surface: 5037   10.5 kg.
            §§86; 91; 121; 140; 149; 160
            2GS:80   clay sickle fragments (cf. Ch. 5.2; Fig. 313)
            2GS:82   clay ring (Ch. 5.3)
            2GS:83   flints (Ch. 5.7)
Sub-surface: 5039   3.75 kg.
            §§86; 98; 118

2G63

Entire square occupied by homogeneous clean whitish fill, mixed with red and greenish lumps, a continuation of the S side of 2G53. For the relationship to the soil further W, see under 2G62.

Surface: 5065   12.75 kg.
            §84
            2GS:116   flint (Ch. 5.7)
Sub-surface: 5066   6.75 kg.

2G64

Entire square occupied by the clean whitish fill observed in 2G63, with red and green lumps. No features.

Surface: 5071   23.50 kg.
            2GS:115, 117   fifteen clay sickle fragments (Ch. 5.2; Figs. 310; 313)
            2GS:120   flints (Ch. 5.7)
Sub-surface: 5072   8.5 kg.
            §146

2G65

In the SE part of this square the clean whitish fill with red and green lumps gives way to a clean brown area. No features.

Surface: 5090   17 kg.
            §§131; 147; 149
            2GS:148   two grindstone fragments (Ch. 5.6)
Sub-surface: 5091 10 kg.
            2GS:134   fragment of clay axe-head (Ch. 5.3)

2G66

The soil in this square was described as "homogeneous clean brown fill, occasional green and red lumps". No mention is made of a distinction between two types of fill such as we observed in 2G65, but possibly weather conditions made it less easy to see here. The colour ("brown") suggests the material in the SE of 2G65, but the mention of red and green lumps is reminiscent of the whitish fill, so possibly both were indeed present. No features.

Surface: 5108   22 kg.
            2GS:211   unworked piece of stone; not separately listed
Sub-surface: 5109   13.5 kg.
            §84
            2GS:210   two clay sickle fragments (Ch. 5.2; Fig. 311)
            2GS:205   clay spool (Ch. 5.3)
            2GS:158   stone vessel sherd (Ch. 5.5; Fig. 331)
            2GS:159   stone vessel sherd (Ch. 5.5; Fig. 332)
            2GS:209   stone smoother fragment (Ch. 5.6)

2G67

The greater part of the square is still taken up by featureless fill, which cannot be certainly identified with the deposits to N or W. Visible in the SE corner is part of a wall running almost due S for about 11 m. into 2G77. Unfortunately it cannot be associated with any other features, and we can only say of it that it is presumably "late"—i.e. ED I or later.

Surface: 5158   6.25 kg.
Sub-surface: 5159   3.5 kg.
            2GS:266   lump of white-veined stone, no worked surfaces; not separately listed

2G68

Although the mound here begins to drop more sharply towards the productive ED I levels, there are still no features within this square. However, the stratigraphic status of some of the fill is clear: in the N side of 2G68 there is a band of hard, dark soil which directly overlies the bricks of the two N-S enclosure walls (and extends into the S of 2G58). On the

E side of the square there was a clear distinction between this fill and another still darker soil, which overlies the continuation of the W wall of Block D and obscures its southward extension. This soil is therefore presumably later still. However, we were unable to trace any consistent distinction between these two types of fill for any distance westwards.

Surface: 5162   7.25 kg.
              2GS:267   grindstone fragment (11.4 x 9.1 x 4.5; not separately listed)
Sub-surface: 5163   15.75 kg.
              §161
              2GS:271   grindstone (Ch. 5.6)
              2GS:272   perforated stone (Ch. 5.6)

2G69

Lying on the N side of the southern peak of the mound, this square slopes somewhat towards the N and NW, with also a slight slope away to the E. Only in the N and W were there recognizable features, principally the continuation of the complex W wall of Block D; for the detail of this, see above, Fig. 5. About 2 m. further E was another stretch of brickwork, presumably a wall, but unconnected with any other architectural features. It probably belonged with the buildings within Block D, but more than that it is not possible to hazard.

Surface: 5166   7.5 kg.
Sub-surface: 5167   10 kg.
              §123
              2GS:268   grindstone fragment; not separately listed (10.2 x 7.4 x 4.3 cm.; white stone)
              2GS:278   piece of worked black stone; not separately listed (H. 6.4; Di. of base ca. 9 cm.; circular end and possibly deliberately faceted sides)

2G70

Only a few small recent pits, and a small ashy patch in the N. Even the line of the modern ditch was not visible here, although it does reappear further S.

Surface: 5002   0.75 kg.
              2GS:25   stone smoother fragment (Ch. 5.6)
              2GS:5   flint (Ch. 5.7)
Sub-surface: 5005   7.25 kg.
              §§91; 112; 118; 121; 122; 141; 146; 159
              2GS:12   clay sickle fragment (Ch. 5.2; Fig. 312)
              2GS:8   grindstone fragment (Ch. 5.6)
              2GS:14   flint (Ch. 5.7)
              2GS:11   copper fragments (Ch. 5.8)
              2GS:9, 13   shells (Ch. 5.8)

2G71

Apart from several recent, sand-filled pits, some with reed linings, the only feature requiring comment is the transition from normal brown fill in the W of the square to the crusty white soil already mentioned in the S of 2G61 and 62.

Surface: 5022   5.5 kg.
Sub-surface: 5024   8.75 kg.
              §§85; 109; 116
              2GS:39   grindstone fragment (Ch. 5.6)

2G72

Most of the square is taken up by hard whitish fill (cf. under 2G73), but in the S there is a patch of brown fill which may be intrusive.

Surface: 5038   6.5 kg.
              §§86; 104; 111; 118; 146
Sub-surface: 5040   3 kg.
              §§116; 136; 161

2G73

No features recorded in this square. The soil was again hard, whitish material with green and reddish lumps, and it was noted in this case that this is indeed the same fill as found further N and E, into the S half of 2G53-55, and further W (including 2G61, 62 and 71). Note again, as already observed under 2G62, that there were more surface sherds than "sub-surface". These indications all support the theory that this area of the mound is composed at the surface by deliberate fill below an eroded building level.

Surface: 5068   11 kg.
              §127
Sub-surface: 5069   2.5 kg.
              §148

2G74

Entire square occupied by the whitish fill with red and green lumps (cf. under 2G73).

Surface: 5073   14.25 kg.
Sub surface: 5074   2.25 kg.

2G75

The whitish fill here gives way to an area of brown soil, shared with 2G65. We have no information about stratigraphic relationship.

Surface: 5088   11 kg.
                  §146
Sub-surface: 5089   2 kg.
                  §127
                  2GS:136   flint (Ch. 5.7)

2G76

Soil described as clean brown fill, and presumably identical with that in the E side of 2G75. There is a small patch of burnt soil in the NE corner of the square.

Surface: 5106   13.5 kg.
                  §154
                  2GS:196   perforated stone (Ch. 5.6)
Sub-surface: 5107   ca. 10 kg. (weight estimated only)
                  2GS:293   grey ware jar (see Ch. 4.4; the rest of the sub-surface pottery was accidentally bagged with this jar and hence not weighed while scales were present)
                  2GS:292   stone pounder (Ch. 5.6)

2G77

No features save for the S end of the stretch of wall mentioned above under 2G67.

Surface: 5160   8 kg.
                  §128
Sub-surface: 5161   2 kg.
                  2GS:273   animal figurine fragment (Ch. 5.3)
                  2GS:261   fragment of black stone; not separately listed

2G78

No features recorded in this square.

Surface: 5164   14.5 kg.
Sub-surface: 5163   3 kg.

2G79

This square is divided into the featureless fill of its N half, which it shares with the squares to N and W, and the looser soil in its S part, which belongs with the large pit described under 2G89.

Surface: 5168   11.5 kg.
                  2GS:263   stone bowl sherd (Ch. 3.5; Fig. 340)
                  2GS:274   flint (Ch. 5.7)
Sub-surface: 5169   5.75 kg.

2G80

Apart from numerous recent pits, mostly with remnants of reed linings, there were no features. Towards the NE a small rectangular cut was made to check the stratigraphy, and this showed bands of yellow sandy soil sloping steeply from E down to the W. These are probably from the E bank of the ditch, which was otherwise not observed here, perhaps being obscured by a great depth of washed soil from further up the mound.

Surface: 5001   3 kg.
                  §86
                  2GS:2   stone vessel fragment (Ch. 5.5; Fig. 321)
                  2GS:3   copper fragments (Ch. 5.8)
Sub-surface: 5004   9 kg.
                  §§106; 115
                  2GS:7   stone pounder fragment (Ch. 5.6)
Sub-surface (cut in NE):   5012   3.5 kg.

2G81-86

These squares were not cleared. Note only the following object picked up from the surface of 2G85, at the point marked on the plan:

                  2GS:190   inscribed potsherd (Ch. 4.4)

2G87

No features of interest were noted in this square, save for a large patch of burnt soil, though not so intensely burnt that it could be considered a hearth or other form of fire installation (4.20 x 4.40 m.).

Surface: 5176   5 kg.
Sub-surface: 5177   0.5 kg.

2G88

This square lies on the SW flank of the S peak of the mound; once again we were unable to detect any features.

Surface: 5174   14.5 kg.
                     §§83; 147; 150
                     2GS:269   chipped stone blade (not flint); not separately listed
Sub-surface: 5175   2 kg.
                     2GS:268   stone grinder fragment; white stone (10.2 x 7.4 x 4.3 cm.; not separately listed)

2G89

Although once more there were no architectural features in this square, nor any clue as to what causes the mound to rise here to its southern peak, one feature was conspicuous, and indeed occupied virtually the entire square: this was a huge pit with relatively loose sandy fill and a quantity of potsherds in it. The E edge of the pit overlaps into 3G, and could be followed N into 2G79, but unfortunately its limit to the W was not clear to us, nor in the S, where it was certainly eroded away. It is this pit which is responsible for the concentration of solid-footed goblets in these squares, strangely placed almost at the centre of the greatest concentration of bevelled-rim bowl sherds. The pit is helpful for our dating of the mound as a whole: its date must be assumed to fall within ED I, to judge from the solid-footed goblets, but it cuts into layers of fill which lie above the walls of Blocks C and D (in 2G68), and these walls are securely dated themselves to the ED I period, by way of their links with Block A. We have therefore at least three building phases in ED I, all within the lifetime of the solid-footed goblet.

Surface: 5170   18.75 kg.
Sub-surface: 5171   9.5 kg.
                     §156
                     2GS:288   rim of pottery jar found entire in situ; Di. at rim 13.3 cm., but H. extant only 5 cm.;
                            not separately listed
                     2GS:257 and 276   flints (Ch. 5.7)
                     2GS:277   animal bones (Ch. 5.8)
                     2GS:260   shell (Ch. 5.8)

2G90

A large number of small pits filled with sandy soil and often showing remains of reeds comprise the features in this square. A soil change was also noted close to the W edge, and with regard to the line of the recent ditch in the squares to the N, this was probably one edge of it. The same double line was indeed observed on the uncleared surface further to the S, in 2F, so that it may reasonably be expected to re-emerge at this point. A small test hole was dug in the NE of the square to a depth of only some 10 cm., without appreciable results.

Surface: 5000   2.75 kg.
Sub-surface: 5003   6.5 kg.
                     §87
                     2GS:6   flint (Ch. 5.7)
Cut in NE corner: 5009   unweighed
                     §§97; 119; 149

2G91-96

These squares were not cleared.

2G97

This square lies on the gently sloping SW side of the southern peak. Note the large amount of pottery from the surface, a situation matched in the 3G squares.

Surface: 5178   31.25 kg.
                     §§86; 151
                     2GS:284   incised sherd (Ch. 4.4)
                     2GS:282   unworked piece of reddish stone; not separately listed
                     2GS:283   unworked piece of blackish stone; not separately listed
Sub-surface: 5179   8 kg.
                     §§83; 88; 161

2G98

No features recorded. In a patch of ashy soil in the NE corner of the square were found side-by-side two miniature jars (see below). The heavy concentration of surface sherds continues here from 2G97.

Surface: 5180   22 kg.
                     §§127; 147; 148; 160
                     2GS:286   three small unworked fragments of stone; not separately listed
Sub-surface: 5181   4.75 kg.
                     2GS:281   miniature pottery jar (Ch. 4.4)
                     2GS:280   miniature stone jar (Ch. 5.5; Fig. 293)
                     2GS:287   fragment of animal figurine (Ch. 5.3)
                     2GS:279   flints (Ch. 5.7)

2G99

A sharply sloping gully runs through this square from the high point in 2G89, exposing different layers. On the W side is an area of blackish debris which would normally be attributed to a courtyard floor. Where this is cut into by the gully, it can be seen to lie above a much cleaner, clayey layer, which constitutes a deliberately laid floor for an earlier building phase levelled off. As can be seen from the contours, the appearance of recognizable architectural features at this height (that is, ca. +6.50) is paralleled in the 3G squares. Towards the E of the square we enter the lower end of the big ED I pit mentioned under 2G89, although its lower edge was hard to define precisely.

Surface: 5172 11 kg.
Sub-surface: 5173 19 kg.
§54

3G50

The majority of the square consists of clean brown fill, with a large patch of ashy soil—not a hearth—in the SW corner. Just to the N of this, a stretch of wall with a clear N face but its S face uncertain, and running parallel to it, a longer stretch of some 8 m. of wall, 0.60 m. wide. The resulting corridor, 1.50 m. in width, is filled with dirtier occupation debris than the rest of the square.

Surface: 5916 24.75 kg.
§§2; 13; 17; 24; 27; 35; 38; 39; 42; 48; 49; 51; 56; 70
Sub-surface: 5917 7 kg.
§76

3G51

In the W half of this square the brown fill of 3G50 continues, giving way in the eastern half to a blacker ashy deposit. In the S this change was associated with a clear wall running NW-SE, although its W face was hard to detect by comparison with the brown fill. At a distance of 4.40 m. further E there was a second clear colour change, where the black ashy soil is interrupted by a strip of brown soil some 0.70 m. in width, which runs for at least 11 m. into 3G62. Given the alignment of this strip only one interpretation seems plausible: that it represents the line of a wall. Although no bricks could be distinguished, it was established that the brown strip rests in fact in a shallow depression, a few centimetres in depth, in the black ashy soil which continues beneath it unbroken. What this must be, therefore, is the very base of a wall, and the depression must be either a deliberate foundation trench, or caused by the sinking of the soil under the weight of the wall. The surviving top of the strip where it crosses into 3G52 was at +5.97, and it may therefore quite reasonably be associated with the wall further W, which stands as high as +6.29 m.

Surface: 5918 31 kg.
§§13; 27; 31; 35; 45; 51; 58; 68
Sub-surface: 5919 1 kg.
§§66; 78
3GS:34 stone pounder (Ch. 5.6)
3GS:35 stone grinder (Ch. 5.6)

3G52

As described under 3G51, the black soil continues beneath the wall line in the W of 3G52 and more than halfway across the square. It gives out, presumably because of the slope of the mound, about 3 m. from the E edge of the area cleared by us, and at just this point, lying at +5.62 m., is a clear wall composed of rectangular bricks measuring 40 x 19 cm. To the N this wall is probably obscured by the continuation of the black soil from the W. It was thought likely that this wall is connected with an ill-defined area of rectangular brickwork seen in the NW corner of 3G73, but since we did not clear 3G63 this remains only a speculation. It is interesting that although we are already as low as +5.50 m. here, the surface traces are as clear as anywhere on the mound, whereas in other parts the traces below about +6.00 can be very meagre.

Surface: 5928 10 kg.
§§3; 7; 35; 68
3GS:30 flint (Ch. 5.7)
Sub-surface: 5929 unweighed (but 3 sherds retained:)
§§28; 51; 65; 71

3G60

Most of this square has the relatively clean brown fill mentioned already under 3G50 and 51. In the NW corner is part of an ashy patch shared with 3G50, and near to it the base of an oval kiln measuring 2.00 x 1.40 m.; this showed signs of firing at high temperatures, including vitrified wasters (FI 78/7). [This kiln was excavated in 1981.]

Surface: 5908 9.5 kg.
§§18; 19; 68
Sub-surface: 5909 7.75 kg.
§§6; 7; 17; 36; 45; 51; 60; 69; 72; 78
3GS:42 flint (Ch. 5.7)

3G61

Like 3G60, almost certainly occupied by brown fill, with the exception of the NE corner, where there was a change to the black ashy soil of 3G52. We could not see any sign of the wall which presumably ran through the square at this point from 3G51. If we were already below its foundation, one must assume that the fragment of wall in 3G62 is of a different phase, since the ground here is lower still. Close to the W side of 3G61 is a second oval kiln (FI 78/8), measuring some 2.30 x 1.50 m., and including in its filling many vitrified wasters (cf. FI 78/7 in 3G60). [This kiln too was excavated in 1981, and the vitrified potsherds from it all seemed to be of Uruk date, adding to the uncertainty about the dating of the surface levels in this square.]

Surface: 5910 26 kg.
§§2; 13; 17; 37; 42; 51; 59; 70; 72; 78
3GS:33 flints (Ch. 5.7)
Sub-surface: 5911 5.75 kg.
§§37; 45; 64; 68; 70
3GS:40 stone smoother (Ch. 5.6)
3GS:39 flint (Ch. 5.7)

3G62

In the NW the black soil continues from 3G52, and with it the shallow trench which we attribute to an eroded wall; it looks as though we may have here a corner, the wall turning to the E. In the E side of the square the browner soil runs up to the face of a wall already recorded in 3G52, and built of rectangular bricks. However, the fragment of walls in the SW corner did not seem to be of the same brick, and aligns rather suggestively with the wall in 3G51. No clear divisions were observed in the brown fill, either here or in 3G61, and the stratigraphic relationship of these various fragments of wall can only be settled by excavation.

Surface: 5920 15.25 kg.
§§3; 7; 12; 13; 33; 46; 59; 64; 67; 69; 70; 74
Sub-surface: 5921 6 kg.
§§13; 19; 21; 23; 36; 37; 38; 46; 51; 64; 72
3GS:46 two pieces of white stone, probably from a stone pounder; not separately listed

3G70

Most of this square was taken up by brown fill with the occasional brick. In the extreme SE corner is a wall from the structure principally lying in 3G81, q.v., and after removal of some 0.10 m. of brown fill an alignment of four bricks quite probably in situ emerged closer to the centre of the square. Also underlying the brown fill was the dog-leg wall on the N side of the square; this may have been contemporary with the walls in 3G81, and like them it is obscured on the W by overlying fill. While it could, to judge from its height, also belong with the walls in 3G50, which we incline to attribute to the ED I Block D, we must note that the surface of 3G70 was one of those very thickly strewn with Uruk pottery, which must have derived from the fill overlying or lying against these walls. In the N of 3G70 the type of brick was not identified; if it is an ED I wall, we should probably assume that it is a foundation placed in a trench.

Surface: 5912 39.75 kg.
§§9; 16; 26; 32; 33; 37; 38; 42; 51; 56; 63; 64; 67; 68; 69; 71
3GS:23 and 25 flints (Ch. 5.7)
Sub-surface: 5913 13.75 kg.
§§3; 4; 7; 12; 15; 23; 24; 27; 41; 42; 43; 44; 45; 46; 51; 53; 56; 62; 63; 68; 69; 70; 71; 72
3GS:29 jar base (Ch. 4.4)
3GS:28 stone cube (Ch. 5.6)

3G71

The brown fill on the E side of 3G70 continues into this square. For the features in the SW corner see under 3G81. There is still a relatively heavy concentration of sherds in the surface batch (as opposed to the sub-surface), and one is led to imagine that the fill on the surface is of Uruk date.

Surface: 5914 20.5 kg.
§§35; 37; 45; 47; 70
3GS:43 stone pounder (Ch. 5.6)
3GS:27 unworked lump of metalliferous stone (?); not separately listed
Sub-surface: 5915 3.5 kg.
§§9; 12; 13; 17; 38; 42; 45; 51; 55; 56; 58; 66; 68; 69; 71
3GS:36 red-painted jar (Ch. 4.4)
3GS:37 stone grinder fragment (Ch. 5.6)

3G72

In the brown fill on the W side is a circular hearth (Fl 78/9), otherwise the fill continues up to the walls as planned. Clearly these walls are either broken or incompletely recovered, but the alignment strongly suggests that they belong with the wall fragments in 3G62, and this is the more plausible because a small gully breaks the surface at the N side of 3G72, accounting for the discontinuity of the wall line.

Surface: 5922 25 kg.
§§25; 39; 51; 52
3GS:32 stone pounder(?) (Ch. 5.6)
3GS:31 flints (Ch. 5.7)
Sub-surface: 5923 3 kg.
§§12; 13; 36; 37; 59; 69

3G73

The continuation of the wall from 3G72 was marked only by rather ill-defined lines, and is doubtful. In the N of the square there is an area of rectangular bricks as shown; these are possibly to be associated with the bricks at the E side of 3G52 and 62, but heavy rain prevented us from recovering their exact limits or alignment. It is worth noting that while a level on the 3G52 bricks gave +5.62 m., the height at the NW corner of 3G73 was +5.81, an acceptable discrepancy for walls of the same phase. We observed no sign of the change in stratum which must be assumed between these rectangular bricks and the walls further S in 3G72 and 3G73.

Surface: 5930 [not recorded]
Sub-surface: 5931 [not recorded]

3G80

The only feature in this square is a small stretch of wall towards the SE corner, the bricks of which, to judge from their irregular laying, must have been plano-convex. Otherwise the soil was described as "greenish pottery-filled rubble"; however, the W side of the square was cut by the late pit, which no doubt accounts for most of the solid-footed goblets in this square, which had a heavy cover of predominantly Uruk sherds.

Surface: 5904 34.5 kg.
§§3; 8; 14; 57; 75; 77
3GS:15 grindstone fragments (Ch. 5.6)
3GS:14 flints (Ch. 5.7)
Sub-surface: 5905 26.25 kg.
§§14; 15; 16; 17; 19; 29; 32; 33; 37; 39; 40; 43; 44; 45; 47; 50; 51; 54; 56; 57; 64; 66; 68; 71; 75; 78
3GS:16 stone counter(?); roughly hemispherical piece of fine-grained grey-black stone, smooth flat base and many rubbed facets on upper side, part of which is broken (Di. 2.2; H. 1.3 cm.; not separately listed)
3GS:10 flint (Ch. 5.7)

3G81

In the NW corner, extending into 3G70 and 71, was a clear but rather complex area of brickwork, standing out unusually well as yellow brick against red and ashy fill. Within a room enclosed by these walls was a hearth or perhaps an oven of 1.40 m. diameter (Fl 78/10). The wall face on the W side was obscured by the rubbly soil sloping down from the summit of the mound, and would be in 3G80. In the SW corner of the square is a stretch of wall running roughly NW-SE and clearly built of plano-convex bricks, measuring 0.15 x 0.08 m. in cross-section and so probably laid on end here. This stretch of wall very likely belongs to the same structure as the fragment in the SE of 3G80. Just to the E, as marked on the plan, we found the bases of two pottery vessels in situ; also from the SW corner, and probably from the same room, came three stone vessels. This suggests that at this point we are in fact at the level of a floor on which these items were resting. Since the walls to N and to S are not well aligned, it is possible that they belong to other phases.

[The above stands as written in 1980; in 1981 we excavated in 3G81 in order to recover a sample of Uruk pottery. The E wall of the room in which the stone vessels etc. were found was located, and it was confirmed that the bricks are at the very base of the walls, only a single course surviving. The walls in the N are earlier, of Uruk date.]

Surface: 5906 28 kg.
§§8; 14; 16; 27; 30; 36; 37; 44; 47; 56; 72; 73; 75
Sub-surface: 5907 5.25 kg.
§§65; 69
3GS:1 (=3G81:248) pottery (Ch. 4.4)
3GS:2 (=3G81:247) pottery (Ch. 4.4)
3GS:22 sherd counters (Ch. 5.3)
3GS:17 stone jar (Ch. 5.5)
3GS:18 stone bowl (Ch. 5.5; Fig. 342)
3GS:19 bituminous stone bowl (Ch. 5.5; Fig. 343)
3GS:2 shell (Ch. 5.8)

3G82

Except for the walls on the E side, which are discussed under 3G83, and the large quantity of surface sherds, there was nothing remarkable about this square.

Surface: 5924 43.5 kg.
§§4; 5; 11; 14; 23; 27; 36; 37; 49; 66; 67; 69; 71
Sub-surface: 5925 6 kg.
§§1; 5; 19; 27; 36; 38; 39; 44; 65; 69; 73

3G83

Shared with 3G82 is a curious brick feature with a straight wall running E-W, off whose N face is built a semicircular feature of about 3.30 m. diameter. Although the W side is lost, the junction of the two at the E was clear, and within the semicircle the soil was noticeably dirtier. Further to the SE is another small fragment of wall also aligned due E-W, and the same is true of the walls in the SE corner, suggesting that these may all be of one phase. It was noticed that the bricks in the SE corner lie directly above an area of rectangular bricks similar to those in 3G52 (not shown on plan as heavy rain prevented accurate recording). Note finally that we are here beyond the very heavy cover of surface sherds.

Surface: 5932 10 kg.
§§2; 7; 33; 37; 67; 74
3GS:47 large clay cone (Ch. 5.1; Fig. 297)
Sub-surface: 5933 [not recorded]

3G90

This square slopes relatively steeply down to the S, and its NW corner is cut by the ED I pit. Otherwise there is nothing to say about it, except to point out that it was this square from which a selective surface collection of sherds was taken in 1976, so that the surface sherd weight recorded in 1978 is doubtless somewhat lower than it should have been. Also in this preliminary collection were three clay cone fragments and some pieces of clay sickle: these have not been incorporated with the 1978 figures used for the distribution maps.

Surface: 5900 20.25 kg. (but see above!)
§§4; 8; 14; 31; 32; 34; 37; 42; 47; 54; 58; 66; 78
Sub-surface: 5901 8.75 kg.
§§31; 36; 38; 47; 50; 53; 54; 70; 78
3GS:4 clay cone (Ch. 5.1; Fig. 301)
3GS:6 flints (Ch. 5.7)
3GS:5 shell (Ch. 5.8)

3G91

No features recorded.
Surface: 5902 23.75 kg.
§§47; 51; 70
Sub-surface: 5903 3 kg.
§§43; 66
3GS:7 shell (Ch. 5.8)

3G92

No features recorded.
Surface: 5926 13.25 kg.
§§1; 12; 13; 36; 44; 51; 56; 64; 74; 78
Sub-surface: 5927 8 kg.
§§6; 13; 49; 61
3GS:24 two clay cone fragments (see Ch. 5.1; Fig. 299)

3G93

In the W, the fill with many surface sherds probably continued, but with the drop in the ground some features are exposed on the E side. In the NE corner is the small fragment of architecture continuing from 3G83, which seems to lie as described under 3G83 on top of earlier rectangular brickwork. On the N side of the square is a small lump of brickwork which resembled that in 3G83 close by, and probably belongs with it. Finally, there was a rather dubious line of bricks towards the SE corner which is worth mentioning only because it too is on an E-W alignment.

Surface: 5934 12 kg.
§§13; 60
Sub-surface: 5935 4 kg.
§§2; 55; 58; 66; 71
3GS:44 stone bowl sherd (Ch. 5.5; Fig. 344)

Chapter 4

THE POTTERY

4.1 *Note on the presentation of the pottery*

Most of the pottery report was written by Ellen McAdam after studying the sherd material on site in 1979. Her work inevitably does not take into account sherd material discarded during the seasons of 1977 and 1978, nor did she have the opportunity of studying the larger items which were numbered and taken to the Iraq Museum. The whole vessels and other similar items are therefore listed, according to their 2G or 3G numbers, on pp. 82-6 in catalogue form. The discarded material consisted of the non-diagnostic body sherds, most of the "mass-produced types", and the occasional large pieces whose size was disproportionate to their interest, and most of which came from the rims and walls of very large bowls (over 1 m. in diameter). The evidence of the mass-produced types is discussed on pp. 44-52, and is taken from the notes made when the pottery was originally washed, weighed, and sorted.

Since virtually none of this pottery has a stratigraphically pure provenance, the reader might well be excused for wondering whether it justifies such an extended treatment. As explained in Chapter 1 already, we believe that it does for two reasons: in the first place the distribution of the mass-produced types, when recorded quantitatively, offers an interesting opportunity to check some of the underlying assumptions of surface collection, while in second place the remaining sherds effectively present us with a varied corpus of Uruk and ED I pottery as represented at Abu Salabikh. Of course it is true that we have an exact provenance only for a few whole vessels, but the accumulated evidence from the entire surface demonstrates that the very great majority of the surface and sub-surface material belongs to these periods. Furthermore, it is certain that the Uruk pottery is concentrated at the south-east corner of the area cleared. Consequently the sherds from 3G squares are considered by Mrs. McAdam in the "Uruk" part of her sherd report, while her "Early Dynastic" section is based primarily on the material from the western squares of 2G. It was clear even after a first swift look at the material that distinctions would emerge between the two periods, but it will be as well to warn once again that the occurrence of a sherd in our "Uruk" or "Early Dynastic" squares is not any sort of proof of its date—as can be seen by considering the distribution chart for bevelled-rim bowls (Figs. 22-3). It will be clear that the sherds used by us to define the general date of areas of the mound are virtually only the mass-produced types, and so that the less frequent types with which the main body of the pottery report is concerned are "dated" by reference to their association with bevelled-rim bowls, solid-footed goblets, etc.

An indication of the quantity of sherds recovered from each square is given in the previous chapter by the sherd weights, as recorded before the discard of any body sherds or of the mass-produced types. Since the sherd material is treated only as two main groups, we have not discussed in detail the pottery coming from each square, although cross-references to individual sherds referred to here are included in the previous chapter. Since they are selected as characteristic of one group or the other, their specific provenance is not of great significance, but nevertheless the square from which each sherd came is mentioned; it may prove of interest in the case of unusual pieces, especially when it is possible that the square may be excavated one day. We should add that in a few cases the conditions at Abu Salabikh had the better of us, in that over a period of 12 months or less the salts broke up the surface of the sherds and with it the batch number marked on them, making it totally or partially illegible.

4.2 *The mass-produced types and their distribution* (J. N. Postgate)

To introduce this section we can hardly do better than quote verbatim the words of H. J. Nissen, discussing the "Early Mass-produced Pottery Types": "Sherds of these wares were the primary basis for our distinction of the periods from Late Uruk through Early Dynastic I, and hence deserve a special discussion. They belong to three main types of open bowls, which can be well separated from each other chronologically. On a number of sites they make up 50% or more of the total sherd collection, providing an opportunity to date these sites from the sherds of the mass-produced types only. From what we know, the "beveled-rim bowls" are confined to the Uruk period and give way abruptly to the "conical cups" at the beginning of Jemdet

Nasr; the latter remain in mass use through Early Dynastic II. The tallest variant form of these conical cups, the "solid-footed goblet", makes its appearance at the beginning of Early Dynastic I and becomes the hallmark of that period, disappearing at its end." (Adams & Nissen 1972, 99).

Nissen's remarks on the value of these types for the dating of sites is confirmed by our experience on the West Mound. Lacking any closed stratigraphic context for the surface sherds, we were obliged to make use of the presence of these diagnostic types as almost our only indicator of date, but the dating they suggested was in all cases confirmed by sub-surface observations and other finds. We are clearly in no position to refine the relative dating of the mass-produced types themselves, that being a task to be undertaken with carefully excavated samples, and are therefore dependent on Nissen's own observations as recorded at Warka (Nissen 1970, 132-42), as well as the well accepted Diyala sequence and the position at Nippur, as described by Hansen 1965.

Bevelled-rim bowls As always, these are crudely made vessels, and ours tally with Nissen's suggestion that they were made in a mould, and finished off on the inside by hand (Nissen 1970, 137). Three examples are illustrated here (Figs. 13-15; 2GS:215, 2GS:150, 2GS:143). Our normal bevelled-rim bowl seems to have had a diameter of 16 cm. and a height of 9 cm., but variations do occur (e.g. H. ca. 6.5 cm. in 3G72 sub-surface). The following measurements were taken during the preliminary sorting, but will give a fair general idea:

Di. ca. 16 cm.	H. ca. 9 cm.	3G60 sub-surface (2 examples)
Di. ca. 16 cm.	H. ca. 9.2 cm.	3G70 sub-surface (2 examples)
	H. ca. 6.5 cm.	3G72 sub-surface
	H. ca. 9.5 cm.	2G82 sub-surface; 2G97 sub-surface

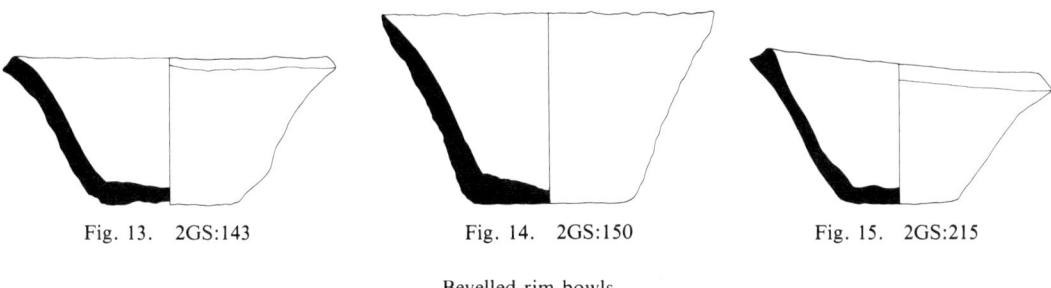

Fig. 13. 2GS:143   Fig. 14. 2GS:150   Fig. 15. 2GS:215

Bevelled-rim bowls

Although the fabric of the bowls was generally buff-coloured, it was our impression that there was a higher proportion of sherds with a greenish tinge in the surface (as opposed to the sub-surface) batches, which could be attributed to the higher temperature at which those sherds which better survived the destructive effects of the salts concentrated at the surface of the mound must have been fired. Sherds with a terracotta red fabric, such as 2GS:143, were much less common, but this variation is presumably also a consequence of firing temperature. However, since we did not record the fabric of every sherd, we cannot give figures for the relative frequency of the different colours of the fabric.

For the chronological implications of the bevelled-rim bowl we must refer once again to Nissen (e.g. in Adams & Nissen 1972, 99 ff.). It is assigned at Warka to the Late Uruk period, and apparently ceases rather abruptly with the transition to "Jemdet Nasr" ("Mit Schicht 34 hört plötzlich das Überwiegen dieser Keramikart auf", Nissen 1970, 138). On the Warka Survey the absence of both bevelled-rim bowls and solid-footed goblets was taken as a sign of the transitional phase between Uruk and Early Dynastic, i.e. Jemdet Nasr, and Adams saw no cause to question this more recently (Adams 1981, 126). With our unstratified material it is clearly impossible to comment on this observation as applied to Abu Salabikh, but we should note that on the North-East Mound, in levels we are inclined to attribute to the beginning of ED I, there were still sherds from bevelled-rim bowls, albeit rather fine and small by comparison with the majority from the West Mound (cf. *Iraq* 42, 96).

We are not here concerned with the bevelled-rim bowl as a component of the material culture, but unashamedly with its value as a chronological indicator. For a recent discussion of the question of function, we can refer to Le Brun 1980.

Solid-footed goblets and similar No complete examples of the solid-footed goblet were recovered from the West Mound, because their high and relatively slender walls are unusually fragile. Nevertheless, the base of these vessels is unmistakable, and the type was plentiful in some squares. During the course of our clearing of the surface in 1977, our first encounter with ED I pottery in any quantity at Abu Salabikh, it became clear that we had been classing together as "solid-footed goblets" the bases of two types of vessel which can in fact be distinguished as long as enough of the base is preserved. These two basic types are illustrated in Fig. 16: the genuine solid-footed goblet has indeed a narrow, solid foot which spreads out a little towards its string-cut base, whereas the other type with sides almost as steep is perhaps better described as a "tall cup" (cf. Wright 1969, 64: "narrow cups"). There is in fact a fairly continuous spectrum of types from the genuine solid-footed goblet at one end to the conical bowls discussed below; but we would accept Wright's verdict that "in the possessions of a domestic unit at a given time there seem to have been a few preferred proportions from this possible range of variation" (1969, 63). There is the further point that, unlike the conical bowls (even quite steep-sided ones), no-one can have expected the solid-footed goblet, nor probably the tall cup either, to stand upright unsupported, so that they can only have been suited for the imbibing of liquids—a use reflected in later ED banqueting scenes. The conical bowls, on the other hand, would have served to hold food as well as drink at any date.

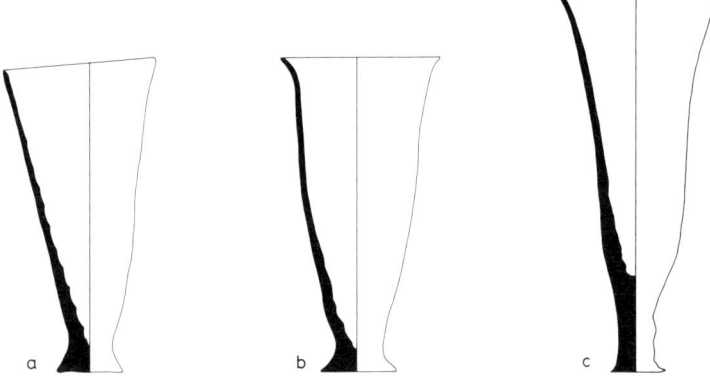

Fig. 16. Solid-footed goblet types (a: AbS 1458, *Iraq* 40, 86-7; b: AbS 1459, *Iraq* 40, 86-7; c: OUS:13, from Gr. 160 on NE Mound).

The solid-footed goblet is generally accepted as a type fossil of the ED I period, from the Diyala to Ur and Warka (cf. Adams & Nissen 1972, 103). Observers agree that it began at the beginning of ED I, increased to its greatest frequency towards the middle of that period, and died out again before ED II. No such observations seem to have been offered for the "tall cup", although at Warka at least it seems to have covered much the same time span. In square 2G23, by the west wall of Room 12, a small cut made to investigate a feature turned up over 100 rim sherds from conical bowls and solid-footed goblets (a distinction was not always possible), but also 37 unmistakable bases from solid-footed goblets, not any from tall cups; at the time the pottery sorter remarked that this was exactly comparable to the position on the North-East Mound, and since that site was founded after the Uruk period and probably inhabited after ED I, this could be seen as a hint that the genuine solid-footed goblet remained in mass production later than the very similar tall cup. But this certainly requires confirmation from stratified sequences. It could however glean some support from the comment of Delougaz, that "it would appear that the earlier specimens are less often distorted, are slightly shorter, and have a somewhat wider foot than the later ones" (Delougaz 1952, 57).

Conical bowls For the tidy-minded, conical bowls are a much less satisfactory subject than bevelled-rim bowls or solid-footed goblets. As a mass-produced type they persist into the late ED III period, and a vessel of conical shape and with a string-cut base is already encountered in the Uruk period, although Nissen would have the "conical cup" proper beginning only in the Jemdet Nasr period, in succession to the bevelled-rim bowl. During ED II and ED III, at least at Abu Salabikh, the conical bowls are quite standardized, although there is the occasional much smaller example. On the West Mound, however, we have a considerable variety in both size and quality. Our preliminary recording of the sherds, most of which were discarded, does not distinguish all these variations, nor would this have been possible with any except the best preserved pieces: with vessels so similar, a detached base or rim is insufficient for a detailed classification. Nevertheless, the wide range of sizes demanded some attention, so that sherds from unusually large bowls were noted. The following list shows the occurrence of these sherds by their squares, with diameters of individual bases where these were noted.

	Surface			*Sub-surface*	
Square	No. of sherds	Diams.	Square	No. of sherds	Diams.
			2G18	1	8.0
			2G19	13	
			2G28	1	
			2G29	2	
2G34	2				
2G43	1				
			2G54	1	
			2G55	2	
			2G58	12	
2G59	5	8.0			
2G64	1				
			2G69	2	7.1; 7.2
			2G98	1	
3G50	2				
			3G70	3	
3G71	7	6.0			
			3G80	3	
3G82	8	6.4; 8.7	3G82	4	
			3G90	5	
3G91	16		3G91	4	
3G92	7		3G92	9	6.0; 6.4; 6.6; 6.8
			3G93	1	7.0

Our largest recorded base was from the surface of 3G82, with a diameter of 8.7 cm., and as a general rule those with a diameter of more than 6.5 would certainly be considered "large", those between 6.0 and 6.5 normally too. No complete profile was reconstructed, but one bowl from 3G72 surface had a rim diameter of ca. 18 cm., well above the normal size for an ED II or III conical bowl, while a sherd from 3G93 sub-surface, which very nearly had a complete profile, had a base diameter of 7 cm. and a height of 15 cm. These large bowls were not differentiated only by their size, although their base diameters were usually the only easily recorded feature. The walls of these bowls were often heavily ribbed, in a way quite foreign to smaller, finer bowls, and well illustrated by the pot reproduced in Delougaz 1952, Plate 20 d; while the wall of the vessel right up to the rim is usually if not always proportionately thicker than in the smaller examples.

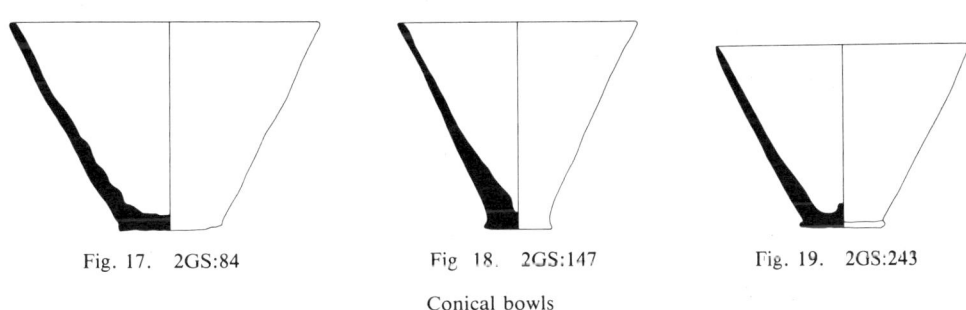

Fig. 17. 2GS:84   Fig 18. 2GS:147   Fig. 19. 2GS:243

Conical bowls

Smaller conical bowls The more usual smaller bowls are recognizably the forerunners of the ED II and ED III conical bowls, both in size and in quality and style of manufacture. Again we have a wide range in size, which is perhaps best illustrated by batch 5927 from 3G92, sub-surface, containing base sherds with diameters of: 2.5; 4.0; 4.2-4.8; 4.5; 4.6; 5.5; and the "large" bases of 6.0 to 6.8 cm. diameter already cited above. On the whole, though, we can say that the average smaller bowl has a base diameter of around 3.5 to 5.5 cm. The occasional smaller base may have come from a much finer type, rim sherds of which were sometimes noted, resembling the fine conical bowl rims from Level III in our Area E deep sounding.

Other dimensions may be illustrated by the profiles in Figs. 17-19, with rim diameters of 13.0

to 16.5 cm., and heights of 9.0 to 11.0 cm. The shape of these vessels, which all come from the "ED side" of the mound, varies a little, and is uniformly steeper-sided than any conical bowl of ED III date, but it will surely be agreed that they are quite distinct from the solid-footed goblets and "tall cups" with which they are contemporary.

"Cut-rim" bowls During the clearance of the eastern end of the mound in 1978, we became increasingly aware of the existence of a variety of conical bowl of medium size, whose rim was not of the normal, rounded, "plain" type, but was distinctly bevelled. To avoid confusion, we labelled these "cut-rim bowls". As with the large conical bowls, it would be deceptive to present their distribution in chart form, since in 1977 and early 1978 we may not have been sufficiently aware of them to record them separately, and because it is only the rims that are diagnostic, but it does seem worth placing the observed occurrences on record here:

	Surface		*Sub-surface*
2G08	1	2G08	3
2G19	1		
2G48	1		
2G49	2	2G49	5
2G59	14	2G59	27
		2G67	1
		2G69	4
2G78	1		
2G79	1		
2G88	1		
2G99	1		
3G52	1		
3G60	4	3G60	1
3G62	1		
3G70	1		
3G72	6		
3G80	5		
3G81	7	3G81	3
3G82	16	3G82	6
		3G91	2
3G92	2	3G92	6
		3G93	1

This reveals a cluster in squares 2G49, 59, 69 and 3G60, and another in 3G81, 82, and 72, making it fairly certain to our minds that these bowls were in use at the same time as the bevelled-rim bowls. Indeed, in their form they seem to represent a stage transitional between the bevelled-rim bowl and the conical bowl with plain rim, and this may not be fortuitous. As far as one can tell, this form is not recorded from other sites such as Warka or the Diyala cities. However, it is present in the Inanna Temple sounding at Nippur, according to information kindly supplied by R. Zettler on the basis of a study by G. Algaze. Any more detailed discussion must obviously await the publication of the Nippur material, or at least some stratified evidence from Abu Salabikh itself.

Distribution charts Having described the mass-produced types and their accepted chronological significance, we may turn to consider their distribution across the mound's surface and the reasons for it.

Sherd weights (Figs. 20-1) The potsherds from each operation were weighed after washing so as to give us a rough estimate of the quantity for each square. This estimate is perforce only rough, to within the nearest half kilogram or so, and the quantities recovered must have depended to some extent on how closely the workmen in the relevant square were supervised. Moreover, the quantity of sub-surface sherds was of course dependent in some degree on how deep it was necessary to penetrate in order to recover usable features, and this varied from one part of the mound to another. However, the resultant distribution chart is not without interest. Taking first the surface sherds (Fig. 20), we notice at once the heavy concentration of sherds in 3G, which was immediately apparent to anyone walking across the mound before we began the clearance. The surface of 3G82 yielded 43.5 kg. of sherds, or nearly half a kilogram per square metre. These squares coincide with the dark, dirty deposits which are thought to be of Uruk date. It is no surprise to find a low frequency of sherds on the skirts of the mound: down the west edge, and on the north-east side below the 6.00 m. contour, but it is perhaps a little surprising to see how few sherds came from 2G04 and 2G03, also 2G13 and 14, where the very clear ED I walls lay directly beneath the surface. An explanation for this may be that the layers

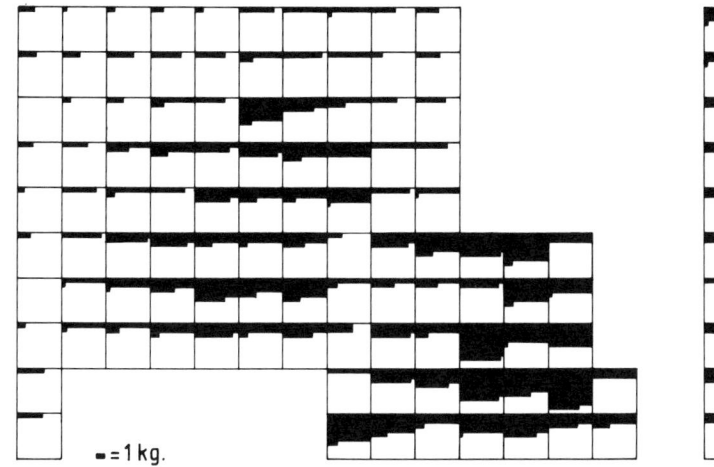

Fig. 20. Sherd weight distribution—Surface.

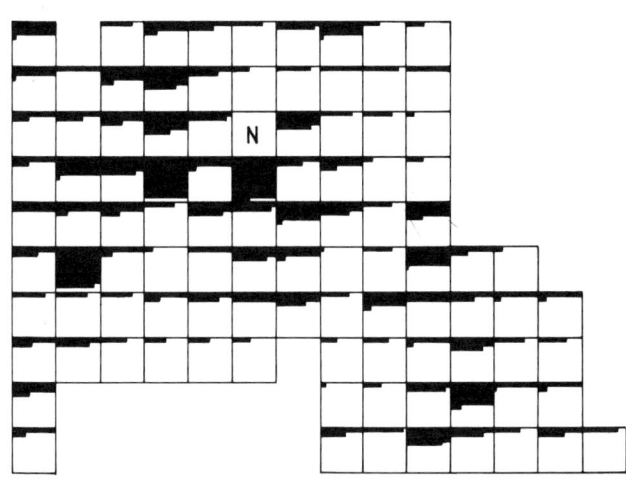

Fig. 21. Sherd weight distribution—Sub-surface.

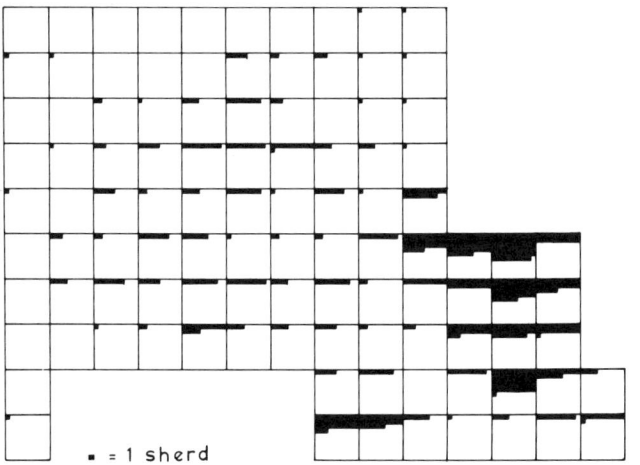

Fig. 22. Bevelled-rim bowl sherds distribution—Surface.

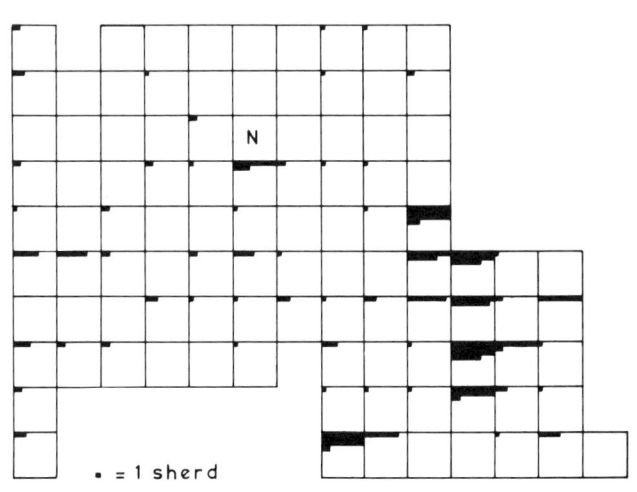

Fig. 23. Bevelled-rim bowl sherds distribution—Sub-surface.

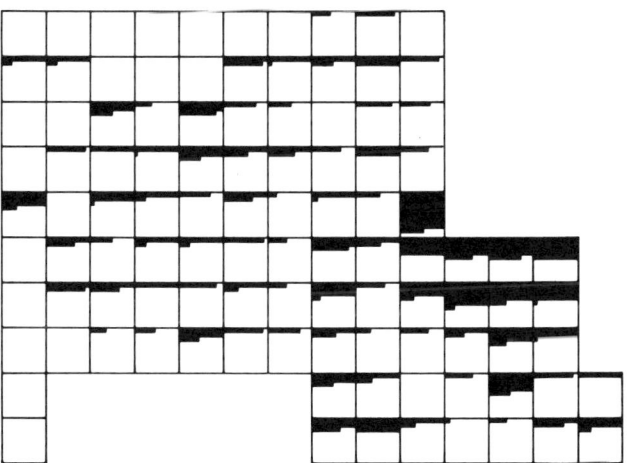

Fig. 24. Bevelled-rim bowl sherds plotted against total sherd weight—Surface.

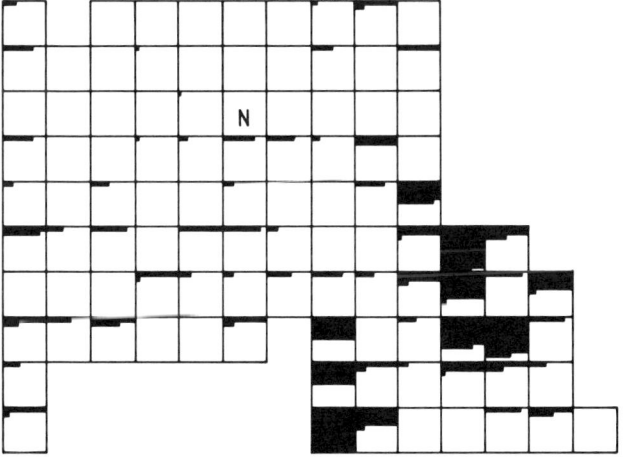

Fig. 25. Bevelled-rim bowl sherds plotted against total sherd weight—Sub-surface.

NB. some batches of potsherds went unaccountably astray and were not weighed or sorted: from the Surface 5930 (3G73), and from the Sub-Surface 5035 (2G01), 5099 (2G25), 5107 (2G76), 5929 (3G52), 5931 (3G73) and 5933 (3G83). These squares are omitted from the relevant distribution charts, except for 2G25 (Sub-Surface) which is marked with an N to indicate that the figures are lacking.

eroded, which presumably once contained the sherds to be found lying on the surface, will have been the walls and fill of the rooms—not the floors—and if the fill was largely composed of building debris, one would not in fact expect it to be rich in sherds. One should contrast these squares with the area south of the double enclosure wall, where we found no sign of architecture, but the surface sherds were more numerous (e.g. 2G62-66, 72-76): whether this was an open area used for rubbish, or, as we rather suspect, an artificial terrace using fill brought from elsewhere, it is easy to see how it could have yielded a higher concentration of sherds.

Turning to the sub-surface weights (Fig. 21), we find a rather different situation. In theory, this should not surprise us, since it is presumably the case that sherds *on* the surface had their provenance in whatever soil deposits have been eroded, whereas those *beneath* the surface do at least belong stratigraphically within the layers one is actually clearing away, and may very well reflect differences in the type of deposit, as well as in date. Moreover, while the sherds are still underground their distribution within the soil must have suffered less disturbance, and have been less liable to the averaging-out agents experienced on the surface. Hence we should not be discomfited if differences between squares are more extreme, and we should expect the sherd distribution to reflect more closely the nature of the deposits we have planned on the surface. So on the eastern flank of the mound it looks as though we may already have passed through the level of heavy concentration, since 3G91, 81, 71, 61, 92, 82, 72, and 62 yielded much less sub-surface pottery, although 3G80 and 2G99, being higher up on the 6.50 m. contour, are still rich in sherds. The squares south of the double enclosure wall yield less than those along the west side of the mound—an inversion of the surface collection—but we must bear in mind that slightly more earth could have been scraped from the west side. However, the quantities of sherds from 2G33, 35, and 51 cannot be explained in this way: most of the pottery in 2G51 came from the large pit and much of it was conical bowl sherds. In 2G33 no particular type predominated, but the bulk of the pottery came from a rubbish tip, to judge from the staining of the sherds, while a high proportion of the sherds from 2G35 came from solid-footed goblets, a type which is renowned for occurring in heavy concentrations. In all these cases it is probable that the concentration of sherds results from the presence of rubbish deposits, whether in an actual pit or in a relatively horizontal layer. Another such pit was observed in 2G79-99, and its effects are more evident when we come to consider the distributions of bevelled-rim bowls and solid-footed goblets.

Bevelled-rim bowls (Figs. 22-3)   The distribution of bevelled-rim bowl sherds is of course our prime justification for considering the eastern side of the mound as predominantly of Uruk date. The surface and sub-surface charts show much the same picture, perhaps with rather fewer stray sherds in the sub-surface batches, as one might expect. Two points may be noted in particular: the *presence* of some bevelled-rim bowl sherds in the rather barren squares towards the middle of 2G, where the ED I architecture is buried by later fill, and to the south of the double enclosure wall, and the *absence* from 2G02-04 and 12-14, where we have ED I walls at the surface, and from 2G68, 69, 78, 79, 88 and 89—here all the more striking because of the heavy bevelled-rim bowl concentrations to north, south and east.

Bevelled-rim bowl sherds plotted against weight (Figs. 24-5)   The number of bevelled-rim bowl sherds in any square—or indeed, of any sherd-type—is clearly only significant when seen in relation to total quantity. The reader can of course compare each distribution chart with the weight charts (Figs. 20-1), but we thought it desirable to present this relationship visually in at least one case. In Figs. 24 and 25 we have done this in the following way: assuming each square to contain a total of 100 units, then each unit represents the number of bevelled-rim bowl sherds in the square (n) divided by the total recorded weight in kg (w), multiplied by 25. A completely blacked-in square of 100 units would therefore be an indication that $\frac{n}{w} = 4$. Thus for instance 2G35 sub-surface contained 14 bevelled-rim bowl sherds, and its total sherd weight was 47 kg. The resulting value of 7.5 is reached by dividing 14 by 47 and multiplying by 25: $\frac{14}{47} \times 25 = 7.4468$. This is of course a quite meaningless and artificial figure, but it seemed the best way to illustrate the difference between a straight count of the sherds, as in Figs. 20-1, and their relative frequency. But the reader should resist the temptation to deduce from Fig. 25, for instance, that in 2G97 the bevelled-rim bowl sherds made up 100% of the total count.

The resultant chart really accentuates the impression given by Figs. 22-3: there remains a significant concentration in the 3G area, and certain blank spots remain blank. Perhaps the

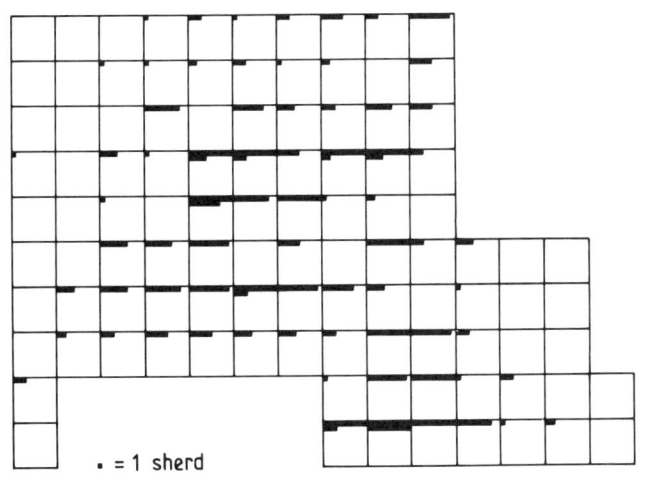
Fig. 26. Solid-footed goblet sherds distribution—Surface.

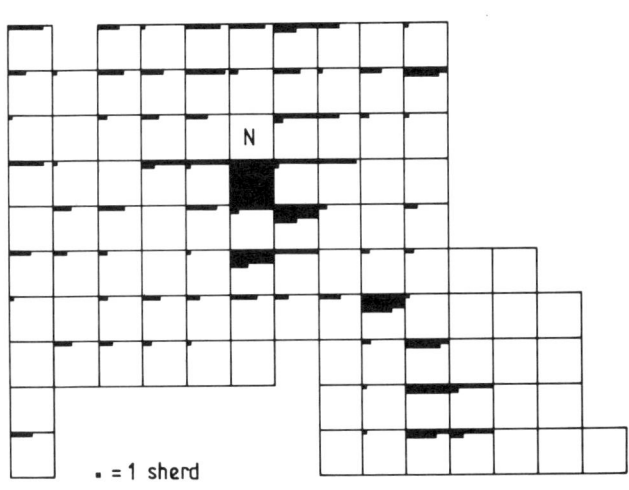
Fig. 27. Solid-footed goblet sherds distribution—Sub-surface.

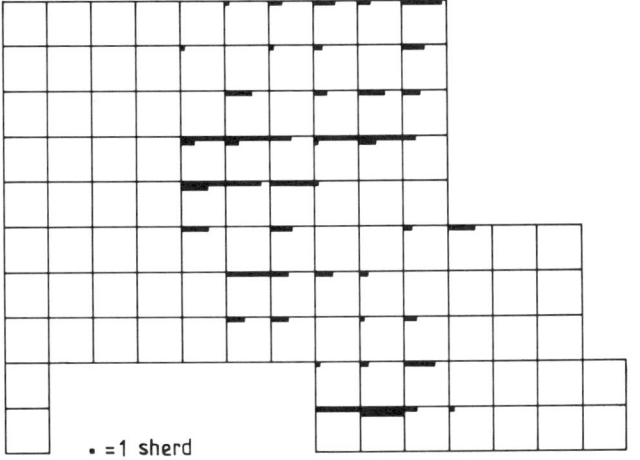
Fig. 28. 'Tall cup' sherds distribution—Surface.

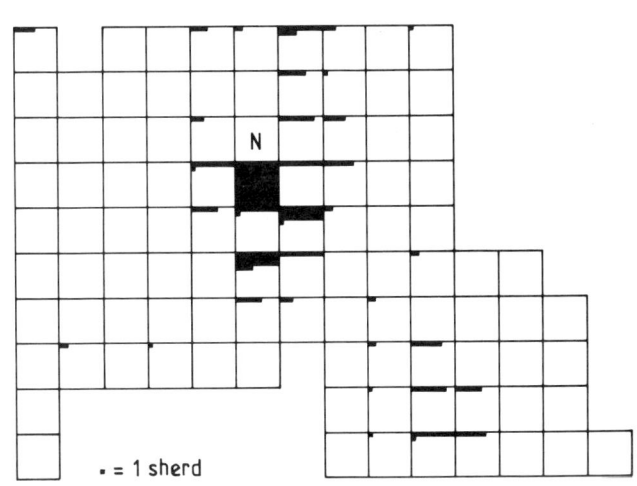
Fig. 29. 'Tall cup' sherds distribution—Sub-surface.

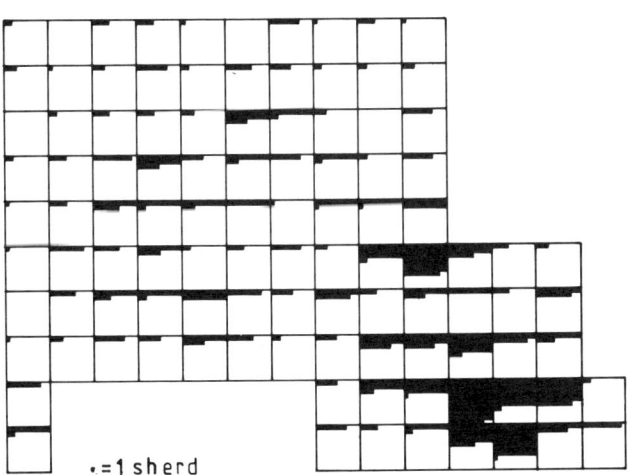
Fig. 30. Conical bowl sherds distribution—Surface.

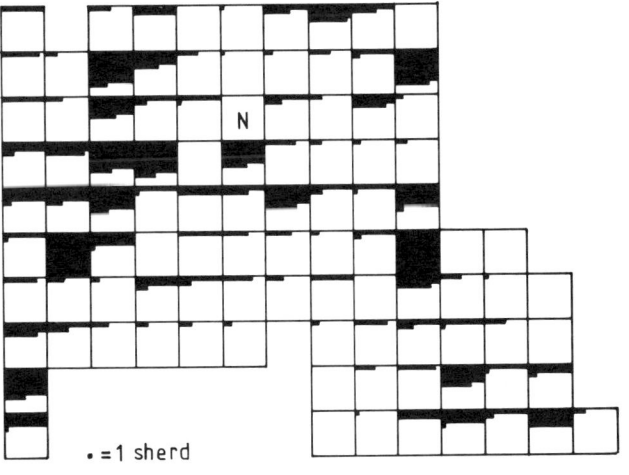
Fig. 30a. Conical bowl sherds distribution—Sub-surface.

NB. in Figs. 27 and 29 the numbers for 2G35 cannot be shown fully, being in excess of 100; in fact the figure is 160 for Fig. 27 and 150 for Fig. 29.

most interesting result is that the sub-surface distribution appears noticeably more extreme than that of the surface sherds.

Solid-footed goblets and similar (Figs. 26-9)   We give first the total of both "genuine" solid-footed goblets, and the variants, or "tall cups" (Figs. 26-7). Figs. 28-9 show the occurrence of sherds from the tall cups, but it is not complete because we did not start recording them separately until we had completed studying the first four rows of 10 m. squares from the west, as shows clearly on the chart; the occurrences in 2G00 and 2G71 were, exceptionally, noted, and show at least that the "tall cups" did indeed exist in this part of the mound.

There is nothing of particular note in the surface distributions, except of course for the total absence of these types from almost all the 3G squares. A comparison of the sub-surface distribution reveals two things: first, that we can say nothing very convincing about the comparative distribution of the tall cup and the solid-footed goblet proper; and secondly, that the blank spot noted in the bevelled-rim bowl distributions above, in 2G68, 69, 78, 79, 88, and 89, corresponds with the existence of solid-footed goblets and tall cups. This complementary distribution is the result of the large rubbish pit in these squares, which also cuts the west edge of 3G and accounts for the sherds in 3G80 and 90.

Conical bowls (Figs. 30-30a)   We attach little significance to the distribution of conical bowl sherds, because of the variety of types to which they might have belonged, as described above. Nevertheless, we do give this chart here so that the reader may see at a glance the occurrence of such sherds, and compare them quantitatively with the other mass-produced types. Figures for the occurrence of "large conical bowls" and "cut-rim bowls" are given already above, but these are included in the totals here as well.

Clay sickles and cones   We have also made similar distribution charts for these two types of artefact which are conventionally accepted as indicators of the Uruk period (see Figs. 295-6, 303-4). They are reproduced in Chapter 5 in the appropriate sections, and are generally in line with the sherd distributions.

4.3 *Pottery from the surface of the West Mound* (Ellen McAdam)

Introduction The catalogue of pottery types which follows this introduction was compiled after a short study season in 1979. Although I then examined every available batch, lack of time made detailed study of the fabrics or of the precise distribution of different types over the mound impossible, although all the major types have been listed and, where possible, illustrated. The material from the "Uruk" and "ED I" squares is listed separately, but the inclusion of a type in either section is of course no guarantee of its date and the examples listed under each type represent only a sample of squares in which it occurred, not a complete list.

The effect of the salt had probably destroyed or obscured a number of features such as paint or burnishing and on occasion it was impossible to determine even the original colour and temper of the sherd. A short account of the fabrics in the two areas of the mound appears at the beginning of their respective catalogue sections; although my study was necessarily a cursory one, it revealed that there were differences between the Uruk and ED I squares, with a smaller proportion of over-fired sherds and a preponderance of one fabric type in the latter.

Almost all the material dealt with is in the form of sherds, mainly rim sherds. It is difficult to compare these, which possess only one or two distinguishing features, with complete vessel types from other sites, defined by a whole range of characteristics. I have therefore confined myself as far as possible to a comparison of the two areas identified by the distribution of the mass-produced wares, drawing parallels from other sites only for the most distinctive sherds.

Bowls The most striking difference between the bowls from the Uruk and ED I squares was in the incidence of decoration. Decorated bowl sherds from the Uruk squares were very unusual; of the two illustrated, one is from a shallow, possibly oval dish with incised cross-hatching on the rim (§19, Fig. 54). Similar dishes were found in Late Uruk contexts at Habuba Kabira (Sürenhagen 1975, Tab. 22 nos. 1, 2 and 3), Warka (Nissen 1970, Taf. 103 no. 42/1) and the Warka area (Adams & Nissen 1972, fig. 30 ag; fig. 42, 64 etc.). The other decorated bowl sherd (Fig. 51) resembles those from the ED I squares (§99, Figs. 169-72; 148-9), which are from large bowls with incised decoration on the rim or with incised or impressed decoration on the outside below the rim, either on an applied rib or on the body of the pot; the bowl shown in Fig. 170 also carries pattern-burnishing on its inner surface. Large bowls with similar decoration occur in ED I levels at Nippur (McCown, Haines & Biggs 1978, Pl. 48 Nos. 6-9) and Warka (Nissen 1970, Taf. 53 no. 6/10 and Taf. 46 nos. 3/57-9), and in late Jemdet Nasr levels at Susa (Steve & Gasche 1971, Pl. 27 nos. 25 and 27).

Sharply carinated bowls in the Uruk squares show considerable variation in size and rim shape (§13, Figs. 46-8); comparable types occur in Late Uruk contexts at Habuba Kabira (Sürenhagen 1975, Tab. 20 no. 15; Tab. 22 no. 78) and at Warka (Haller 1932, Taf. 19 A v'). At Abu Salabikh the type seemed to survive into ED I and become more standardized in size and shape (§§87-9, Figs. 160-2); it also enjoys a long life at Susa (Steve & Gasche 1971, Pl. 29 no. 2; Pl. 26 nos. 14, 15, 17, 18; Pl. 24 no. 5). The internally-sloping rim of Fig. 162 seems to be a characteristic of the ED I squares; see also §83, Figs. 145-9.

Jars Both areas produced a wide range of neckless or short-necked jars with a variety of simple rim forms (§§23-8, Figs. 56-61; §§103-6, Figs. 176-9), paralleled in both Late Uruk and ED I levels at Warka (Nissen 1970, Taf. 105 nos. 34-9) as well as in the Late Uruk at Habuba Kabira (Sürenhagen 1975, Tab. 24-7). It is perhaps hardly surprising that such simple, easily-made forms should be longer-lived, although combinations with certain forms of decoration are distinctive. The Grey Ware neckless rolled rim jar with two finger-impressed ribs from the ED I squares (§106, Fig. 179) is very similar to Grey Ware jars from the Late Uruk site of Tell Rubeidheh in the Hamrin valley (unpublished). The neckless jar with flat cut rim (§28, Fig. 31) resembles examples from Warka and the surrounding area (Haller 1932, Taf. 18 A, c'; Adams & Nissen 1972, Fig. 30 g); it is not found in the ED I squares and appears to belong to the Late Uruk.

The band rim is another long-lived form (§§31-5, Figs. 64-9; §§112-15, Figs. 185-91), becoming more standardized in the ED I squares, where there is less variation within the different sub-types. In some examples it was clear that the rim had been formed by folding over the top of the neck to produce the strengthening band, but in others a similar shape had been obtained by moulding the clay around the rim; salt encrustation made it difficult to determine the method used in each case. At Warka the fold-over method was a feature of the earlier levels, the moulded types being later copies (Nissen 1970, 144; Taf. 106 no. 70; Taf. 107 no. 81; and Taf. 59, 60, 69). One of the examples from the ED I squares at Abu Salabikh (Fig. 187) is decorated with a row of finger-nail impressions set in a horizontal band of reserved slip at the base of the neck.

Everted-rim jars are present in both Uruk and ED I squares (§§43-45, Figs. 79-84; §§119-22, Figs. 196-201), but whereas in the Uruk squares the sherds are from medium-sized jars, sometimes decorated (e.g. Figs. 79 and 83), in the ED I squares they tend to be from larger, thicker-walled vessels. Parallels are to be found at Warka (Haller 1932, Taf. 19 C m', s'-p'; Taf. 20 C y, z, b', c', and Nissen 1970, Taf. 57, 9/9; Taf. 58, 9/16, 9/20; Taf. 67, 18/14-17; Taf. 101, 40/18, 40/21; Taf. 96, 39/85, etc.), and in the Diyala (Delougaz 1952, Pl. 142 A.516.270; Pl. 179 C.516.373; Pl. 192 D.514.370a and b).

Lugs and handles Strap-handled jars with combed decoration occurred in both areas (§51, Figs. 91 and 92; §127, Figs. 205 and 206); three of the examples illustrated were in Grey Ware. Jars with horizontal comb decoration similar to that shown in Fig. 205 were found in the Warka area (Adams & Nissen 1972, Figs. 64 no. 13 and 73 no. 6), and at Warka itself (Nissen 1970, Taf. 98, 39/109) in Late Uruk contexts. There seem to be no parallels for the handled jars with cross-hatched comb decoration. The surface of the handle was often decorated with grooves or finger-nail impressions which would have given a firmer grip (§51, Figs. 93-5; §127, Fig. 177); decorated strap-handles occur at Warka (Haller 1932, Taf. 18 C q), in the Warka area (Adams & Nissen 1972, Fig. 58 no. 26) and at Susa (Steve & Gasche 1971, Pl. 29 no. 14), and it seems to be a Late Uruk feature. Each area produced one example of a cable handle (§52, Fig. 96; §128), but rim swellings were noted only from the Uruk squares (§53, Fig. 97).

Tab rims were found in both Late Uruk and ED I squares (§54, Fig. 98; §130, Figs. 208 and 209), although according to Adams & Nissen (1972, 103; Fig. 30, u) this is a type restricted to the ED I; certainly the example from the Uruk squares illustrated in Fig. 98 has a type of panelled reserved slip decoration usually thought of as ED I. Tab rims have been found in ED I levels at Nippur (Hansen 1965, Fig. 36), in the Diyala (Delougaz 1952, Pl. 63, 13), and at Warka (Nissen 1970, Taf. 107 no. 93).

Lugs were surprisingly rare when one considers the large numbers of four-lugged jars found at other sites in both Late Uruk and ED I periods (Delougaz 1952, 39-41 and 53-5; Hansen 1965, Figs. 11a+b, 12, 14, 21, 25, 33; Nissen 1970, Taf. 107 nos. 97 and 98; Adams & Nissen 1972, Fig. 30 ad; Haller 1932, Taf. 19 D b, c; Sürenhagen 1975, Tab. 6 and 7; Le Breton 1957, Figs. 10 and 12; etc.). The example of an unpierced lug with black paint illustrated from the Uruk squares is probably a stray 'Ubaid sherd (§55, Fig. 99). The jar with horizontally-pierced lugs on a finger-nail impressed rib (§56, Fig. 79) is very like one from Nippur illustrated by Hansen (1965, Fig. 11a); it is in the characteristic Uruk sealing-wax red washed and burnished ware. The jar shown in Fig. 82, however, which is also from the Uruk squares, is a distinctive ED I type with parallels in the Diyala and at Warka; although it was badly damaged and the drawing is a partial reconstruction enough remained to show that it closely matched Delougaz's description of jars with "a notched ridge forming a gutter below the rim . . . the lugs are attached to, or just below, the ridge" (1952, 53; Pls. 40-2, 191; see also Adams & Nissen 1972, Fig. 77 and Nissen 1970, Taf. 107 no. 104). In addition to the two ED I single-lug jars shown in Plate VIIIa, b (§133), the ED I squares produced a carinated jar with unpierced lugs on a row of herring-bone finger-nail impressions (§131, Fig. 210) and a pierced oval lug in a band of incised cross-hatching (§132, Fig. 211) reminiscent of some of the four-lugged jars from other sites listed above. The miniature jar drawn in Fig. 272 is probably imitating a four-lugged jar with a band of incised decoration.

Spouts Apart from the three instances of decoration around spouts from the ED I squares (§141, Figs. 218; 220-1), there seemed to be few differences between spouts from the two areas.

Decoration on jars Reserved slip decoration, while certainly practised in the Late Uruk period at Abu Salabikh, seems to have become more popular in the ED I period, especially in combinations of diagonal and horizontal stripes or with rows of finger-nail impressions (§64, Figs. 70; 72; 85; 98; §§142-4, Figs. 222-8 etc.). A similar development was observed by Adams & Nissen in the Warka area (1972, 103) and by Hansen at Nippur (1965, 208).

Painted decoration, as one would expect in a collection of surface sherds, is not very common in either area (§66, Figs. 99; 110; §146, Figs. 218; 220; 230-4). The possibly 'Ubaid painted sherd with unpierced lug (Fig. 99) from the Uruk squares has already been mentioned; the light green fabric of another painted sherd, this time from the ED I squares (Fig. 230) also suggests that it is an 'Ubaid stray. Of the remainder, the small jar from the ED I squares shown in Fig. 231, with cross-hatched circles between horizontal bands of black paint, is the only one with a discernible pattern; most are decorated with simple designs of bands or stripes of black, purplish or red paint. Two painted sherds picked up on the mound in 1973 have no closer provenance (Figs. 280-1).

Incised decoration was not particularly common, and generally took the form of bands of cross-hatching or of cross-hatched triangles (§68, Figs. 74-5; 82; 112-13; §147, Figs. 236-8; 286). In the Uruk squares bands of incised decoration were often found on the shoulders of jars with out-turned necks (Figs. 74-8), although the lugs so frequently associated with this type of decoration at other sites were lacking (e.g. Haller 1932, Taf. 19 D, b; Le Breton 1957, Figs. 10 no. 29; 11 nos. 20-21; 12 no. 9; Delougaz 1952, Pl. 144 A.604.223; etc.).

In both Uruk and ED I squares combed decoration tended to be found on Grey Ware sherds (§69, Figs. 76-7; 91-2; Plate IV*b*; §148, Figs. 205; 239). There are parallels for the cross-hatched comb decoration from the Warka area (Adams & Nissen 1972, Figs. 37 no. 5 and 50 no. 19), where it is found in Late Uruk assemblages; at Abu Salabikh it continued at least on occasion over the entire surface of the pot, as the base sherd (Fig. 129) from the Uruk squares shows.

Finger-nail and finger impressions, on their own, on applied ribs or in combination with other forms of decoration are found in both areas (§§70-1; §§149-50), but they are far more popular, and occur in greater variety, in the ED I squares. At least one of the sherds with finger-nail impressions from the Uruk squares is almost certainly of ED I date, since it also features excised triangles (Delougaz 1952, 54 and Pl. 43-5). Of the other forms of impressed decoration, the small triangular impressions on two sherds from the Uruk squares (§72, Figs. 124-5) are of interest because they seem to have been made with reeds, a type of decoration also recorded from the Warka area (Adams & Nissen 1972, Fig. 51 no. 21). Rocker pattern occurred in both areas (§72, Fig. 128; §229).

Only one hollow stand sherd was recovered from the Uruk squares, but they were more plentiful in the ED I squares (§76; §159, Figs. 268-71), where they do not differ substantially from ED I stands in the Diyala (Delougaz 1952, 55 and Pl. 45 and 65). The sherd illustrated in Fig. 271 is somewhat more problematic; of Grey Ware, it resembles ED III stemmed dish bases. Stemmed dish sherds in Grey Ware were found in the deep sounding in Area E on the main mound, but our base sherd is not of the simple conical form usually associated with ED III stemmed dishes (Moon 1981, 64 and Fig. 13 no. 80; Delougaz 1952, 85, Pl. 81 a and b). At Nippur and in the Diyala (Hansen 1965, 209; Delougaz 1952, 58), Grey Ware occurs in ED I levels in shapes imitating stone vessels, but at Warka Nissen found that the Grey Ware came mainly from the earlier levels (1972, 147).

Miscellaneous sherds §§78 (Figs. 135-40) and 161 (Figs. 275-9) comprise a heterogeneous collection of sherds, some of which have already been published in *Iraq* 40 [1978] 86-87 and need not be further discussed. Both areas produced sieve bowls (Fig. 282 and Plate VII*a*) with parallels at Warka, in the Warka area, in the Diyala region and at Susa (see on 2GS:70 below). The pouring lugs from the Uruk squares (Figs. 136-7) are like examples illustrated from the Diyala (Delougaz 1952, Pl. 20 a and a′) and Nippur (Hansen 1965, Fig. 3), where they belong in Late Uruk levels. The coarse dishes and trays (Figs. 138-40) have parallels at Warka (Nissen 1970, Taf. 104 no. 19), Nippur (Hansen 1965, Fig. 8) and Habuba Kabira (Sürenhagen 1975, Tab. 23), which also indicate a Late Uruk date; the coarse dishes with internal channel, on the other hand, are at home in ED I contexts (Figs. 275; 287; Nissen 1970, Taf. 104 no. 18). The curious "knob lids" (Plate VII*b*) found in the ED I squares are an ED I-II phenomenon, with similar objects in the Diyala region, at Warka and at Nippur. They are usually thought to be jar-stoppers, although it seems an unnecessarily elaborate form of closure. Finally, parallels have yet to be found for the two baked clay objects shown in Figs. 278-9; similar decoration is found in modern Iraq on unbaked clay storage bins and shelves, and finger-impressed ribs sometimes encircle tannurs.

* * *

It is clear that the surface collections from the two areas are to some extent mixed, and there was considerable continuity in pottery types between the Late Uruk and ED I periods, but comparisons with other sites suggest that the pottery assemblage from each area provides a reasonable cross-section for the period to which the mass-produced types indicate it belongs. How accurately the surface collections represent the full repertoire of each period can only be established by excavation.

The Uruk Squares

	Fabric
§§1-18	Bowls
§19	Decoration on bowls
§§20-2	Bases
§§23-50	Jars
§§51-6	Lugs, handles, etc.
§§57-63	Spouts
§§64-72	Decoration
§§73-5	Bases
§76	Hollow stands
§77	Miniatures
§78	Miscellaneous

Fabric

Most of the sherds from the West Mound were greenish in appearance, suggesting at first that only very hard-fired or over-fired sherds had survived the destructive effects of the salt. Closer examination, however, revealed that in many cases the green colour was due to surface discoloration by weathering and bore no relationship to the original colour of the fabric. A sample of sherds selected at random revealed quite a wide range of fabrics in proportions which varied between the Uruk and ED I areas of the mound. The significance and accuracy of these results could only be tested by excavation; in particular, one might suspect that the surface sample is indeed biased in favour of the dark green, over-fired fabrics and against shapes and wares habitually fired to low temperatures, such as coarse vegetable-tempered storage jars. Even the hard-fired fabrics had suffered surface damage, so that decorative details such as paint or pattern-burnishing are probably under-represented, and red fabrics seem particularly prone to disintegration under salty conditions. The heavy salt-encrustation also made it difficult or impossible on occasion to determine the nature of the temper. Almost all the surviving sherds other than the mass-produced types were wheel made.

The following types of fabric were distinguished:

1. *Pink/Orange fabric, cream slip:* This is a well-made, hard-fired medium or fine-tempered fabric with a smooth cream surface, much used for vessels with decoration. In some examples it is not entirely certain that the pale surface effect has not been achieved by some device such as wet-smoothing, but in most cases it is clearly a slip. On vegetable-tempered pots this is particularly obvious, because the slip contains a fine grit temper. Vegetable and grit temper occur in approximately equal proportions and overall this pink and cream ware accounted for almost 28% of the sample from the Uruk squares.

2. *Greenish, over-fired fabrics:* These were present in slightly greater numbers than any other type of fabric, accounting for just over 29% of the sample. Many were warped or cracked, with a black core. The majority came from medium or thin-walled vessels with fine or medium temper; grit temper predominated. On a few over-fired sherds a two-tone effect was observed, the dark green giving way to a clearly-defined band of light green or yellow near the rim or the edge of the base. It is not clear whether this was an accident of firing or deliberate, perhaps having to do with the way the pots were stacked in the kiln (see §§67, 74).

3. *Buff fabrics:* The buff wares are softer than the pink and cream, more porous and mainly used for medium-walled, medium-tempered vessels which were less frequently and less neatly decorated than those of pink and cream fabric. Vegetable- and grit-tempered sherds occurred in equal numbers. Buff fabrics formed just under 26% of the sample.

4. *Red fabrics:* (a) Very few sherds of medium, grit-tempered red fabric survived (ca. 4%) and most were from jars. The outer surfaces were lost and the fabric was soft and crumbling.
     (b) A very few sherds of coarse, chaff-tempered red fabric occurred (ca. 3%), mainly from jars or coarse plates. Some had a black core and all were hard but friable.

5. *Grey Ware:* Grey Ware formed a little over 10% of the sample. All the sherds were from well-made, medium-walled jars, usually surface-smoothed and bearing a wide range of decoration, especially finger-nail impressions, comb and rocker decoration. It was particularly difficult to detect the nature of the temper in Grey Ware, but once again it seemed to be divided equally between vegetable and grit.

6. *Red Washed and Burnished:* Only one sherd of this classic Uruk ware found its way into the sample. The fabric was a very hard orange-buff with a fine vegetable temper, the wash a bright sealing-wax red with a high burnish (Fig. 79).

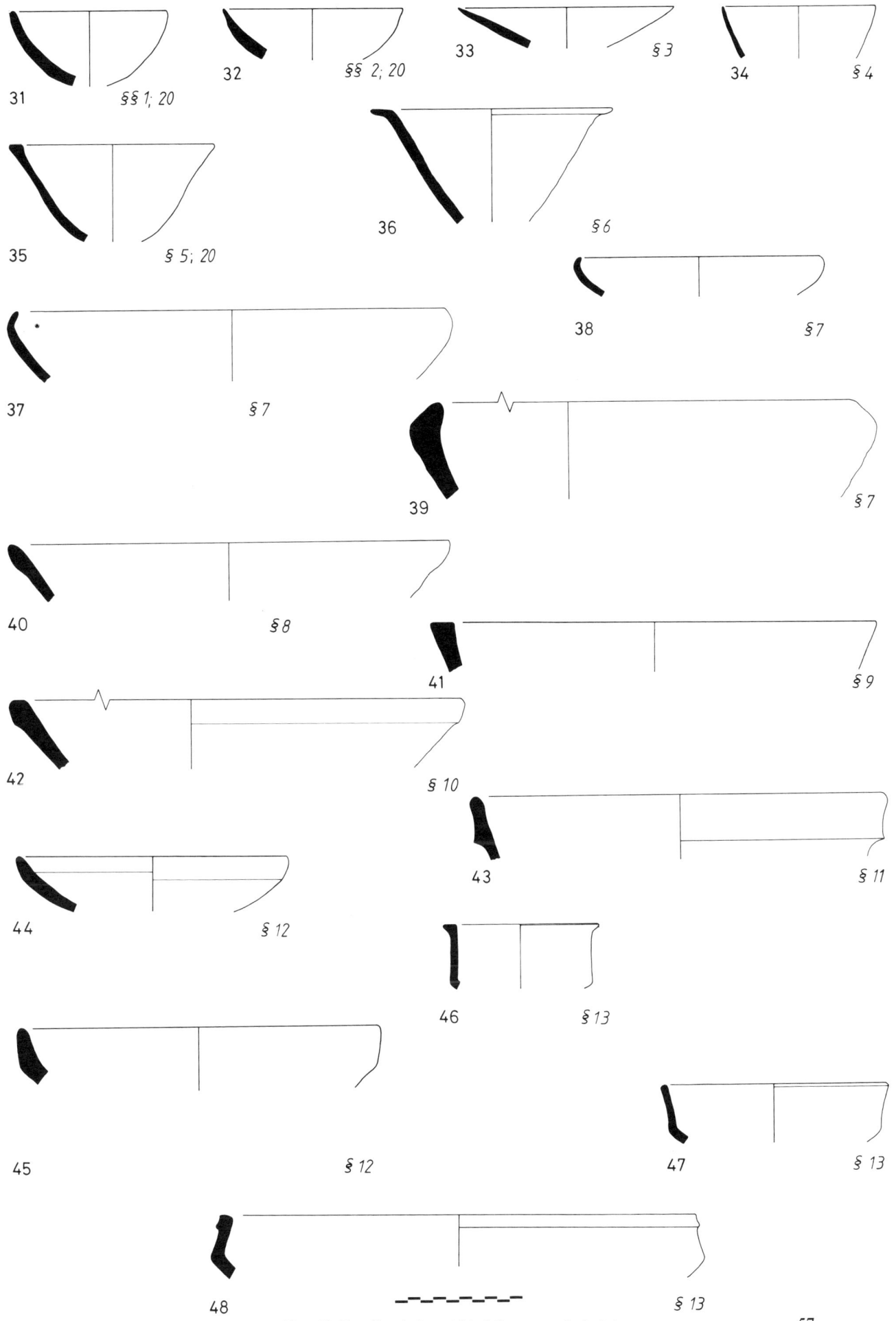

Figs. 31-48. Sherds from "Uruk" squares. Scale 1:4.

Bowls
The classification of bowls from rim sherds alone is easier than that of jars, since the overall shape is more predictable.
 §1 *Curving sides, rounded rim:* A small, round-bottomed, almost hemispherical shape.
    Diam.: 12 cm.
    Examples: 3G92 Surface (Fig. 31); 3G82 Sub-surface.

 §2 *Curving sides, pinched rim:* A small, shallow, probably round-bottomed shape.
    Diam.: 14 cm.
    Examples: 3G93 Sub-surface (Fig. 32); 3G61 Surface; 3G83 Surface; 3G50 Surface.

 §3 *Straight-sided, pointed rim:* A shallow saucer shape, possibly used as a lid.
    Diams.: 17-23 cm.
    Examples: 3G80 Surface (Fig. 33); 3G70 Sub-surface; 3G62 Surface; 3G52 Surface.

 §4 *Straight-sided, rounded rim (small):* A very thin-walled, well-made, conical shape, probably flat-based.
    Diams.: 10-15 cm.
    Examples: 3G82 Surface (Fig. 34); 3G70 Sub-surface; 3G90 Surface.

 §5 *Sinuous sided, flat rim:* Probably round-bottomed.
    Diams.: 13-18 cm.
    Examples: 3G82 Surface (Fig. 35); 3G82 Sub-surface.

 §6 *Straight-sided, internally sloping everted rim:* A conical shape, probably flat-based.
    Diams.: 12-18 cm.
    Examples: 3G60 Sub-surface (Fig. 36); 3G92 Sub-surface.

 §7 *Straight-sided, sharply-incurving rim:* A fairly deep, enclosed bowl found in fabrics ranging from fine to coarse.
    Diams.: 17-44 cm.
    Examples: 3G70 Sub-surface (Fig. 37; a small hole has been bored through the rim); 3G52 Surface (Fig. 38);
        3G70 Sub-surface (Fig. 39); 3G62 Surface; 3G60 Sub-surface; 3G83 Surface.

 §8 *Straight-sided, bulging rim:* Probably a deep, conical shape.
    Diams.: 26-36 cm.
    Examples: 3G80 Surface (Fig. 40); 3G81 Surface; 3G90 Surface.

 §9 *Straight-sided, flat rim:* Probably a deep, conical shape.
    Diams.: 24-35 cm.
    Examples: 3G71 Sub-surface (Fig. 41); 3G70 Surface.

 §10 *Straight-sided, square-topped rim:*
    Diam.: 42 cm.
    Example: 2G39 Surface (Fig. 42).

 §11 *Straight-sided, projecting rim:*
    Diam.: 32 cm.
    Example: 3G82 Surface (Fig. 43).

 §12 *Gently-carinated bowls:*
    Diams.: 21-30 cm.
    Examples: 3G70 Sub-surface (Fig. 44); 3G92 Surface (Fig. 45); 3G62 Surface; 3G71 Sub-surface; 3G72
        Sub-surface.

 §13 *Sharply-carinated bowls:* These vary widely in diameter and rim shape.
    Diams.: 12-37 cm.
    Examples: 3G62 Sub-surface (Fig. 46); 3G92 Surface (Fig. 47); 3G72 Sub-surface (Fig. 48); 3G92 Sub-surface;
        3G61 Surface; 3G93 Surface; 3G51 Surface; 3G62 Surface; 3G71 Sub-surface; 3G50 Surface.

 §14 *Straight-sided, rounded rim (large):* A large, thick-walled conical shape.
    Diams.: 36-40 cm.
    Examples: 3G80 Sub-surface (Fig. 49); 3G80 Surface; 3G82 Surface; 3G81 Surface; 3G90 Surface.

 §15 *Curving sides, everted rim:*
    Diams.: 30-33 cm.
    Examples: 3G80 Sub-surface (Fig. 50); 3G70 Sub-surface.

 §16 *Curving sides, cut rim:* A broad, shallow shape. There is occasionally a finger-nail impressed rib below the rim.
    Diams.: 24-40 cm.
    Examples: 3G80 Sub-surface (Fig. 51); 3G70 Surface; 3G81 Surface.

§17 *Curving sides, projecting or everted rim:* Large, coarse, thick-walled bowls.
　　　Diams.: 28-38 cm.
　　　　　Examples: 3G60 Sub-surface (Fig. 52); 3G61 Surface (Fig. 53); 3G71 Sub-surface; 3G50 Surface; 3G80 Sub-surface.

§18 *Upright-sided bowl, flat everted rim:*
　　　Diam.: 14 cm.
　　　Example: 3G60 Surface (Fig. 54).

§19 *Decoration on bowls:* This is very infrequent in the Uruk squares. For an example of a bowl with a finger-nail impressed rib below the rim see Fig. 51, from 3G80 Sub-surface.
　　　Incised cross-hatching on bowl rim: Fig. 54 (3G60 Surface).
　　　Plum-coloured wash on bowl rim: 3G82 Sub-surface.
　　　Black paint inside bowl: 3G62 Sub-surface (Plate V*a*).

Bowl bases

§20 *Round bases:* These are probably often discarded as body sherds. Some of the smaller bowls were certainly round-bottomed, e.g. Figs. 31, 35 and 32.

§21 *Flat bases:* One large flat base was almost certainly from a bowl because of its carefully-smoothed internal surface: 3G62 Sub-surface (Fig. 55).

§22 *Ring bases:* Not certainly identified.

Jars

§23 *Neckless, plain collar rim:*
　　　Diams.: 7-10 cm.
　　　Examples: 3G82 Surface (Fig. 56); 3G62 Sub-surface; 3G70 Sub-surface.

§24 *Neckless, cut collar rim:*
　　　Diams.: 9-12 cm.
　　　Examples: 3G70 Sub-surface (Fig. 57); 3G50 Surface.

§25 *Neckless, inturned collar rim:*
　　　Diam.: 7.2 cm.
　　　Example: 3G72 Surface (Fig. 58).

§26 *Neckless, out-turned collar rim:*
　　　Diam.: 9 cm.
　　　Example: 3G70 Surface (Fig. 59).

§27 *Neckless, rolled rim:*
　　　Diams.: 11-19 cm.
　　　　　Examples: 3G50 Surface (Fig. 60; row of finger-nail impressions on shoulder); 3G82 Surface and Sub-surface; 3G81 Surface; 3G51 Surface; 3G70 Sub-surface.

§28 *Neckless, flat cut rim:*
　　　Diam.: 21 cm.
　　　Example: 3G52 Sub-surface (Fig. 61; finger-nail impressed rib immediately below rim).
　　　See Haller 1932, Taf. 18 A c'.

§29 *Flaring neck, plain rim:*
　　　Diam.: 10 cm
　　　Example: 3G80 Sub-surface (Fig. 62).

§30 *Straight neck, plain rim:*
　　　Diam.: 9 cm.
　　　Example: 3G81 Surface (Fig. 63).

Band rims: In band rims the top of the rim is turned over to form a strengthening band around the top of the jar, which is usually narrow in relation to the rest of the pot.

§31 *Upright or slightly outward-curving neck, plain band rim:*
　　　Diams.: 11-22 cm.; one unusually small example 3.5 cm. (3G90 Sub-surface; Fig. 65).
　　　Examples: 3G90 Surface (Fig. 64); 3G90 Sub-surface (Fig. 65); 3G51 Surface.

§32 *Upright or slightly outward-curving neck, overhanging rim:*
   Diams.: 9-13 cm.
   Examples: 3G80 Sub-surface (Fig. 66); 3G90 Surface; 3G70 Surface.

§33 *Upright or slightly outward-curving neck, projecting band rim:*
   Diams.: 10-27 cm.
   Examples: 3G80 Sub-surface (Fig. 67); 3G83 Surface; 3G70 Surface; 3G62 Surface.

§34 *Upright or slightly outward-curving neck, dished band rim:*
   Diam.: 10 cm.
   Example: 3G90 Surface (Fig. 68).

§35 *Short, out-turned neck, concave band rim:*
   Diams.: 13-38 cm.
   Examples: 3G50 Surface (Fig. 69); 3G51 Surface; 3G71 Surface; 3G52 Surface.

§36 *Short, out-turned neck, plain rim:* Often in buff fabric with horizontal reserved slip, combing or grooving on shoulder.
   Diams.: 10-16 cm.
   Examples: 3G92 Surface (Fig. 70; horizontal reserved slip on shoulder); 3G82 Sub-surface (Fig. 71; horizontal grooving on shoulder); 3G90 Sub-surface; 3G82 Surface; 3G62 Sub-surface; 3G72 Sub-surface; 3G60 Sub-surface; 3G81 Surface.

§37 *Short out-turned neck, slightly swollen rim:*
   Diams.: 13-15 cm.
   Examples: 3G61 Sub-surface (Fig. 72; diagonal reserved slip below row of finger-nail impressions at base of neck); 3G72 Sub-surface; 3G71 Surface; 3G82 Surface; 3G62 Sub-surface; 3G83 Surface; 3G70 Surface; 3G81 Surface; 3G90 Surface; 3G61 Surface; 3G80 Sub-surface.
   See Hansen 1965, 13.

§38 *Short, out-turned neck, bulbous rim:*
   Diams.: 11-19 cm.
   Examples: 3G71 Sub-surface (Fig. 73); 3G62 Sub-surface; 3G82 Sub-surface; 3G70 Surface; 3G50 Surface; 3G90 Sub-surface.

§39 *Out-turned neck, cut rim:* Often buff fabric with band of incised cross-hatching on shoulder.
   Diams.: 6-34 cm.
   Examples: 3G80 Sub-surface (Fig. 74; incised cross-hatching on shoulder); 3G50 Surface; 3G72 Surface; 3G82 Sub-surface.
   See Delougaz 1952, Pl. 164 B.663.213; Haller 1932, Pl. 19 D b.

§40 *Out-turned neck, inward-sloping rim:*
   Diam.: 12 cm.
   Example: 3G80 Sub-surface (Fig. 75; band of incised cross-hatching on shoulder, perhaps another underneath).

§41 *Out-turned neck, flat rim:*
   Diam.: 11.5 cm.
   Example: 3G70 Sub-surface (Fig. 76; Grey Ware with cross-hatched comb decoration).

§42 *Out-turned neck, projecting cut rim:* Several examples decorated with cross-hatched combing or with incision.
   Diams.: 11-16 cm.
   Examples: 3G70 Sub-surface (Fig. 77; cross-hatched combing); 3G71 Sub-surface (Fig. 78; Grey Ware, incised); 3G50 Surface; 3G90 Surface; 3G70 Surface; 3G61 Surface.

§43 *Out-turned neck, sloping everted rim:*
   Diams.: 8-15 cm.
   Examples: 3GS:36 from 3G71 Sub-surface (Fig. 79; red wash and burnish, four-lug jar with finger-nail impressed shoulder rib); 3G70 Sub-surface (Fig. 80; Grey Ware); 3G80 Sub-surface; 3G91 Sub-surface.
   See Hansen 1965, Fig. 11.

§44 *Neckless, squashed everted rim:*
   Diams.: 10-17 cm.
   Examples: 3G82 Sub-surface (Fig. 81); 3G80 Sub-surface (Fig. 82; with four(?) rectangular double- or triple-pierced lugs on rib forming a gutter below the rim; see Delougaz 1952, Pls. 40-2 and 191); 3G81 Surface; 3G92 Surface; 3G70 Sub-surface.

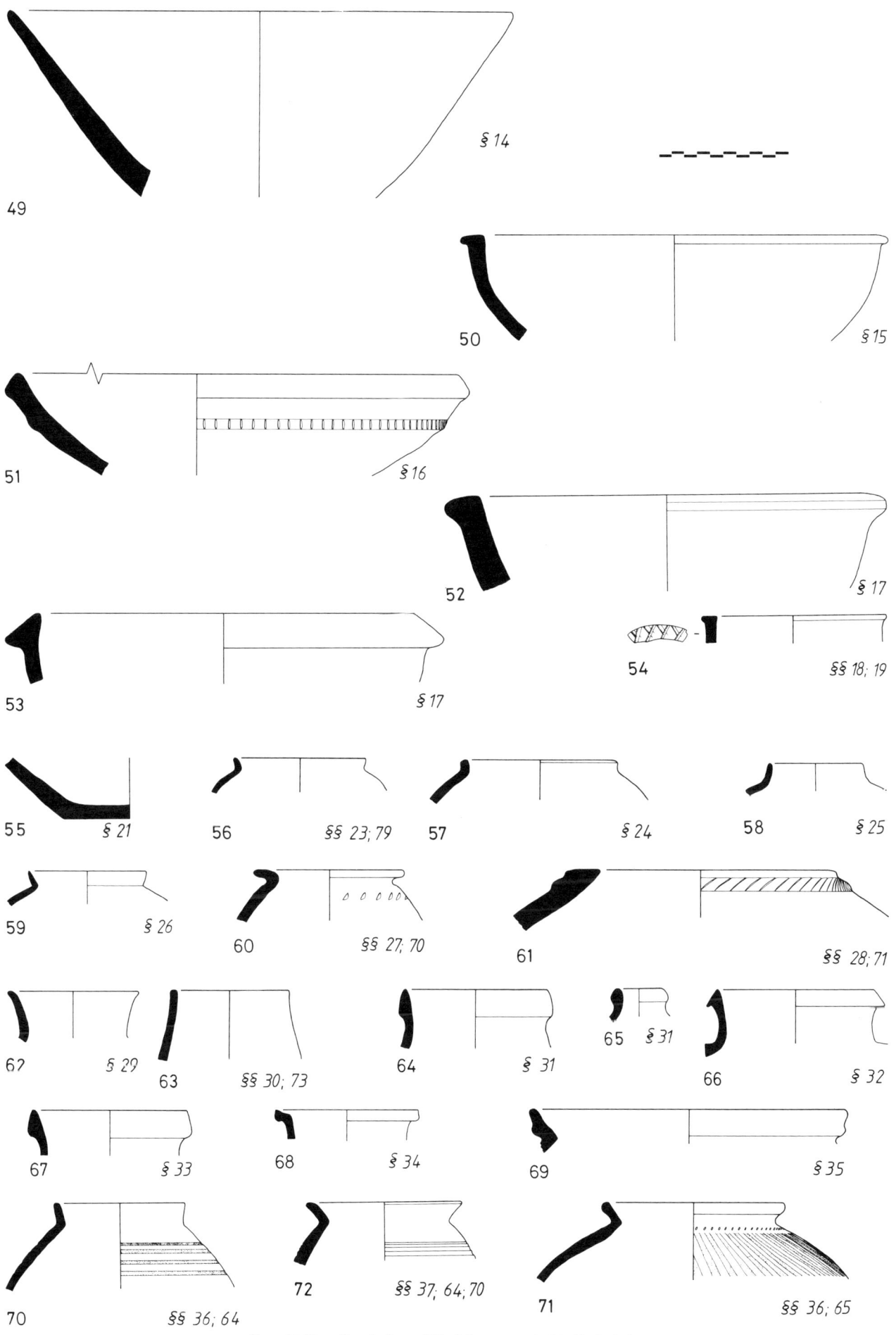

Figs. 49-72. Sherds from "Uruk" squares (ctd.). Scale 1:4.

§45 *Short, out-turned neck, rounded everted rim:*
    Diams.: 16-22 cm.
    Examples: 3G71 Surface (Fig. 83; Grey Ware, row of finger-nail impressions at base of neck); 3G70 Sub-surface (Fig. 84); 3G71 Sub-surface; 3G80 Sub-surface; 3G60 Sub-surface; 3G61 Sub-surface; 3G51 Surface.

§46 *Small, squat jars with out-curving necks and flat projecting rims:*
    Diams.: 10-11 cm.
    Examples: 3G62 Sub-surface (Fig. 85; diagonal reserved slip); 3G70 Sub-surface; 3G62 Surface.

§47 *Straight or slightly inward-turning neck, square-topped rim:*
    Diams.: 12-15 cm.
    Examples: 3G80 Sub-surface (Fig. 86); 3G91 Surface; 3G90 Surface & Sub-surface; 3G81 Surface; 3G71 Surface.

§48 *Outward-curving neck, round-topped rim:*
    Diam.: 13 cm.
    Example: 3G50 Surface (Fig. 87).

§49 *Straight neck, flat-topped projecting rim:*
    Diams.: 12-19 cm.
    Examples: 3G82 Surface (Fig. 88); 3G92 Sub-surface; 3G50 Surface.

§50 *Very large coarse jars:*
    Diams.: 36-80 cm.
    Examples: 3G80 Sub-surface (Fig. 89); 3G80 Sub-surface (Fig. 90); 3G90 Sub-surface.

Lugs, handles, etc.

§51 *Strap handles:* These are rarely found attached to the parent jar. Both the examples illustrated are comb-decorated Grey Ware.
    Jar diams.: 7-10 cm.
    Examples: 3G70 Surface (Fig. 91); 3G70 Sub-surface (Fig. 92; Plate VI*b*).
  There was also a wide range of detached examples.
    Widths: 2-7 cm.
    Examples: 3G61 Surface (Fig. 93; Plate VI*b*; decorated with rows of finger-nail impressions); 3G52 Sub-surface (Fig. 94; Plate VI*b*; decorated with four parallel grooves); 3G72 Surface (Fig. 95; decorated with 3 parallel ribs and finger-nail impressions); 3G70 Surface; 3G71 Sub-surface; 3G92 Surface; 3G50 Surface; 3G51 Surface; 3G80 Sub-surface; 3G71 Sub-surface; 3G62 Sub-surface; 3G91 Surface; 3G60 Sub-surface.
    See Haller 1932, Pl. 18 C q, Wright 1981, 112 Fig. 55h.

§52 *Rope or twisted handles:* Only one example was noted, 3G72 Surface (Fig. 96; Plate VI*b*).
    See Haller 1932, Pl. 18 C p; Delougaz 1952, Pl. 20 b; Adams & Nissen 1972, 100.

§53 *Rim-swellings:* These are obtained by adding a crescent-shaped piece of clay to the rim to produce a flat or slightly raised projection, often decorated with finger-nail impressions.
    Examples: 3G90 Sub-surface (Fig. 97); 3G70 Sub-surface.

§54 *Tab rims:* These have four rectangular projections equally spaced around the rim. Width: 3-5 cm.; Thickness: 1.5-2 cm.; Diams.: 10-15 cm.
    Examples: 3G80 Sub-surface (Fig. 98; horizontal reserved slip crossed at regular intervals by diagonal reserved slip; Plate VI*b*); 3G90 Sub-surface & Surface; 2G99 Sub-surface.
    See Delougaz 1952, Pl. 63, 13; Haller 1932, Pl. 20 C c.

§55 *Unpierced lugs:* These were not numerous.
    Widths: 1.5-3.5 cm.; Lengths: 3-4 cm.
    Examples: 3G93 Sub-surface (Fig. 99; Plate V*a*; VI*b*; light green fabric, oval lug with black painted decoration, probably 'Ubaid); 3G71 Sub-surface.

§56 *Horizontally pierced lugs:* Triangular in shape.
    Widths: 1.5-3.5 cm.; Lengths: 2.5-4 cm.
    Examples: 3G71 Sub-surface (Fig. 79; cf. §43); 3G81 Surface; 3G70 Surface & Sub-surface; 3G50 Surface.
  Broad lug 3.5 cm. wide, 1 cm. high: 3G92 Surface.
  Jar with 4(?) rectangular double- or triple-pierced lugs on rib forming gutter below rim (badly damaged): 3G80 Sub-surface (Fig. 82; cf. §44).

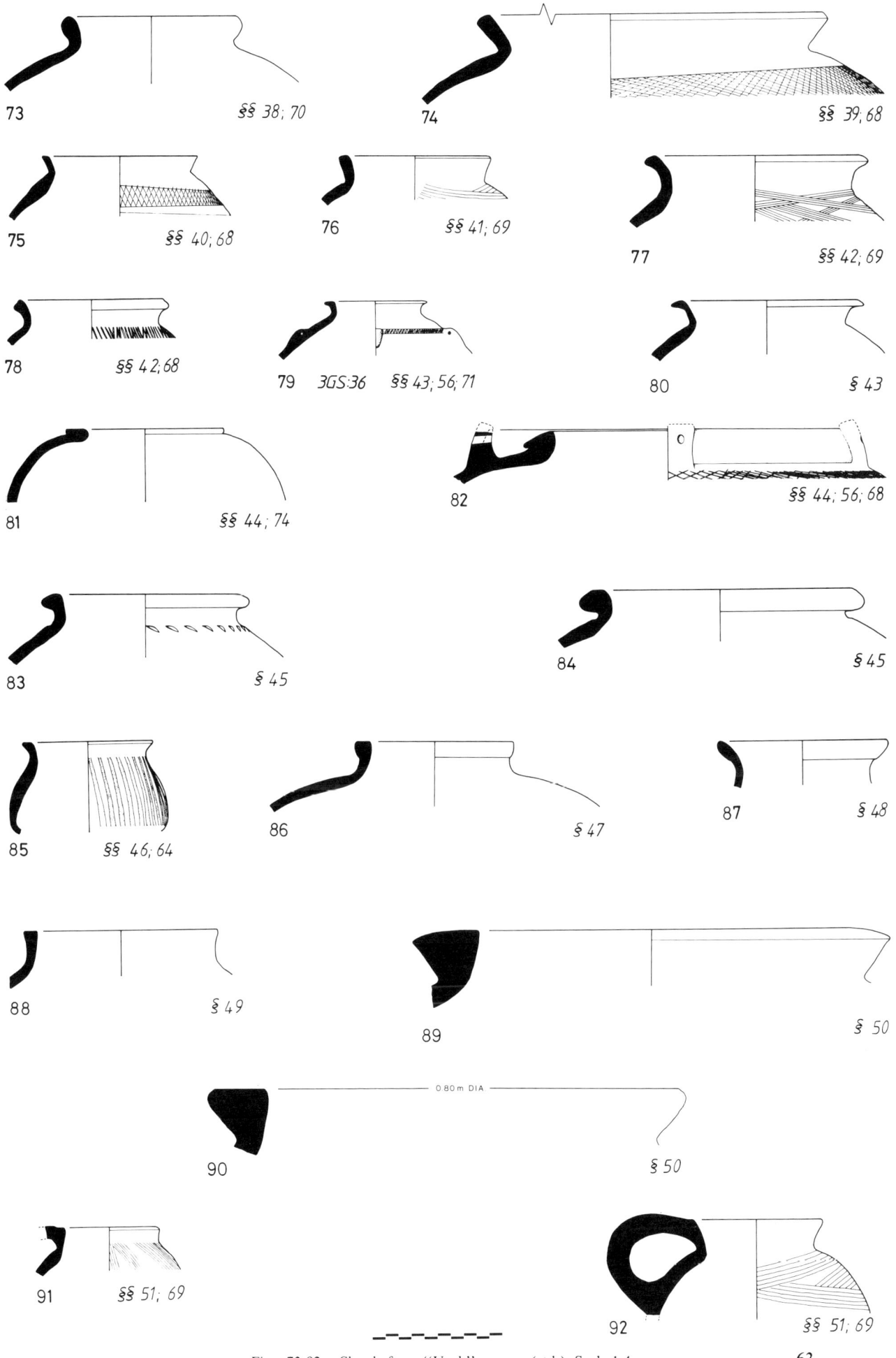

Figs. 73-92. Sherds from "Uruk" squares (ctd.). Scale 1:4.

63

Spouted jars: Most spouts tapered towards the end; some had a distinct droop. The usual method of attachment was to smooth clay from the jar body up into the spout, but in a sherd from 3G93 Surface (Fig. 106), the process has been reversed.

§57 *Small tapering spouts:*
Lengths: 3-3.7 cm.; Diam. at base: 2.6 cm.
Examples: 3G80 Surface (Fig. 100); 3G80 Sub-surface.

§58 *Medium tapering spouts (usually rather squat):*
Lengths: 3.5-5 cm.; Diam. at base: 3.5-4.7 cm.
Examples: 3G90 Surface (Fig. 101); 3G71 Sub-surface (Fig. 102); 3G93 Sub-surface (Fig. 103); 3G51 Surface.

§59 *Large tapering spouts:*
Lengths: 4.6-6 cm.; Diam. at base: 4.8-5.3 cm.
Examples: 3G72 Sub-surface (Fig. 104); 3G62 Surface; 3G61 Surface.

§60 *Drooping spouts:*
Lengths: 3.5-4.5 cm.; Diam. at base: 2.5-4.5 cm.
Examples: 3G60 Sub-surface (Fig. 105); 3G93 Surface (Fig. 106).

§61 *Trumpet-shaped:* 3G92 Sub-surface (Fig. 107).

§62 *Long, thin:* 3G70 Sub-surface (Fig. 108).

§63 *Attached to rim:* 3G70 Sub-surface (Fig. 109); 3G70 Surface.

Decoration on jars

§64 *Reserved slip decoration:* The heavy encrustation of salt may have disguised the presence of reserved slip decoration in some instances.
Horizontal reserved slip: On jar shoulder: 3G92 Surface (Fig. 70).
Diagonal reserved slip: More frequent than horizontal reserved slip; on jar shoulders and bodies.
Examples: 3G62 Sub-surface (Fig. 85); 3G61 Sub-surface (Fig. 72; below row of finger-nail impressions); 3G70 Surface (around spout); 3G62 Surface.
Horizontal and diagonal reserved slip together: Very neatly executed, with regularly-spaced diagonals crossing the horizontal reserved slip.
Example: 3G80 Sub-surface (Fig. 98).
See Adams & Nissen 1972, Fig. 30 r.

§65 *Grooving:* Found on jar shoulders, 1-4 mm. wide and 1-2 mm. apart.
Examples: 3G82 Sub-surface (Fig. 71); 3G81 Sub-surface.
Parallel grooves on strap handle: 3G52 Sub-surface (Fig. 94).

§66 *Paint:*
Unpierced lug, light green fabric with black paint: 3G93 Sub-surface (Fig. 99; Plate V*a*; VI*b*).
Horizontal bands of black paint on jar shoulder: 3G82 Surface (Fig. 110; Plate V*a*).
Horizontal bands of purplish paint on jar shoulder: 3G90 Surface.
Black bituminous paint on coarse vessel: 3G91 Sub-surface.
Red wash and burnish: 3G71 Sub-surface (see §43); 3G51 Sub-surface.
Plum-coloured wash: 3G80 Sub-surface.

§67 *Two-tone effect, dark/light green, perhaps firing accident:* See above, p. 56; Plate IV*b*, bottom right.
Examples: 3G62 Surface (Fig. 132); 3G83 Surface (Fig. 111); 3G70 Surface; 3G82 Surface.

§68 *Incised decoration:* Found on jar shoulders, usually in bands of cross-hatching bounded by horizontal lines. In some of the better-preserved examples the effect appeared to have been produced by pressing some sort of fibrous material such as a grass-stalk or straw onto the clay. The bands are often rather uneven. The fabric is usually buff, medium-fine grit- or vegetable-tempered.
Incisions (vertical) on jar shoulder: 3G71 Sub-surface (Fig. 78; Grey Ware).
Bands of cross-hatched incision:
Examples: 3G80 Sub-surface (Fig. 82); 3G80 Sub-surface (Figs. 74 and 75); 3G61 Sub-surface; 3G60 Surface; 3G51 Surface; 3G70 Sub-surface; 3G52 Surface; 3G71 Sub-surface.
Cross-hatched incised triangles: 3G70 Surface (Fig. 112; Plate IV*b*); 3G70 Sub-surface; 3G60 Surface.
Cross-hatched incision with deeply excised triangles and row of finger-nail impressions: 3G70 Sub-surface (Fig. 113; Plate IV*b*).
See Delougaz 1952, Pl. 45.

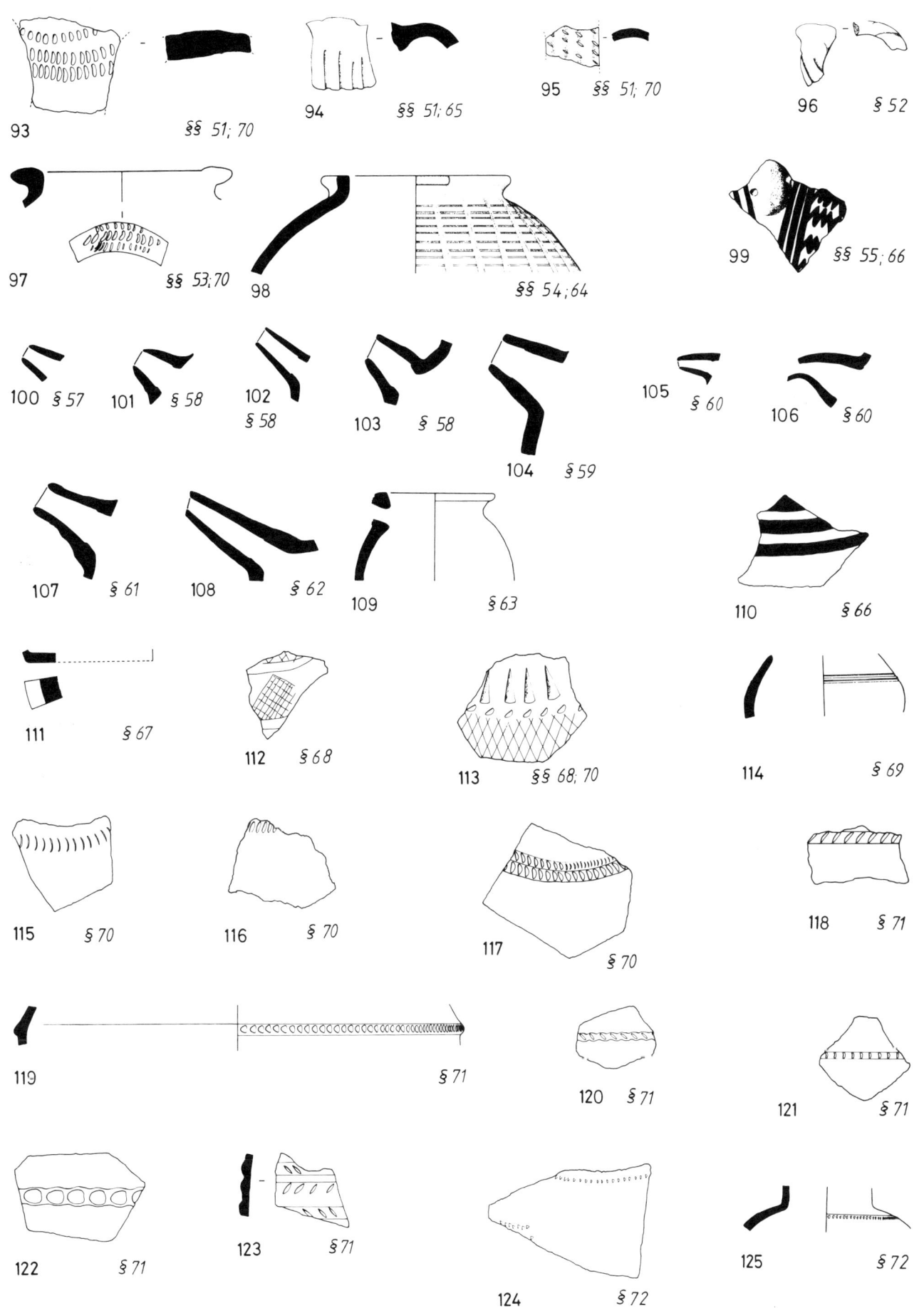

Figs. 93-125. Sherds from "Uruk" squares (ctd.). Scale 1:4.

§69 *Combed decoration:* Most of the comb decoration takes the form of irregular cross-hatching on the shoulder and probably all over the jar, since combed bases were found. Combs with three, four, and six teeth 1.5-3 mm. apart were detected. Combed decoration is most frequently found on Grey Ware jars, but some examples were of buff fabric, medium vegetable- or grit-tempered.

Horizontal comb decoration on jar shoulder: 3G81 Sub-surface (Fig. 114; Plate IV). .

Cross-hatched comb decoration: 3G70 Sub-surface (Fig. 77); 3G70 Sub-surface (Fig. 76; Grey Ware); 3G60 Sub-surface; 3G82 Surface; 3G71 Sub-surface; 3G72 Sub-surface; 3G62 Surface.

Cross-hatched comb decoration on handled jars: 3G70 Surface (Fig. 91), 3G70 Sub-surface (Fig. 92)—both Grey Ware.

Cross-hatched comb decoration on jar base: 3G82 Sub-surface (Fig. 129; Plate IV*b*; Grey Ware).

Impressed decoration: Most of the impressed decoration took the form of finger or finger-nail impressions, but a wide range of effects was produced depending on how deeply and at what angle the impression was made. Much of it was carried on applied ribs at shoulder carinations.

§70 *Rows of finger-nail impressions:* These are usually impressed directly into the pot at the base of the neck, sometimes in association with other motifs such as diagonal reserved slip.

Examples: 3G61 Sub-surface (Fig. 72; with diagonal reserved slip); 3G70 Sub-surface (Fig. 115; Grey Ware); 3G70 Sub-surface (Fig. 116); 3G50 Surface (Fig. 60); 3G71 Surface (Fig. 73; Grey Ware).

In two rows at base of jar neck: 3G70 Sub-surface.

With incised cross-hatching and deeply-excised triangles: 3G70 Sub-surface (Fig. 113).

In rows on strap handle: 3G61 Surface (Fig. 93); 3G91 Surface (Fig. 95).

In rows on rim swelling: 3G90 Sub-surface (Fig. 97).

In two rows between 3 horizontal lines: 3G62 Surface (Fig. 117; Plate IV*b*).

§71 *Finger-nail impressed ribs from jar shoulder carinations:*

Examples: 3G71 Sub-surface (Fig. 79; see §43); 3G82 Surface (Fig. 118; Plate IV*b*); 3G70 Surface (Fig. 119); 3G80 Sub-surface (Fig. 120; Plate IV*b*); 3G70 Surface (Fig. 121); 3G52 Sub-surface (Fig. 61).

Finger-impressed ribs: 3G93 Sub-surface (Fig. 122; Plate IV*b*).

Three ribs: 3G70 Sub-surface (Fig. 123).

§72 *Other impressed decoration:*

Triangular (reed ?) impressions at base of jar neck and perhaps around spout: 3G60 Sub-surface (Fig. 124; Grey Ware).

Triangular impressions under horizontal line at base of jar neck: 3G81 Surface (Fig. 125; Plate IV*b*).

Rough chevrons from base of jar neck: 3G70 Sub-surface (Fig. 126; Plate IV*b*; Grey Ware).

Row of lozenges in low relief: 3G61 Surface (Fig. 127; Plate IV*b*).

Rocker pattern: 3G62 Sub-surface (Fig. 128; Plate IV*b*; Grey Ware). See Hansen 1965, Figs. 1 and 2; Haller 1932 Pl. 19 D a.

Jar bases

§73 *Rounded bases:* These are probably very often discarded as body sherds. The jar shape from 3G81 Surface (Fig. 63) was probably round-bottomed, by comparison with examples from elsewhere. From 3G82 Sub-surface (Fig. 129) is a rounded base with comb decoration. See also the small carinated jar from 3G70 Sub-surface (3GS:29; Fig. 130).

§74 *Flat bases:* Simple flat bases were by far the most numerous.

Examples: 3G92 Surface (Fig. 131); 3G62 Surface (Fig. 132; with two-tone effect); 3G83 Surface (Fig. 81; with two-tone effect).

§75 *Ring bases:*

Examples: 3G80 Sub-surface (Fig. 133); 3G80 Surface; 3G81 Surface.

§76 *Hollow stands:* Only one example was found: 3G50 Sub-surface.

§77 *Miniatures:* Miniature bowl with sharply incurving rim; very thin, greenish fabric: 3G80 Surface (Fig. 134).

§78 *Miscellaneous:*

Sieve bowl: 3G92 Surface (Fig. 135). See Haller 1932, Pl. 20 B d´.

Pouring lips: 3G61 Surface (Fig. 136); provenance unknown (Fig. 137; with pierced lug). See Delougaz 1952, Pl. 20 a and a´; Hansen 1965, Fig. 3.

Coarse flat plate, perhaps jar stopper; diam. ca. 30 cm.: 3G51 Sub-surface (Fig. 138). See Delougaz 1952, Pl. 20 and p. 39.

Coarse flat plate with hole 2.2 cm. in diam. and protuberance near rim; diam. 13.5 cm.: 3G90 Sub-surface (Fig. 139).

Coarse, straight-sided fragment, ca. 14 cm. long; perhaps from rectangular tray: 3G60 Sub-surface (Fig. 140).

Clay U-sectioned drainage channels or gutter fragments were common. Width ca. 6-10 cm.; Height ca. 4.5-6 cm. Usually of light green, medium-coarse overfired fabric.

Examples: 3G80 Sub-surface; 3G90 Surface, etc.

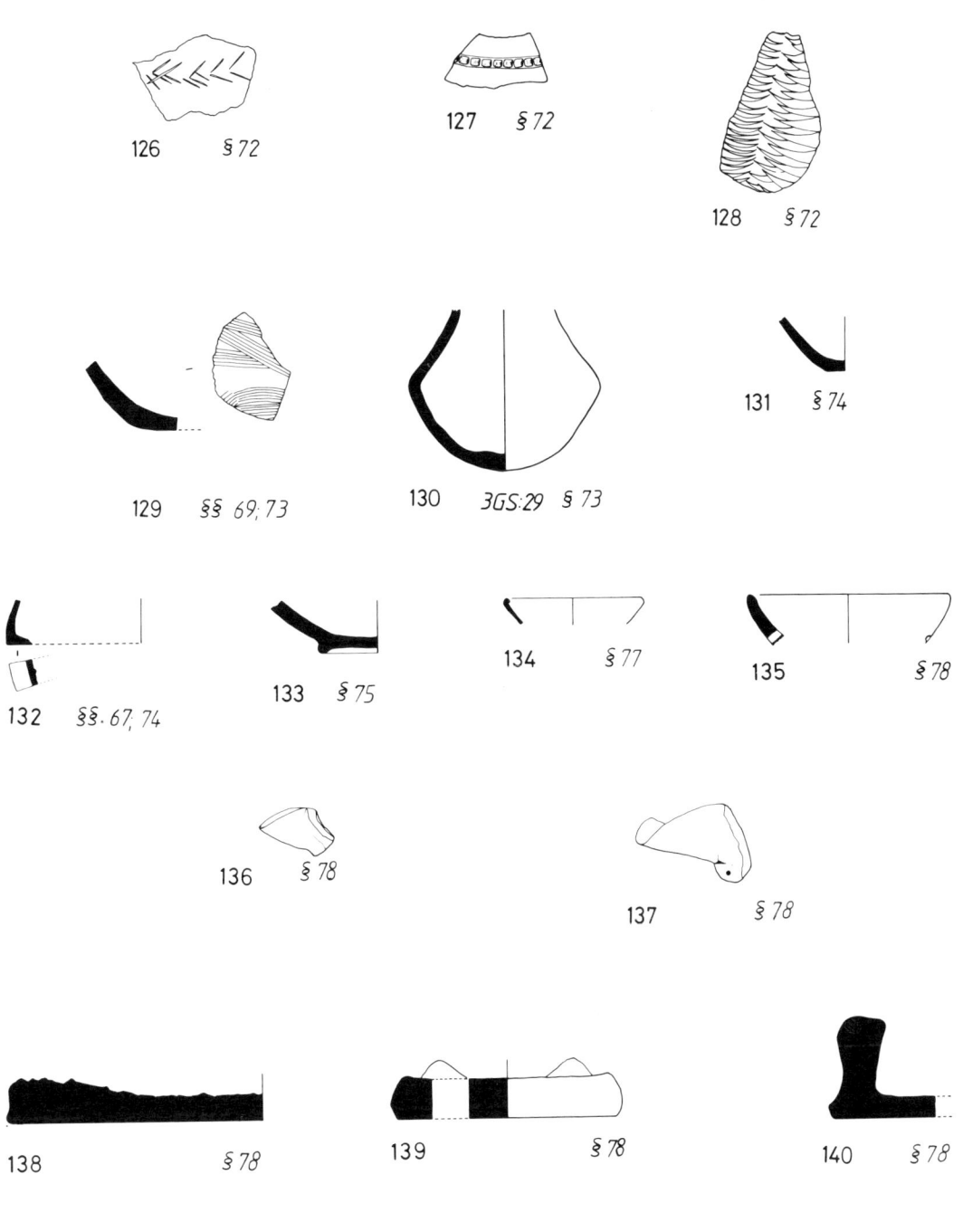

Figs. 126-140. Sherds from "Uruk" squares (ctd.). Scale 1:4.

The ED I squares

	Fabric
§§79-98	Bowls
§99	Decoration on bowls
§§100-2	Bases
§§103-26	Jars
§§127-33	Lugs, handles, etc.
§§134-41	Spouts
§§142-55	Decoration
§§156-8	Bases
§159	Hollow stands
§160	Miniatures
§161	Miscellaneous

Fabric

In the pottery from the Uruk squares grit and vegetable tempers were represented almost equally; in the ED I squares grit tempers predominate, forming nearly 65% of the sample, while vegetable tempers have dwindled to just over 17%. The proportion of over-fired sherds has also declined, while one fabric type has begun to dominate the sample.

1. *Pink/orange fabric, cream slip:* As in the Uruk squares, this fabric is well-made and hard-fired with a smooth cream slip, much favoured for decorated pots. In the ED I squares, however, the vast majority of pink and cream sherds are tempered with fine-medium grit, and this type of fabric alone accounts for over 35% of the entire sample, pink and cream fabrics in general representing 53%.

2. *Greenish over-fired:* Over-fired sherds still occur in considerable numbers, but rather less so than in the Uruk squares at 23% of the sample. A number of bowls occur in this fabric, several with a coarse vegetable temper, but it is mainly seen in medium-walled vessels, the majority having a medium grit temper. The "two-tone" effect is still seen.

3. *Buff fabric:* Sherds of buff fabric have declined to 13% in the ED I squares. The majority of sherds come from medium-walled, grit-tempered vessels but there are several examples of larger vessels with coarse vegetable temper.

4. *Red fabric:* All the sherds in the sample were of the soft, crumbling variety; most were medium grit-tempered with only two sherds of medium vegetable temper. They represent a little under 8% of the sample.

5. *Grey Ware:* Grey Ware sherds formed less than 3% of the sample from the ED I squares. All were medium grit-tempered. A few were burnished.

6. *Red wash and burnish:* Again, this ware was represented by one sherd, a ring base, similar in colour and fabric to the 4-lugged jar from the Uruk squares.

Bowls

§79 *Curving sides, rounded rim:*
    Diam.: 34 cm.
    Example: 2G23 Sub-surface (Fig. 141).

§80 *Curving sides, rounded pinched rim:* A shallow, saucer-like shape, probably round-bottomed.
    Diams.: 12-14 cm.
    Examples: 2G42 Surface (Fig. 142); 2G41 Sub-surface.

§81 *Curving sides, pinched rim:* A shallow saucer-like shape, probably round-bottomed.
    Diam.: 13 cm.
    Example: 2G35 Surface (Fig. 143).

§82 *Straight-sided, rounded rim:* A very thin-walled, well-made conical shape, probably flat-based.
    Diams.: 10-14 cm.
    Examples: 2G04 Sub-surface (Fig. 144).

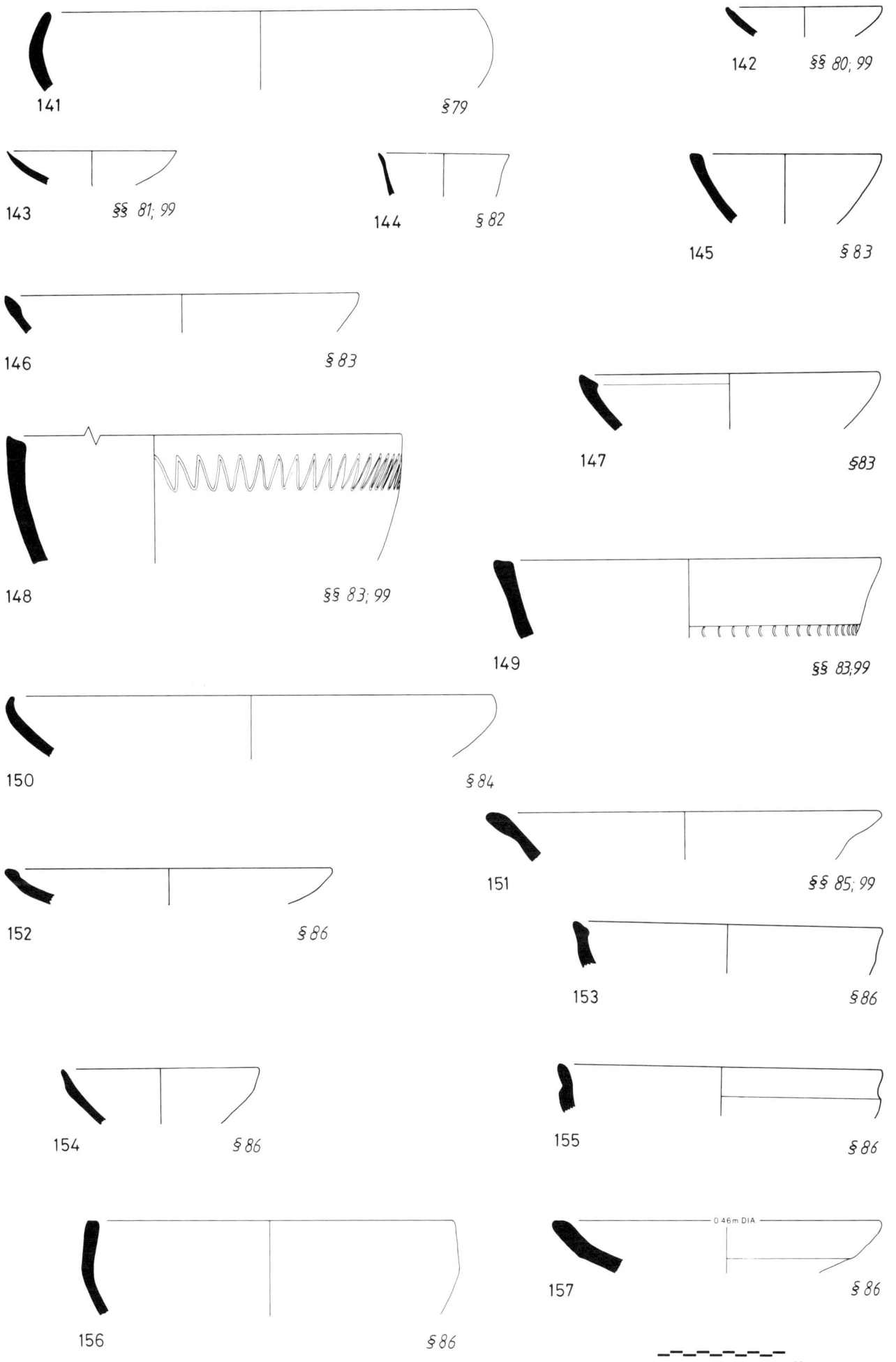

Figs. 141-157. Sherds from ED squares. Scale 1:4.

§83 *Straight or slightly curving sides, internally sloping rim:* A deep conical shape. The large examples are sometimes decorated.
   (Small) diams.: 15 cm.
   Examples: 2G52 Sub-surface (Fig. 145); 2G51 Sub-surface.
   (Medium) diams.: 23-27 cm.
   Examples: 2G97 Sub-surface (Fig. 146); 2G88 Surface (Fig. 147); 2G55 Surface.
   (Large) diams.: 30-38 cm.
   Examples: 2G23 Sub-surface (Fig. 148; incised zig-zag on outside below rim); 2G13 Sub-surface (Fig. 149; row of fingernail impressions beneath horizontal incised line on outside).

§84 *Straight-sided, sharply incurving rim:*
   Diams.: 19-37 cm.
   Examples: 2G11 Sub-surface (Fig. 150); 2G63 Surface; 2G66 Sub-surface.

§85 *Straight-sided, bulging rim:*
   Diams.: 30-40 cm.
   Examples: 2G22 Sub-surface (Fig. 151); 2G31 Sub-surface; 2G71 Sub-surface; 2G51 Sub-surface.

§86 *Gently-carinated bowls:* A heterogeneous group with an enormous variety of rim forms.
   Diams.: 15-46 cm.
   Examples: 2G72 Surface (Fig. 152); 2G62 Surface (Fig. 153); 2G62 Sub-surface (Fig. 154); 2G11 Surface (Fig. 155); 2G00 Sub-surface (Fig. 156); 2G80 Surface (Fig. 157); 2G31 Sub-surface (Fig. 158); 2G25 Sub-surface (Fig. 159); 2G97 Surface (with perforation below carination).

§87 *Sharply-carinated bowls with everted rim:* The sharply-carinated bowl is less frequent and more standardized than in the Uruk squares.
   Diams.: 19-26 cm.
   Examples: 2G90 Sub-surface (Fig. 160); 2G03 Sub-surface; 2G42 Surface.

§88 *Sharply-carinated bowl with flat rim:*
   Diam.: 28.5 cm.
   Example: 2G97 Sub-surface (Fig. 161); [the 1981 excavation showed that this rim comes from a type of Uruk bowl (note the location of 2G97) with a sharp triangular open ("split") spout—see *Iraq* 44 (1982), 116, Fig. 4:10].

§89 *Sharply-carinated bowl with internally-sloping rim:*
   Diam.: 30 cm.
   Example: 2G45 Surface (Fig. 162).

§90 *Curving sides, cut rim:* A shallow saucer-like shape.
   Diam.: 17 cm.
   Example: 2G50 Sub-surface (Fig. 163).

§91 *Straight-sided, cut rim (medium):* Very like the mass-produced Conical Bowl in shape, but well-made and carefully finished.
   Diams.: 20-23 cm.
   Examples: 2G00 Sub-surface (Fig. 164); 2G70 Sub-surface; 2G62 Surface; 2G61 Surface.

§92 *Straight-sided, cut rim (large):*
   Diams.: 30-50 cm.
   Examples: 2G32 Sub-surface (Fig. 165); 2G42 Sub-surface; 2G30 Sub-surface.

§93 *Straight-sided, slightly projecting rim:* Well-made, conical shape.
   Diam.: 20 cm.
   Example: 2G51 Sub-surface (Fig. 166).

§94 *Straight-sided, rounded rim:* A large, medium to thick-walled conical shape.
   Diams.: 30-40 cm.
   Examples: 2G12 Sub-surface (Fig. 167); 2G13 Sub-surface; 2G51 Sub-surface; 2G12 Sub-surface; 2G33 Surface.

§95 *Incurving sides, rolled rim:*
   Diams.: 32-38 cm.
   Examples: 2G42 Sub-surface (Fig. 168); 2G33 Sub-surface.

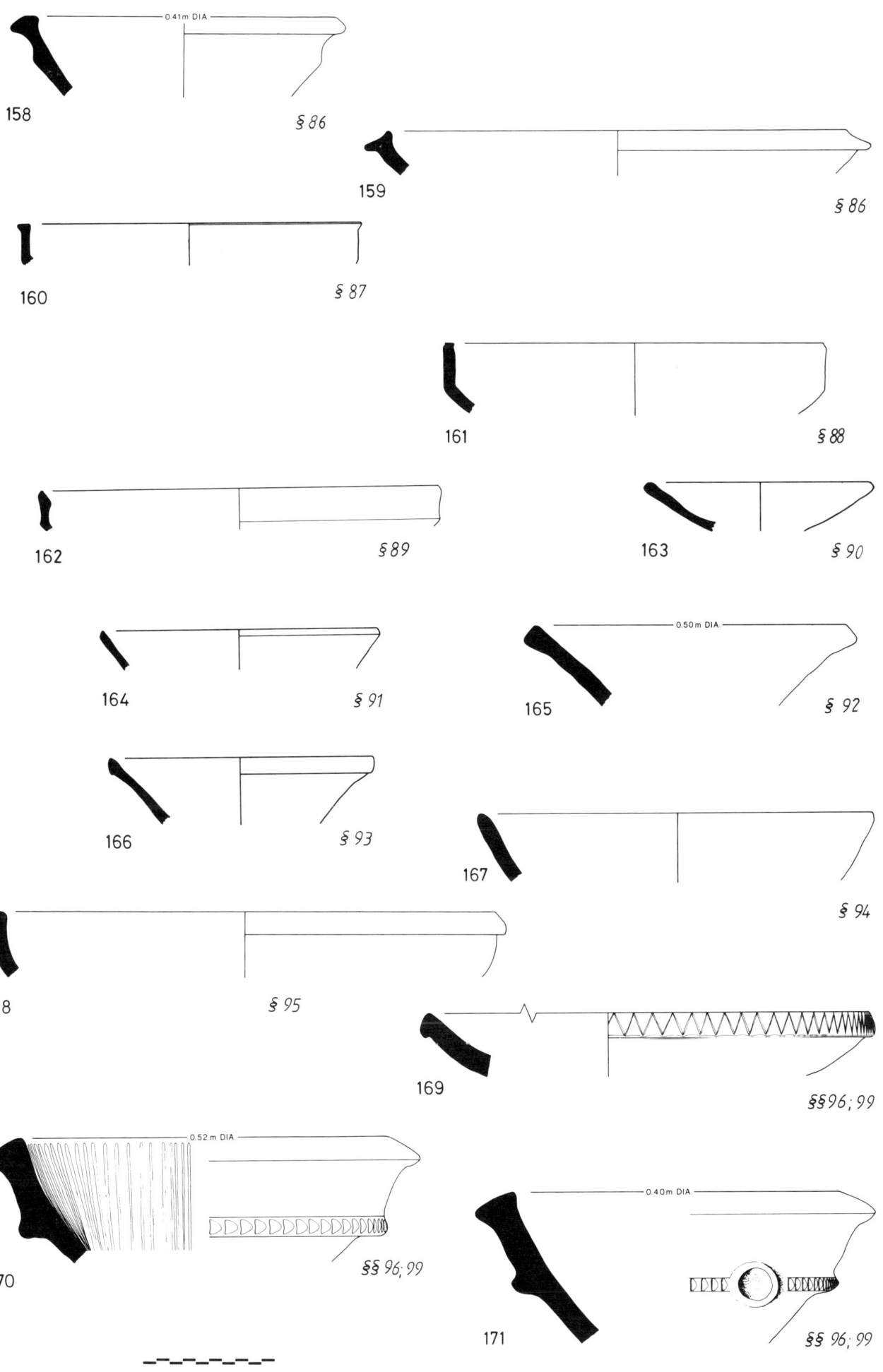

Figs. 158-171. Sherds from ED squares (ctd.). Scale 1:4.

§96 *Curving sides, projecting rim:* A large, open shape which carries decoration on rim or impressed rib.
Diams.: 40-52 cm.
Examples: 2G40 Sub-surface (Fig. 169; incised zig-zag on rim); 2G31 Sub-surface (Fig. 170; finger-impressed rib outside, vertical pattern-burnishing inside); 2G21 Sub-surface (Fig. 171; finger-nail impressed rib with socket outside, Plate VI*a*); 2G41 Sub-surface; 2G33 Sub-surface; 2G32 Sub-surface.

§97 *Straight-sided, projecting rim:*
Diams.: 35-40 cm.
Examples: 2G13 Sub-surface (Fig. 172; incised cross-hatching on rim); 2G90 Sub-surface (Fig. 173); 2G51 Sub-surface (Fig. 174).

§98 *Large coarse bowls with flat-topped rim:*
Diams.: 45-60 cm.
Examples: 2G12 Sub-surface (Fig. 175); 2G33 Surface; 2G62 Sub-surface.

§99 *Decoration on bowls:* This was more frequent in the ED I than in the Uruk squares. Only large bowls were chosen for decoration; all were over 30 cm. in diameter.
Incised decoration on rims: 2G40 Sub-surface (Fig. 169); 2G13 Sub-surface (Fig. 172).
Finger-nail impressed rib: 2G31 Sub-surface (Fig. 170; vertical pattern burnishing inside); 2G21 Sub-surface (Fig. 171; with socket); 2G33 Sub-surface; 2G27 Sub-surface.
Row of finger-nail impressions with incised horizontal line: 2G13 Sub-surface (Fig. 149).
Incised zig-zags: 2G23 Sub-surface (Fig. 148); see McCown, Haines and Biggs 1978, Pl. 48 4-12 and p. 26.

Bowl bases
§100 *Round:* Several of the smaller bowl types were most probably round-bottomed, e.g. 2G35 Surface (Fig. 143); 2G50 Sub-surface (Fig. 151); 2G42 Surface (Fig. 142).

§101 *Flat:* The majority of bowls probably had a simple flat base.

§102 *Ring:* Ring bases from bowls were not certainly identified.

Jars
It is difficult to classify on the basis of rim sherds alone, but on the whole the jars from the ED I squares appeared to belong to a narrower, more standardized range than those from the Uruk squares.

§103 *Neckless, plain collar rim:*
Diams.: 10-19 cm.
Examples: 2G40 Sub-surface (Fig. 176; horizontal comb decoration on shoulder); 2G51 Sub-surface; 2G40 Sub-surface; 2G32 Surface; 2G10 Sub-surface; 2G21 Sub-surface; 2G12 Sub-surface.

§104 *Neckless, cut collar rim:*
Diams.: 11-26 cm.
Examples: 2G51 Sub-surface (Fig. 177); 2G10 Sub-surface; 2G72 Surface.

§105 *Neckless, flaring collar rim:*
Diams.: 12-16 cm.
Examples: 2G01 Surface (Fig. 178); 2G22 Sub-surface; 2G11 Surface; 2G30 Sub-surface; 2G12 Sub-surface; 2G51 Sub-surface.

§106 *Neckless, rolled rim:*
Diams.: 14-26 cm.
Examples: 2G53 Surface (Fig. 179; Grey Ware, 2 finger-impressed ribs on shoulder); 2G21 Sub-surface; 2G80 Sub-surface; 2G32 Sub-surface; 2G53 Surface.

§107 *Neckless, carinated jar:*
Diams.: 23-26 cm.
Examples: 2G32 Sub-surface (Fig. 180; finger-nail impressed rib at shoulder carination); 2G35 Sub-surface.

§108 *Upright neck, plain rim:*
Diam.: 15 cm.
Example: 2G20 Sub-surface (Fig. 181).

§109 *Flaring neck, plain rim:*
Diams.: 6-14 cm.
Examples: 2G61 Sub-surface (Fig. 182); 2G32 Sub-surface; 2G71 Sub-surface; 2G03 Surface; 2G51 Sub-surface; 2G42 Sub-surface; 2G33 Surface.

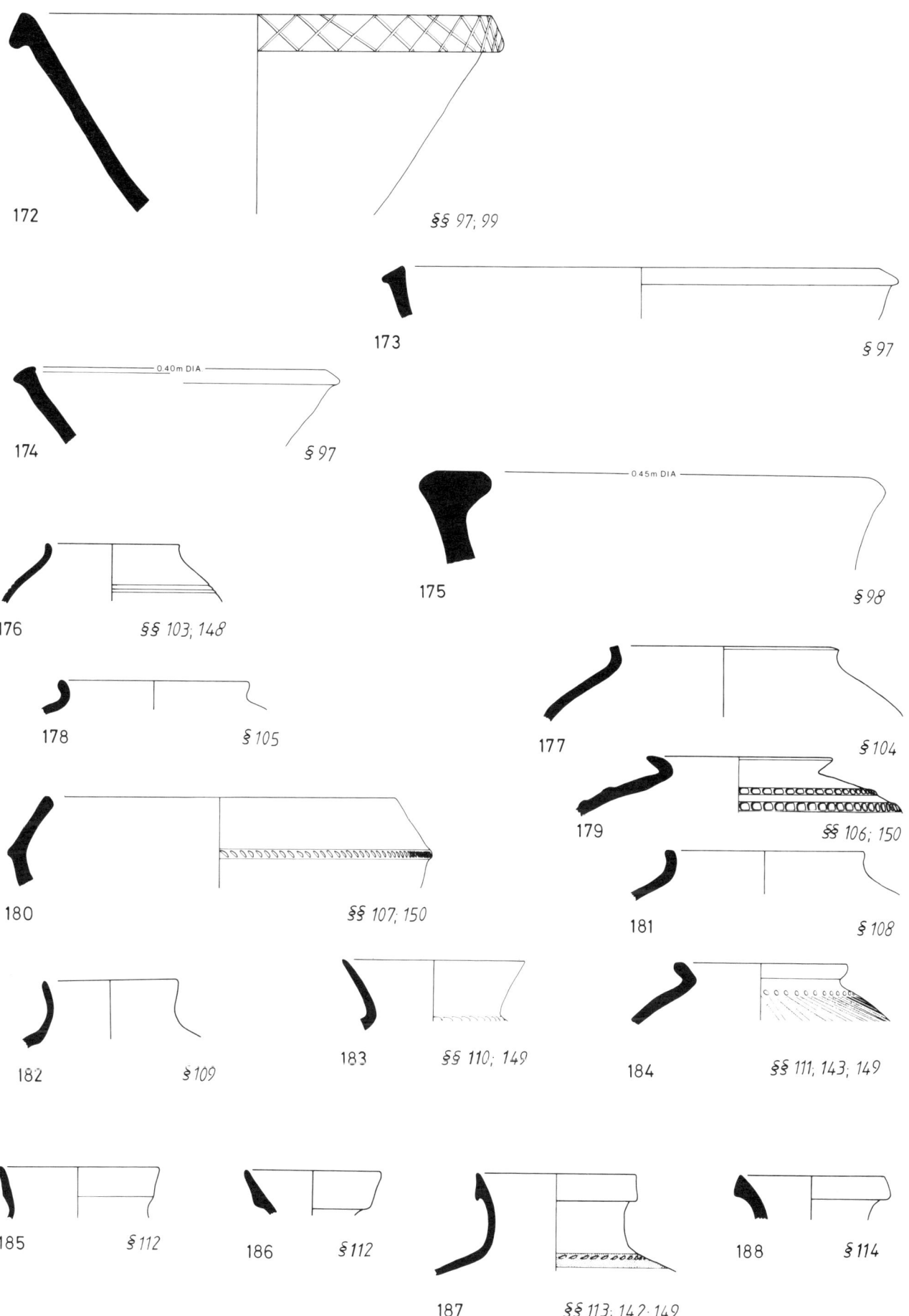

Figs. 172-188. Sherds from ED squares (ctd.). Scale 1:4.

§110 *Out-turned neck, plain rim:*
　　Diam.: 13.5 cm.
　　Example: 2G00 Sub-surface (Fig. 183; row of finger-nail impressions around base of neck).

§111 *Short, out-turned neck, plain or slightly swollen rim:*
　　Diams.: 14-17 cm.
　　Examples: 2G42 Sub-surface (Fig. 184; diagonal reserved slip below row of finger-nail impressions at base of neck); 2G50 Sub-surface; 2G72 Surface; 2G13 Sub-surface.

Band Rims

§112 *Upright or slightly outward-curving neck, plain band rim:*
　　Diams.: 10-14 cm.
　　Examples: 2G51 Sub-surface (Fig. 185); 2G51 Sub-surface (Fig. 186); 2G03 Sub-surface; 2G70 Sub-surface; 2G32 Sub-surface; 2G22 Sub-surface.

§113 *Upright or slightly outward-curving neck, overhanging band rim:*
　　Diams.: 11-12 cm.
　　Examples: 2G12 Sub-surface (Fig. 187; band of horizontal reserved slip with row of finger-nail impressions at base of neck); 2G03 Sub-surface; 2G22 Sub-surface; 2G41 Sub-surface; 2G33 Sub-surface.

§114 *Upright or slightly outward-curving neck, projecting band rim:*
　　Diams.: 8-15 cm.
　　Examples: 2G30 Surface (Fig. 188); 2G22 Sub-surface (Fig. 189); 2G33 Surface; 2G40 Sub-surface; 2G03 Surface; 2G52 Surface; 2G12 Surface.

§115 *Upright or slightly outward-curving neck, dished band rim:*
　　Diams.: 12-15 cm.
　　Examples: (short) 2G20 Sub-surface (Fig. 190); 2G40 Sub-surface; 2G23 Surface; 2G11 Surface and Sub-surface; 2G26 Sub-surface (Fig. 214; spouted).
　　　　(long) 2G20 Sub-surface (Fig. 191); 2G80 Sub-surface; 2G03 Surface.

§116 *Out-turned neck, flaring rim:*
　　Diams.: 13-32 cm.
　　Examples: 2G51 Sub-surface (Fig. 192); 2G72 Sub-surface; 2G50 Sub-surface; 2G42 Surface; 2G71 Sub-surface; 2G21 Surface.

§117 *Out-turned neck, cut rim:*
　　Diams.: 14-16 cm.
　　Examples: 2G51 Sub-surface (Fig. 193); 2G33 Sub-surface; 2GS:92 (Fig. 194 from 2G13, Sub-surface).

§118 *Out-turned neck, projecting cut rim:*
　　Diams.: 7-16 cm.
　　Examples: 2G70 Sub-surface (Fig. 195); 2G41 Sub-surface; 2G50 Surface; 2G12 Surface; 2G72 Surface; 2G62 Sub-surface; 2G51 Sub-surface; 2G10 Sub-surface.

§119 *Upright or slightly out-turned neck, sloping everted rim:*
　　Diams.: (small) 9-16 cm.
　　Examples: 2G42 Sub-surface (Fig. 196); 2G32 Sub-surface; 2G01 Surface; 2G12 Sub-surface; 2G33 Surface; 2G41 Sub-surface; 2G33 Sub-surface; 2G90 Sub-surface.
　　Diams.: (large) 17-23 cm.
　　Examples: 2G33 Surface (Fig. 197); 2G13 Sub-surface; 2G41 Sub-surface; 2GS:293 (Fig. 198 from 2G76 Sub-surface).

§120 *Out-turned neck, blunt everted rim:*
　　Diams.: 17-18 cm.
　　Examples: 2G00 Sub-surface (Fig. 199); 2G50 Surface; 2G51 Sub-surface.

§121 *Straight or out-turned neck, flat everted rim:*
　　Diams.: 8-18 cm.
　　Examples: 2G51 Sub-surface (Fig. 200; Grey Ware); 2G61 Sub-surface; 2G70 Sub-surface; 2G62 Surface.

§122 *Neckless, squashed everted rim:*
　　Diams.: 14-38 cm.
　　Examples: 2G70 Sub-surface (Fig. 201).

§123 *Outward-curving neck, round-topped rim:*
　　Diam.: 16 cm.
　　Example: 2G69 Sub-surface (Fig. 202).

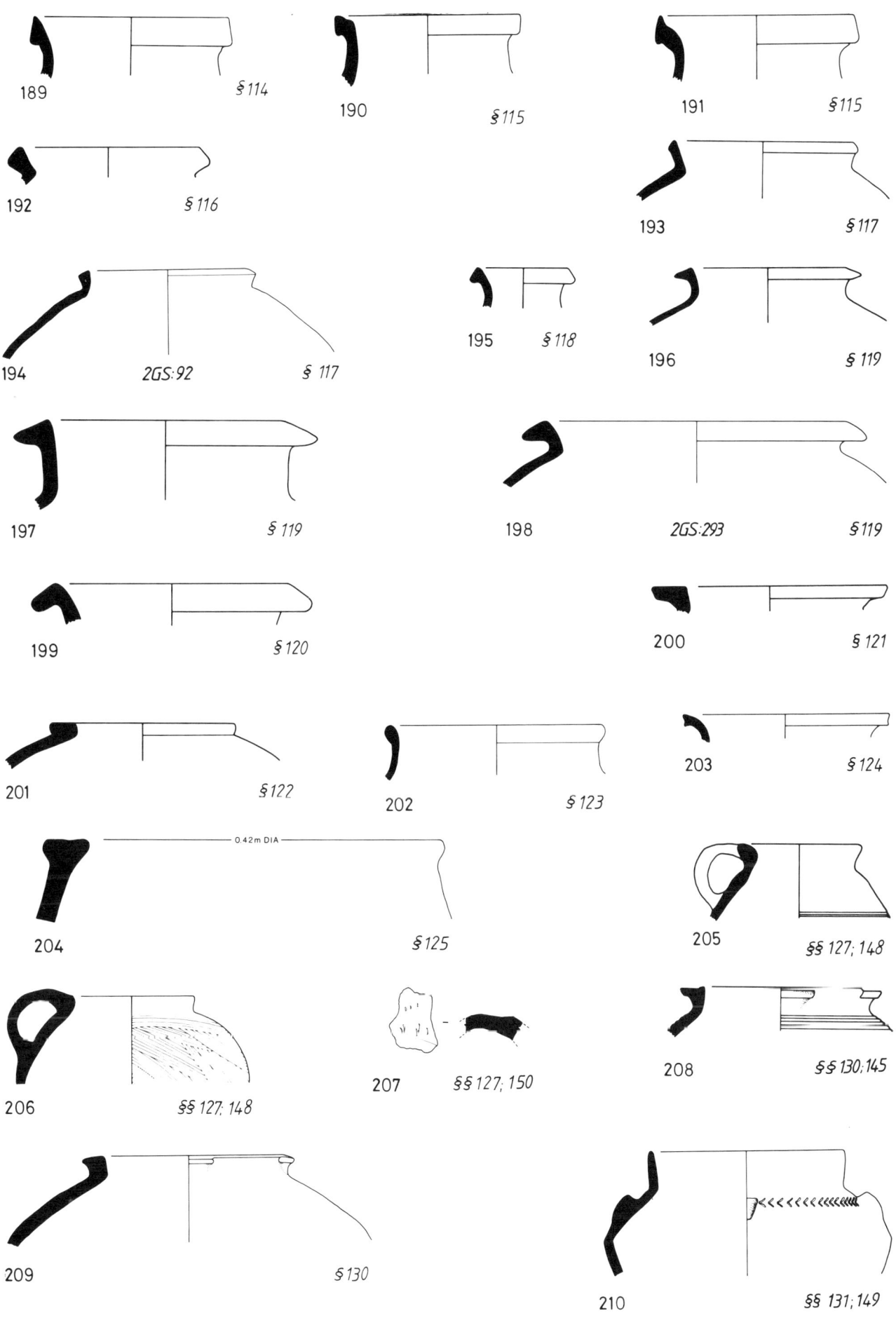

Figs. 189-210. Sherds from ED squares (ctd.). Scale 1:4.

§124 *Outward-curving neck, concave rim:*
    Diam.: 16 cm.
    Example: 2G18 Sub-surface (Fig. 203).

§125 *Large coarse jars with flat-topped rim:*
    Thickness of walls: 1.5-3 cm.
    Diams.: 40-48 cm.
    Examples: 2G33 Surface (Fig. 204); 2G13 Sub-surface; 2G42 Sub-surface.

§126 *Two large, semi-complete carinated jars, ring-based:*
    2GS:101 (Fig. 285) with single beak-lug and finger-nail impressed ribs, and 2GS:104 (Fig. 286) with single spool-lug, excised triangles and bands of cross-hatched incision. See below, pp. 83-4 and Plate VIII; Delougaz 1952, Pls. 41-2.

Lugs, handles, etc.

§127 *Strap handles:*
    Widths: 2.5-5.5 cm.
    Diams. of jars: 9.5 cm.
    Examples: 2G42 Sub-surface (Fig. 205; Grey Ware, horizontal comb decoration); 2G98 Surface (Fig. 206; cross-hatched comb decoration).
        Detached from jar rim: 2G16 Surface (Fig. 207; irregular finger-nail impressions); 2G04 Sub-surface; 2G55 Sub-surface; 2G73 Surface; 2G24 Surface; 2G75 Sub-surface.

§128 *Rope handles:* One example from 2G77 Surface (with rough incised decoration); see Adams & Nissen 1972, 100.

§129 *Round handles:* These were not found attached to rims.
    Diams.: 2-2.6 cm.
    Examples: 2G48/58/49/59 Sub-surface; 2G58 Sub-surface.

§130 *Tab rims:* These have four rectangular projections evenly spaced around the rim.
    Width: 3-5.3 cm.
    Thickness: 1.5-2.1 cm.
    Diams.: 12.5-16 cm.
    Examples: 2G31 Sub-surface (Fig. 208; horizontal grooving on the shoulder); 2G14 Sub-surface (Fig. 209); 2G42 Sub-surface; 2G36 Sub-surface; 2G06 Surface and Sub-surface; 2G37 Sub-surface.
    See Delougaz 1952, Pl. 63, 13; Haller 1932, Pl. 20 C c.

§131 *Unpierced lugs:* Triangular unpierced lugs, 2.5 x 1.6 cm. On shoulder of carinated jar, with a row of herring-bone finger-nail impressions between the lugs: 2G65 Surface (Fig. 210).

§132 *Pierced lugs:* None of the horizontally-pierced lugs was found attached to a sherd large enough to include the rim, with the exception of the two single-lug jars (see §126).
    Triangular: Lengths 4-5 cm.
        Examples: 2G60 Sub-surface; 2G52 Sub-surface.
    Oval: Lengths: 3-3.5 cm.
        Widths: 2-2.5 cm.
        Examples: 2G37 Surface (Fig. 211; in band of incised cross-hatching); 2G40 Sub-surface.
    See Delougaz 1952, Pl. 164.

§133 *Single-lug jars:*
    Large jar with excised triangles, incised cross-hatching and finger-nail impressed rib at jar shoulder carination; spool lug (Fig. 286; Plate VIIIb; see *Iraq* 40, 85; Delougaz 1952, Pls. 41-2).
    Large jar with finger-nail impressed ribs; burnished; single beak-lug (Fig. 285; Plate VIIIa; see *Iraq* 40, 86).

Spouted jars

Most spouts tapered towards the end; the example from 2G05 Sub-surface (Fig. 217) has the suggestion of a droop, but the majority appear to point upwards. The usual method of attachment was to smooth clay from the jar body up into the spout; in Fig. 217 the process has been reversed.

§134 *Small tapering spouts:*
    Lengths: 2.8-3.5 cm.
    Diams. at base: ca. 3 cm.
    Examples: 2G51 Sub-surface (Fig. 212); 2G12 Sub-surface.

§135 *Medium tapering spouts:*
    Lengths: 3.5-5.0 cm.
    Diams. at base: ca. 3.5 cm.
    Examples: 2G10 Surface (Fig. 213); 2G21 Sub-surface; 2G22 Sub-surface; 2G51 Sub-surface; 2G03 Sub-surface.

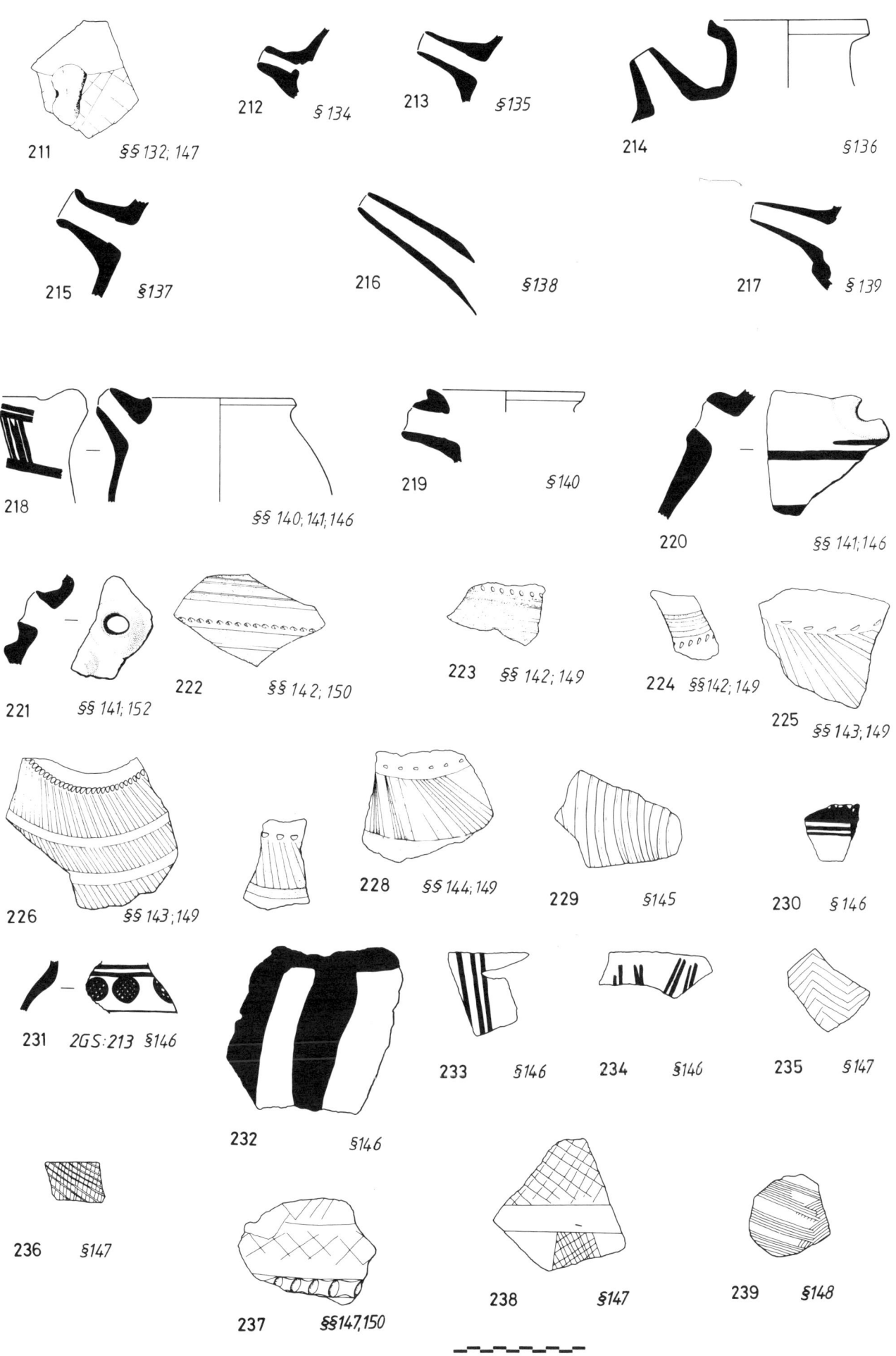

Figs. 211-239. Sherds from ED squares (ctd.). Scale 1:4.

§136 *Large tapering spouts:*
   Lengths: 5.0-5.5 cm.
   Diams. at base: ca. 5 cm.
   Examples: 2G26 Sub-surface (Fig. 214); 2G32 Sub-surface; 2G72 Sub-surface.

§137 *Trumpet-shaped, thickened rim:*
   Example: 2G02 Sub-surface (Fig. 215).

§138 *Long, thin:*
   Example: 2G55 Sub-surface (Fig. 216).

§139 *Drooping:*
   Example: 2G05 Sub-surface (Fig. 217).

§140 *Attached to rim:*
   Example: 2G55 Sub-surface (Fig. 218; fugitive black paint around spout); 2G62 Surface (Fig. 219).

§141 *Decoration around spouts:*
   Examples: 2G70 Sub-surface (Fig. 220; black paint); 2G55 Sub-surface (Fig. 218; black paint); 2G13 Sub-surface (Fig. 221; applied knob).

Decoration on jars

§142 *Horizontal reserved slip:*
   Above and below jar shoulder carination with finger-nail impressed rib: 2G33 Sub-surface (Fig. 222).
   At base of neck, incorporating row of finger-nail impressions: 2G12 Sub-surface (Fig. 187).
   Below row of finger-nail impressions at base of jar neck: 2G12 Surface (Fig. 223).
   Above row of finger-nail impressions on jar shoulder: 2G00 Sub-surface (Fig. 224).

§143 *Diagonal reserved slip:*
   Below row of finger-nail impressions at base of jar neck: 2G42 Sub-surface (Fig. 184); 2G12 Sub-surface (Fig. 225).
   In panels below row of finger-nail impressions: 2G22 Sub-surface (Fig. 226); see Adams and Nissen 1972, Fig. 30 w.

§144 *Diagonal and Horizontal:*
   On jar shoulder below row of finger-nail impressions at base of neck: 2G52 Sub-surface (Fig. 227); 2G12 Sub-surface (Fig. 228).

§145 *Grooving:*
   On jar shoulder below tab rim, 3 mm. apart, 3 mm. wide: 2G31 Sub-surface (Fig. 208).
   Irregular vertical grooving (perhaps imitating metal vessel): 2G35 Sub-surface (Fig. 229).

§146 *Paint:*
   Ubaid-like greenish fabric, black paint: 2G72 Surface (Fig. 230); 2G38 Sub-surface (cross-hatched panel on jar shoulder).
   Black horizontal bands and cross-hatched circles on small jar: 2GS:213 (Fig. 231; Plate V*a*).
   Black band at base of jar neck: 2G36 Surface.
   Coarse black paint around spout: 2G70 Sub-surface (Fig. 220).
   Fugitive black design around spout: 2G55 Sub-surface (Fig. 218).
   Rough black vertical stripes: 2G75 Surface (Fig. 232); 2G23-33 Sub-surface (Fig. 257; with finger-impressed ribs).
   Fine black vertical stripes: 2G64 Sub-surface (Fig. 233).
   Fugitive red paint: 2G33 Sub-surface (Fig. 234); 2G02 Sub-surface; 2G12 Sub-surface; 2G33 Sub-surface; 2G23 Sub-surface.

§147 *Incised decoration:* In some examples the effect appears to have been produced by pressing some sort of fibrous material such as a straw or grass stalk against the clay, while in others it has clearly been produced by drawing a fine point across the surface.
   Incised zig-zags: 2G50 Surface (Fig. 235).
   Herring-bone pattern (on miniature jar): 2G98 Surface (Fig. 272).
   Incised cross-hatching: 2G65 Surface (Fig. 236); 2G37 Surface (Fig. 211; with pierced lug); 2G22 Sub-surface (Fig. 237; on jar shoulder above finger-impressed rib); 2G17 Sub-surface (Fig. 238; bands of incised triangles); 2GS:104 (Fig. 286; Plate VIII*b*; with excised triangles).
   Incised wavy line below two horizontal lines on jar neck: 2G88 Surface.

§148 *Combed decoration:* Combs with 3, 4 and 6 teeth, 2 to 4 mm. apart were detected.
   Horizontal, on jar shoulder: 2G40 Sub-surface (Fig. 176).
   Horizontal, on handled jar: 2G42 Sub-surface (Fig. 205; Grey Ware).
   Cross-hatched, on jar shoulder: 2G73 Sub-surface (Fig. 239; Grey Ware).
   Cross-hatched, on handled jar: 2G98 Surface (Fig. 206).

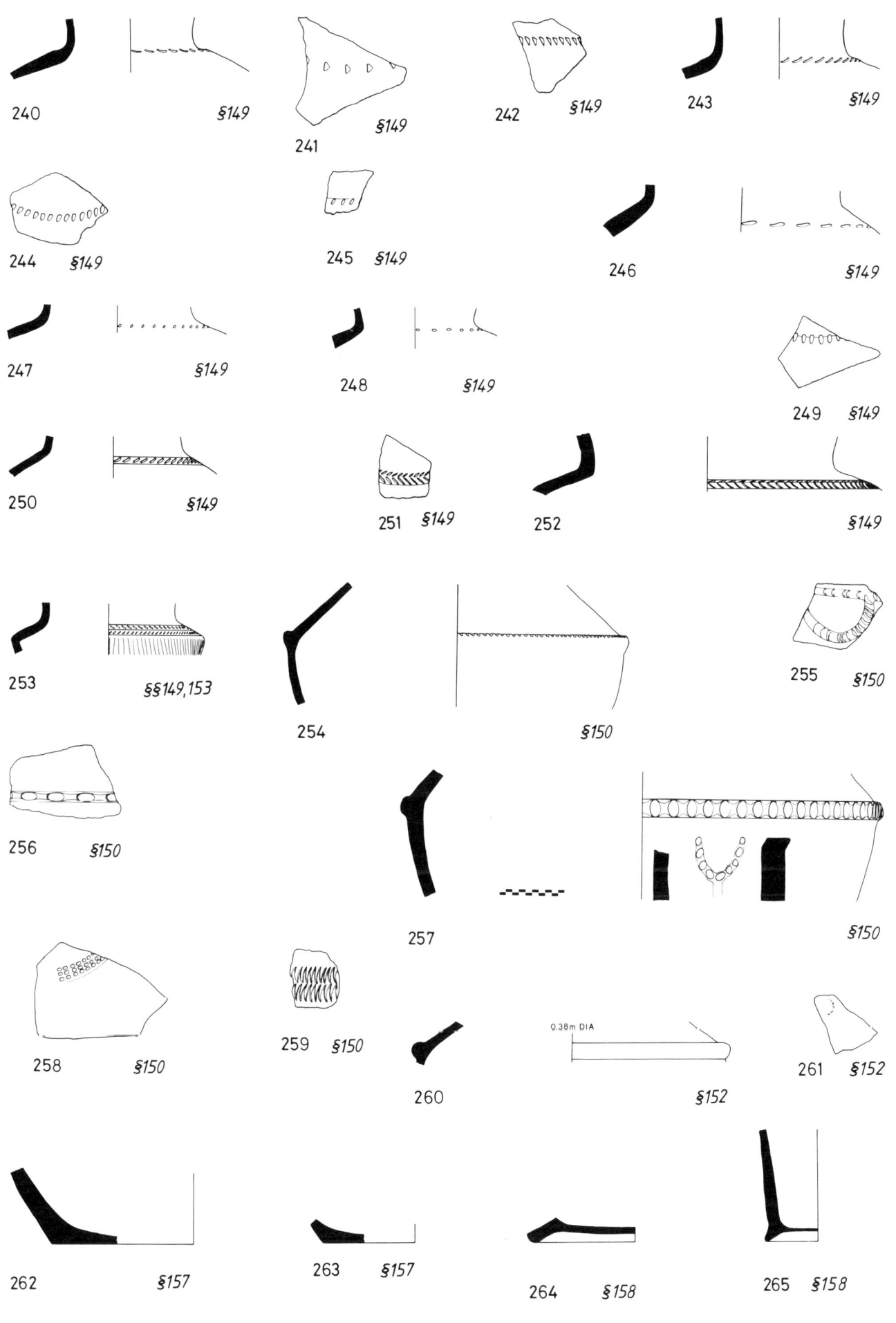

Figs. 240-265. Sherds from ED squares (ctd.). Scale 1:4, except Fig. 257 at 1:8.

Impressed decoration: Finger-nail and finger impressions, either on ribs at shoulder carinations or in rows at the base of the neck, are by far the commonest form of decoration in the ED I squares. The shape and size of the impression varies according to how deeply the nail was pressed into the clay.

§149 *Rows of finger-nail impressions:*
Single rows of finger-nail impressions at base of jar neck: 2G23 Sub-surface pottery group (Fig. 240); 2G41 Sub-surface (Fig. 241); 2G90 Sub-surface (Fig. 242); 2G00 Sub-surface (Fig. 183); 2G12 Sub-surface (Fig. 243); 2G00 Sub-surface (Fig. 244); 2G square uncertain (Fig. 245); 2G00 Sub-surface (Fig. 246); 2G02 Surface (Fig. 247); 2G32 Sub-surface (Fig. 248); 2G03 Sub-surface (Fig. 284).
Single rows of finger-nail impressions with incised horizontal line: 2G12 Sub-surface (Fig. 249).
Single rows of finger-nail impressions between two incised horizontal lines: 2G21 Sub-surface (Fig. 250).
Double row, herring-bone pattern, on jar shoulder with unpierced lugs: 2G65 Surface (Fig. 210).
Triple row on jar shoulder between incised horizontal lines: 2G58 Sub-surface; 2G48/58/49/59 Sub-surface.
Herring-bone pattern with incised horizontal lines: 2G90 Sub-surface (Fig. 251); 2G13 Sub-surface (Fig. 252); 2G23 Sub-surface (Fig. 253; with pattern burnishing below shoulder).
Single row of finger-nail impressions on miniature jar carination: 2G62 Surface (Fig. 273).
Single row of finger-nail impressions with horizontal reserved slip: 2G12 Sub-surface (Fig. 187); 2G00 Sub-surface (Fig. 224); 2G12 Surface (Fig. 223).
Single row of finger-nail impressions with diagonal reserved slip: 2G42 Sub-surface (Fig. 184); 2G12 Sub-surface (Fig. 225); 2G22 Sub-surface (Fig. 226; in panels).
Single row of finger-nail impressions with diagonal and horizontal reserved slip: 2G52 Sub-surface (Fig. 227); 2G12 Sub-surface (Fig. 228).
Finger-nail impressions around base: 2G33 Sub-surface (Fig. 267).
Finger impressions around base: 2G51 Sub-surface (Fig. 266).

§150 *Finger and finger-nail impressed ribs:*
Finger-nail impressed ribs at jar shoulder carinations: 2G32 Sub-surface (Fig. 180); 2G32 Sub-surface (Fig. 254); 2GS:104.
Finger-nail impressed horse-shoe-shaped rib: 2G14 Sub-surface (Fig. 255); 2G88 Surface.
Finger-nail impressions on strap handle: 2G16 Surface (Fig. 207).
Finger-nail impressed rib with horizontal reserved slip: 2G33 Sub-surface (Fig. 222).
Finger-nail impressed ribs (rope imitation) on jar with single beak-lug: 2GS:101 q.v.
Finger-impressed ribs: 2G41 Sub-surface (Fig. 256); 2G23-33 Sub-surface (Fig. 257; with applied finger-impressed "horns" and black paint); 2G22 Sub-surface (Fig. 237; with incised cross-hatching).
Two finger-impressed ribs: 2G53 Surface (Fig. 179; Grey Ware).

§151 *Other impressed decoration:*
Triple row of rectangles above incised line, from spouted jar: 2G47 Sub-surface (Fig. 258).
Rocker pattern on jar body: 2G25 Surface (Fig. 259).
Row of impressed rings below rib on coarse jar: 2G97 Surface.
Irregular stabbed impressions on miniature jar: 2G02 Surface (Fig. 274).

§152 *Plastic decoration:* In addition to the finger-nail and finger-impressed ribs listed above, there was one example of a plain rib at a jar shoulder carination: 2G22 Sub-surface (Fig. 260).
Applied knobs: 2G13 Sub-surface (Fig. 221; from spouted jar); 2G32 Sub-surface (Fig. 261).

§153 *Pattern burnishing:*
Vertical pattern burnishing below jar shoulder: 2G23 Sub-surface (Fig. 253).

§154 *Burnishing:*
On jar with finger-nail impressed ribs and single beak-lug: 2GS:101 q.v.
Burnishing was noted on miscellaneous body sherds, e.g. 2G76 Surface (Grey Ware).

§155 *Excised triangles* on jar with cross-hatched incision and spool lug: 2GS:104, q.v.

Jar bases
§156 *Round:*
A narrow pointed base came from 2G89 Sub-surface.

§157 *Flat:*
Diams.: 14-22 cm.
Examples: 2G24 Sub-surface (Fig. 262); 2G13 Sub-surface (Fig. 263).

§158 *Ring bases:* Ring bases appeared to be more frequent in the ED I squares, being applied especially to fine, well-decorated jars and occasionally carrying decoration themselves in the form of finger or finger-nail impressions.
Examples: 2GS:104, q.v.; 2GS:101, q.v.; 2GS:93, q.v.; 2G23 Sub-surface (Fig. 264; red wash and burnish); 2G13 Sub-surface (Fig. 265; beaker shape); 2G51 Sub-surface (Fig. 266; finger impressions); 2G33 Sub-surface (Fig. 267; finger-nail impressions).

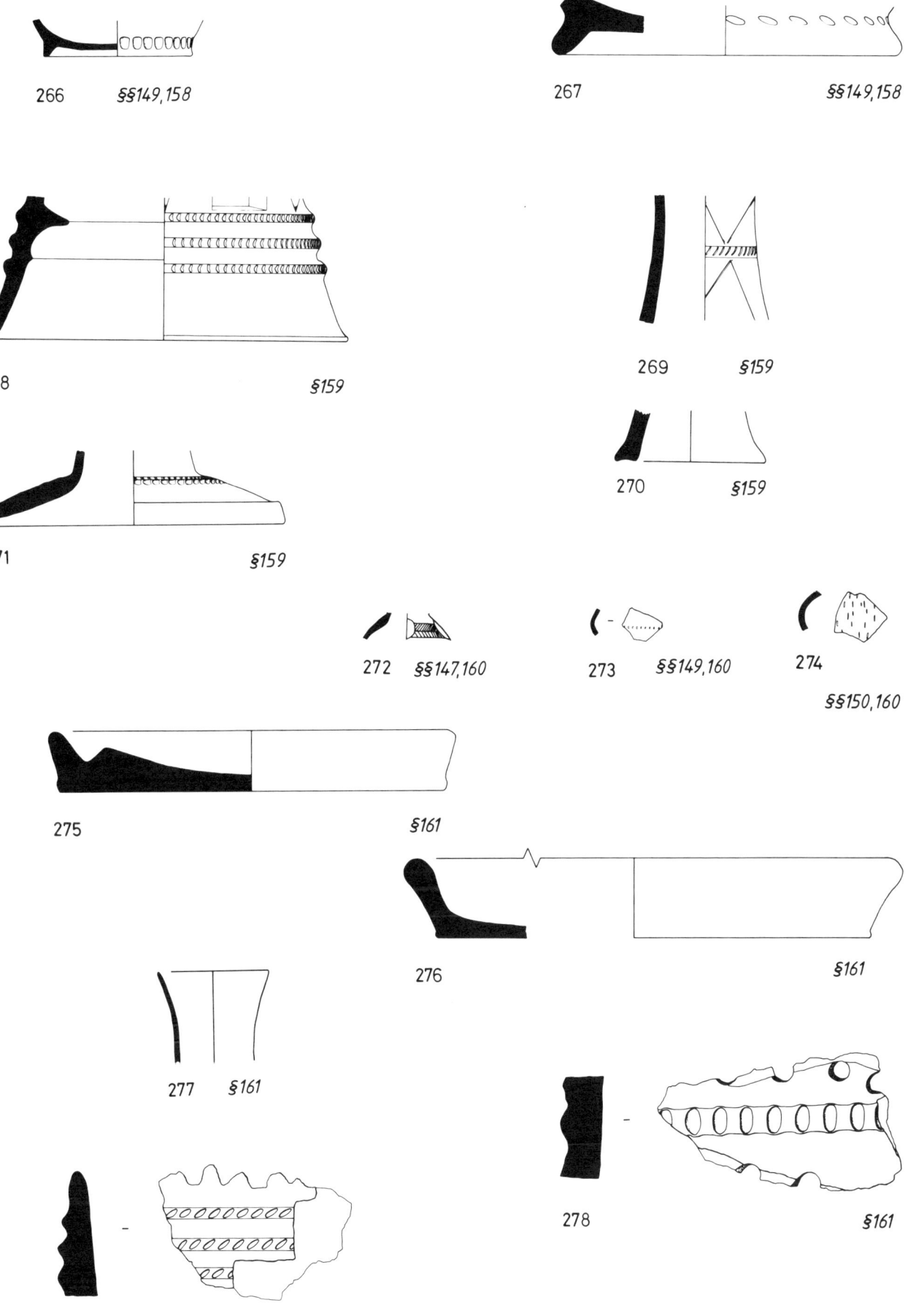

Figs. 266-279. Sherds from ED squares (ctd.). Scale 1:4.

81

§159 *Hollow stands:*
   Base of hollow stand 20 cm. in diam.; internal ledge; two finger-nail impressed ribs; rectangular and triangular fenestrations: 2GS:242, q.v.
   Base of hollow stand 27 cm. in diam.; internal ledge; three finger-nail impressed ribs; rectangular and triangular fenestrations: 2G21 Sub-surface (Fig. 268).
   Stem of hollow stand; row of finger-nail impressions between horizontal incised lines; incised Vs: 2G41 Sub-surface (Fig. 269).
   Base of plain stand(?) 11 cm. in diam.: 2G70 Sub-surface (Fig. 270).
   Base of stemmed dish(?) 22 cm. in diam.; Grey Ware; two rows of finger-nail impressions on two horizontal incised lines at base of stem: 2G26 Sub-surface (Fig. 271).
   Other hollow stand fragments from 2G00 Sub-surface; 2G12 Sub-surface; 2G23 Sub-surface & pottery group; 2G32 Surface; 2G34 Sub-surface; 2G37 Sub-surface; 2G33 Sub-surface; 2G40 Sub-surface; 2G44 Sub-surface; 2G51 Sub-surface.
   See Delougaz 1952, Pls. 45, 172, 174.

§160 *Miniatures:*
   Miniature jar with incised herring-bone decoration between flattened circles, probably in imitation of 4-lugged jar: 2G98 Surface (Fig. 272).
   Miniature jar fragment with row of finger-nail impressions at carination: 2G62 Surface (Fig. 273).
   Miniature jar fragment with irregular stabbed impressions: 2G02 Surface (Fig. 274).
   Miniature jar: 2GS:281, q.v.
   Inscribed miniature jar sherd: 2GS:190, q.v.

§161 *Miscellaneous:*
   Sieve bowls: 2GS:70, q.v.; 2G68 Sub-surface.
   Coarse dishes with internal channel: 2G33 Sub-surface (Fig. 275); 2GS:105, q.v.
   Coarse shallow dish: 2G76 Sub-surface (Fig. 276).
   Rhyton or funnel: 2G13 Sub-surface (Fig. 277; Plate VIa); 2G72 Sub-surface; see Delougaz 1952, Pl. 169, C.077.500; AbS 1450 (*Iraq* 40, 86-7).
   Knob lid: 2GS:85, q.v.; 2G97 Sub-surface.
   Ring-shaped vessel: 2GS:216, q.v.
   Two large flat coarse objects, 2.5-3 cm. thick: 2G22 Sub-surface (Fig. 278; with circular holes and finger-impressed rib); 2G21 Sub-surface (Fig. 279; with serrated edge and three finger-nail impressed ribs). The purpose of these two pieces is obscure, but similar decoration in unbaked clay may sometimes be seen on modern storage bins, etc., in Iraq.
   Drain-ends: 2GS:219, q.v.; 2G04 Sub-surface; 2G05 Sub-surface.
   Circular drain-pipes: 2G07 Sub-surface; 2G38 Sub-surface.

Numbered items of pottery (J. N. Postgate)
This catalogue includes all the whole or nearly whole vessels found during the clearance, as well as a number of other pieces which for one reason or another seemed to merit treatment separately from the main bulk of the sherds. Note that most of these items have already been referred to in the preceding section by E. McAdam.

Miscellaneous Finds 1804/1   Fig. 280
Miscellaneous Finds 1804/2   Fig. 281
   Two painted rim-sherds found on the surface of the West Mound during the contour survey in 1973. They are now housed in the Iraq Museum under "Miscellaneous finds (*multaqaṭat*) 1804".

2GS:70   = AbS 1453   5048   2G22 Sub-surface   Fig. 282   Plate VIIa
   Sieve-based bowl. One large central hole, which has been convincingly explained as the socket for a handle, making this a perforated ladle, and four smaller holes. See §161.
   Rim di. 11.0; H. 5.0 cm.
      Adams & Nissen 1972, 167 Fig. 62:274/25; 101 Fig. 30 ah; Delougaz 1952, Pl. 63:47; Haller 1932, Taf. 20 B d" (prob.); Le Brun 1978, 130:8 (with more examples; Uruk!).

2GS:84   = AbS 1480   5048   2G22 Sub-surface   Fig. 17
   Conical bowl. Brown fabric and surface; grit temper. Several other conical bowls were found nearby, including 2GS:217 q.v.; the remainder not restored.
   Rim di. 15.4-16.6; Base di. 5.2-5.5; H. 10.8-11.3 cm.

2GS:85   = AbS 1461   5056   2G13 Sub-surface   Fig. 283   Plate VIIb
   Globular object with knob; perhaps a net-float? See §161.
   Di. 10.2; H. (extant) 7.0 cm.
      Delougaz 1952, 60 ("a peculiar type of pot cover"; p. 81; Pl. 70 e-i; Haller 1932, Taf. 20 B b' ("grössere Gefässverschlüsse . . .", p. 46); Adams & Nissen 1972, Fig. 74:5; Hansen 1965, 209 ("hollow stoppers"; Inanna Level X); Nissen 1970, Taf. 101.

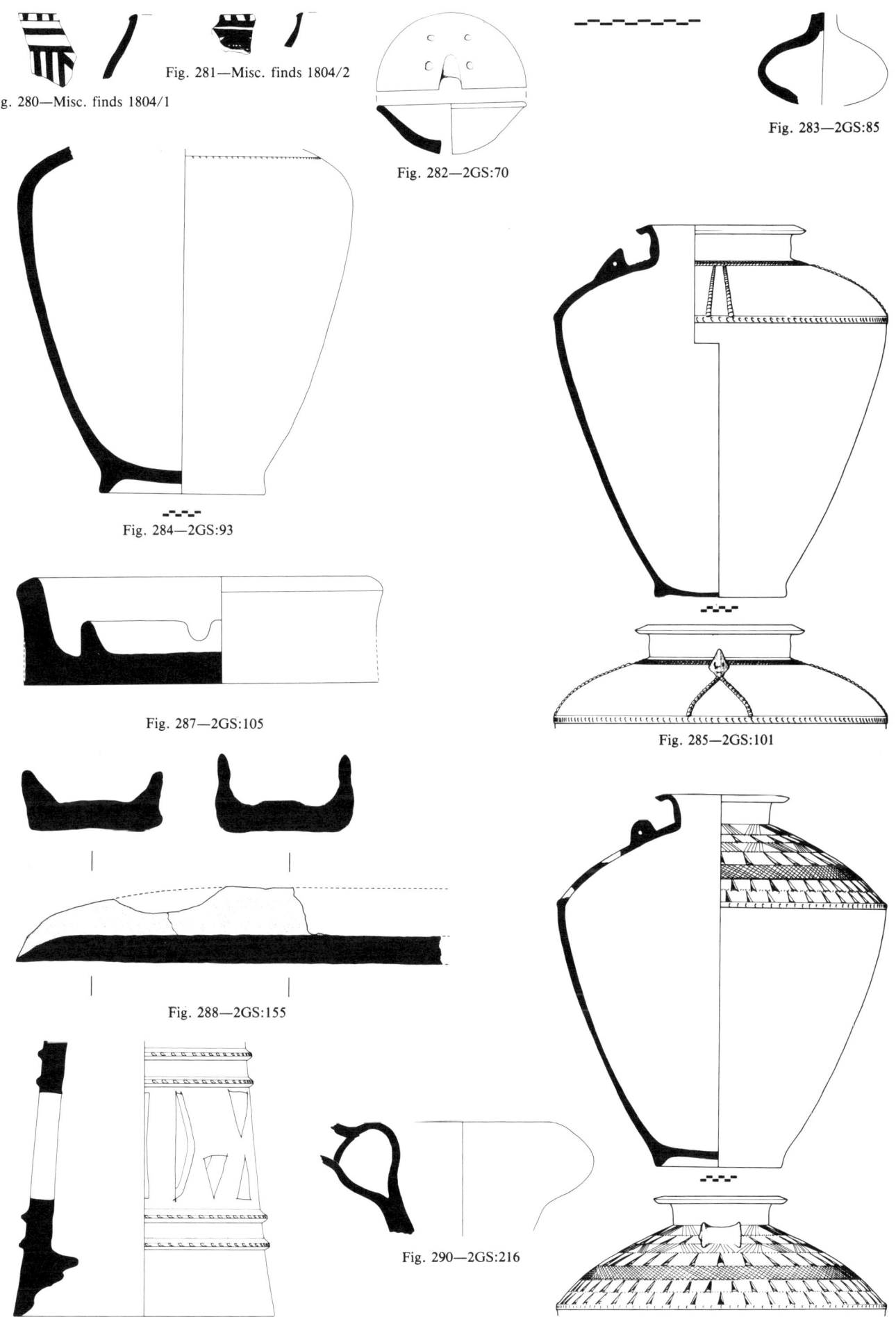

Pottery vessels. Scale 1:4, except Figs. 284-6 at 1:8. (Fig. 289 see p. 85.)

83

2GS:86   5056   2G13 Sub-surface
Tall cup; lower part only. Greenish-yellow fabric. String-cut base with marked spiral traces of manufacture inside.
Di. (max. extant) 7.5; Base di. 3.4; H. (extant) 10.5 cm.

2GS:92   5056   2G13 Sub-surface   Fig. 194
Jar neck. Found in situ in pit in NW corner of square (see plan).
Rim di. 13.5 cm.

2GS:93   = AbS 1463   5055   2G03 Sub-surface   Fig. 284
Large jar, with row of finger-nail impressions on rib at shoulder carination. Rim and neck lost by erosion; friable reddish-brown fabric. Found in Room 8 next to 2GS:101 and 104 qqv.
Di. (at shoulder) 26.2; Base di. 13.0; H. (extant) 26.4 cm.

2GS:99   5029   2G31 Sub-surface   Plate IIIc
Top of large jar, found inverted in situ; see Chapter 3.2 on FI 77/11. Not retained.

2GS:101 = AbS 1475   5055   2G03 Sub-surface   Fig. 285   Plate VIIIa
Large jar with single "Beak lug" and applied rope-like decorative ribs. Medium fine red ware, cream slip out; burnished over whole vessel except rim and neck; inner surface scraped; grit temper. Found in Room 8, with 2GS:93 and 104. A few sherds belonging to this vessel were also found in 1981 in the same area.
Rim di. (outer) 26.8; Base di. 20.8; H. 56.8 cm.
See *Iraq* 40 [1978] 87:2; §126 above.

2GS:104 = AbS 1474   5055   2G03 Sub-surface   Fig. 286   Plate VIIIb
Large jar with excised and incised decoration. Medium coarse reddish fabric, greenish slip out; grit temper. The excised triangles in the upper register are more shallowly excised than those lower down, which are generally cut through the whole thickness of the vessel. Found in Room 8, with 2GS:93 and 101.
Rim di. (outer) 21.2; Base di. 20.0; H. 56.6 cm.
See *Iraq* 40 [1978] 87:1; §126 above.

2GS:105   5030   2G21 Sub-surface   Fig. 287
Coarse flat dish with internal channel. Reddish fabric with brown surface. Inside, a low subsidiary rim, interrupted at one point by a channel, divides the dish into a large central area and a perimeter channel. Found in the NE corner of 2G21.
Rim di. (outer) 28.6; (inner) 22.0; H. of rim (outer) 8.2; (inner) 4.85 cm.
See *Iraq* 40 [1978] 87:7; Nissen 1970, Taf. 104:18; Wright 1969, 72, Fig. 21c; Eridu Fig. 158:65.

2GS:143   5098   2G35 Sub-surface   Fig. 13
Bevelled-rim bowl. Coarse reddish clay.
Rim di. (average) 16.7; Base di. 7.5; H. 7.9 cm.

2GS:147   5098   2G35 Sub-surface   Fig. 18
Conical bowl. Dark greenish fabric.
Rim di. ca. 13 cm.; Base di. 3.4; H. 10.2 cm.

2GS:150   5081   2G34 Sub-surface   Fig. 14
Bevelled-rim bowl. Coarse yellowish clay with darker core. Note the rim, which is tapered to a point rather than actually bevelled.
Rim di. ca. 9 cm.; Base di. ca. 8 cm.; H. ca. 10 cm.

2GS:155   5087   2G04 Sub-surface   Fig. 288
Gutter outflow.
W. 10.5; L. (extant) 33 cm.
Cf. 2GS:219 and §157; Le Brun 1978, 130:13.

2GS:157   5060   2G23 Sub-surface
Solid-footed goblet; rim missing. Red fabric, brown surface; grit temper. It has a genuine solid foot, splayed out at base. It is taller than the solid-footed goblets from the NE Mound illustrated in *Iraq* 40 [1978] 87:4-5, but those from Grave 160 (also at the NE Mound) are probably about the same height (cf. Fig. 16). The rims of this type are so fine that even when the pot appears intact in situ, the actual rim is usually missing.
Rim di. (lost); Base di. 2.8-3.3; H. (extant) 18.6 cm.

2GS:172 = Abs 1481   5113   2G46 Sub-surface
Conical bowl. Reddish fabric and surface; grit temper.
Rim di. 14.7-15.6; Base di. 4.6-5.1; H. 9.8-10.6 cm.

2GS:189   5059   2G33 Sub-surface   Plate IIId
Rim and shoulder of jar. Reddish fabric; grit temper. Wide mouth, with out-turned rim and no neck; wide rounded shoulder, with a single small knob at one point, about 3 cm. from base of neck. Found inverted at point shown on plan, and used as a fire installation (cf. Chapter 3.2, FI 77/12).
Rim di. ca. 15 cm.; H. (extant) 6 cm.

2GS:190 = AbS 1470   2G85 Surface   Fig. 289   Plate VIIIc
Sherd from rim to lower body of a miniature jar with horizontally-pierced shoulder lugs (0.9 cm. below rim), and an inscription roughly incised on the shoulder between two horizontal lines. Inscription is not convincingly deciphered. Surface find in 2G85, a square not otherwise worked, at the point shown on the plan.
W. (extant) 3.2; H. (extant) 3.0; Th. (at break) 0.4 cm.

2GS:213   5127   2G27 Sub-surface   Fig. 231   Plate V*a*
Painted sherd from jar. Green, over-fired clay. Cross-hatched circles.
5.3 x 4.2 cm.
See §146.

2GS:215   5081   2G34 Sub-surface   Fig. 15
Bevelled-rim bowl. Over-fired, greenish fabric. Cf. 2GS:150, from same square.
Rim di. (outer) 16.8; (inner) 15.0; Base di. ca. 6 cm.; H. 7.0-8.5 cm.

2GS:216 = AbS 1483   5127   2G27 Sub-surface   Fig. 290   Plate VIIc
Ring-shaped vessel. Over-fired greenish fabric; grit temper. At one point on the exterior of the vessel is the base of a spout(?) leading from the hollow interior; the lower surface of the ring is rough, perhaps because some further feature was attached there, but this is not certain.
Di. at top (inner) ca. 13 cm.; Max. di. ca. 20 cm.; H. (extant) 8.8 cm.
See *Iraq* 40 [1978] 87:8; no clear parallels noted.

2GS:217   5048   2G22 Sub-surface
Conical bowl. Red fabric, greenish surface; grit temper. Found with 2GS:84.
Rim di. 16.4-17.2; Base (lost); H. (extant) 10.9 cm.

2GS:218   5104   2G12 Sub-surface   Plate IIc
Conical bowl. Very crumbly red fabric; grit temper. Found in situ inside 2GS:219. Not restored.

2GS:219 = AbS 1484   2G12 Sub-surface   Fig. 7   Plates IIc, VIIId
Gutter outflow; final section of tubular drain in 2G12. Red fabric with grit and chaff temper. The base is flat and pierced by four holes, presumably to allow the water to seep away better, and the lip tapers to the edge.
L. (extant) 30 cm.; W. at end 26.5; H. 8.8 cm.
See §161, also 2GS:155. This piece explains the function of similar ones recorded from contemporary sites in the Warka Survey (Adams & Nissen 1972, 214); in 1981 we noted a complete example on the surface of Bismaya (Adab). Also, definitely Uruk in date, at Habuba Kabira (W. Ludwig apud Margueron n.d., p. 73).

Fig. 289. Inscribed miniature jar, 2GS:190.

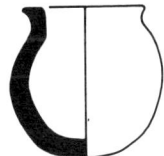
Fig. 292. Miniature jar, 2GS:281.

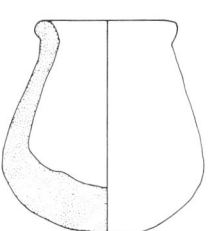
Fig. 293. Miniature jar, stone, 2GS:280.

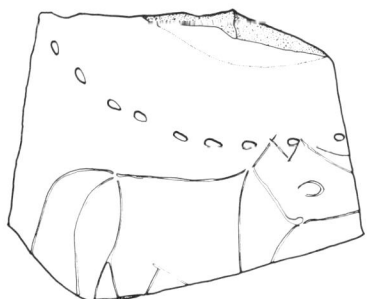
Fig. 294. Incised sherd, 2GS:284.

Miniature jars and incised sherd. Scale 1:2.

2GS:242 5029 2G31 Sub-surface Fig. 291
Hollow stand. Over-fired greenish clay. Part of base only survives.
Base di. 20.0; H. (extant) 21.7; internal ledge's inner rim is at ca. 4 cm. above base (*contra Iraq* 40 "1.5 cm.").
See *Iraq* 40 [1978] 87:3, and 2GS:291.

2GS:243 5077 2G44 Sub-surface Fig. 19
Conical bowl. Buff fabric; carefully finished.
Rim di. ca. 14 cm.; Base di. 4.3-4.5; H. 8.6 cm.

2GS:281 = AbS 1757 5181 2G98 Sub-surface Fig. 292 Plate VII*f*
Miniature jar. Coarse reddish fabric. Discovered next to 2GS:280, a stone jar of similar shape and size.
Rim di. 3.0; Max. di. 4.0; H. 3.9 cm.

2GS:284 = AbS 1795 5178 2G97 Surface Fig. 294 Plate VII*d*
Sherd from jar shoulder with incised outline of an animal, below a row of decorative nicks at base of neck.
8.8 x 10.5 cm.

2GS:291 5060 2G23 Sub-surface
Hollow stands. Main example: reddish fabric, whitish slip out, on base and inside above ledge; rows of excised triangles alternately inverted, separated by double horizontal ribs with finger-nail impressions. Not reconstructed or drawn as few pieces joined.
Base di. ca. 29 cm.; H. of ledge above base 5.6-6.8 cm.
Another example from same provenance was similar, but had a base di. of about 38 cm.

2GS:293 5107 2G76 Sub-surface Fig. 198
Large jar; unrestored sherds only, from upper part. Grey fabric, with wet-smoothed surface; grit temper. One rim sherd only illustrated.
Rim di. ca. 23 cm.

2GS:294 5123 2G47 Sub-surface
Large jar; left in situ (see plan). Complete up to shoulder; top missing. Pink clay, buff slip out; fine even sandy temper. Wide body tapering to a neat flat base.
H. (ext.) ca. 30 cm.; Di. (max.) ca. 50 cm.; Base di. 18-20 cm.

3GS:1 5907 3G81 Sub-surface
Very large conical bowl, left in situ 1978 and re-excavated in 1981, when it was re-numbered 3G81:248; drawing and other details will be published by J. A. Moon in *Iraq 44*. See 3GS:2.

3GS:2 5907 3G81 Sub-surface
Base, much eroded, of large jar; found in situ next to 3GS:1 in 1978 and re-excavated in 1981. See *Iraq* 44, also for the context of these two pots. Re-numbered 3G81:247.

3GS:29 5913 3G70 Sub-surface Fig. 130
Lower part of small jar. Gritty red fabric with black core.
Max. di. 11.3; H. (extant) 9.5 cm.

3GS:36 5915 3G71 Sub-surface Fig. 79
Red-painted jar with four shoulder-lugs, pierced horizontally.
Rim di. (outer) 7.8; (inner) 6.1; H. (extant) ca. 4.7 cm.
See §§41; 58; 68; 73.

Chapter 5

MISCELLANEOUS FINDS

5.1 *Baked clay cones* (Jesper Eidem)   Plate IX*a*
Baked clay cones are found on many southern Mesopotamian sites, and are taken to be diagnostic of the Uruk period. In the Warka Survey Adams & Nissen noted their occurrence on 18 sites ranging from the 'Ubaid to the ED I period (p. 211). Normally they are associated with large, monumental buildings as in Uruk where they make their first appearance in Eanna Level VI. In the Uruk area, however, Adams & Nissen found cones on a number of small sites, which may indicate that this is not always the case. Of the ca. 50 pieces from the West Mound only five are complete, and whereas it is not possible from this very limited material to draw any pertinent conclusions about the types occurring, there does seem to be a considerable variation in size, shape and colour as well as the treatment of the head.

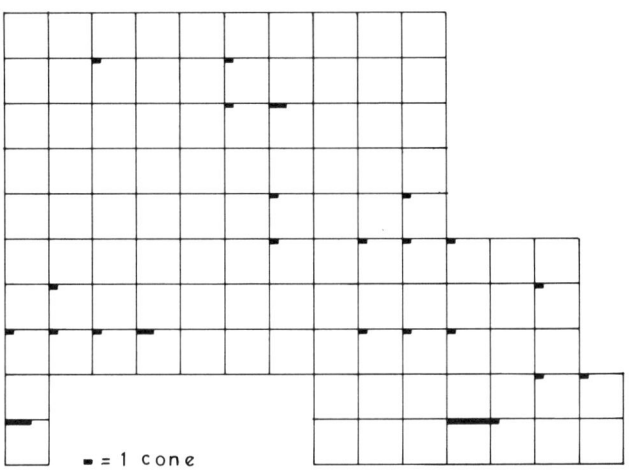

Fig. 295. Clay cones distribution—Surface.

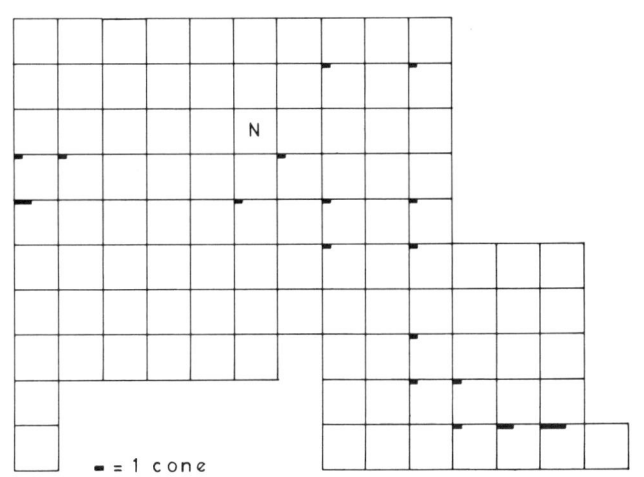

Fig. 296. Clay cones distribution—Sub-surface.

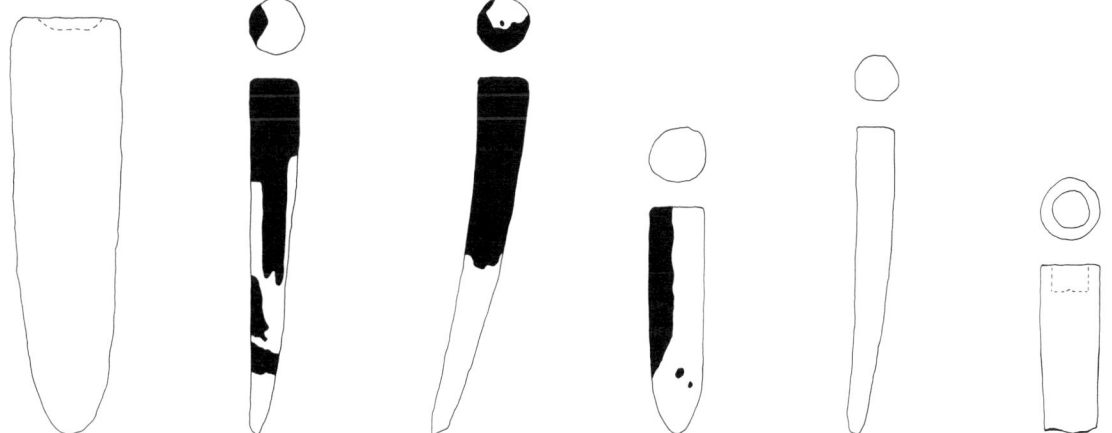

Fig. 297. 3GS:47. Fig. 298. 2GS:289. Fig. 299. 3GS:24. Fig. 300. 2GS:88. Fig. 301. 3GS:4. Fig. 302. 2GS:170.

Clay cones. Scale 1:2.

One specimen (3GS:47; Fig. 297; Pl. IX*a,* top right) of coarse green ware with a very shallow depression in the head measures 11 cm. in length and 2.5 cm. in di. of head; but the majority are of fine hard-baked clay producing a creamy-brown colour, much thinner and probably comparable to 2GS:289 (Fig. 298; Pl. IX*a,* middle left) and 3GS:24 (Fig. 299; Pl. IX*a,* bottom left). A variant type seems to be rather short and almost "torpedo"-shaped (2GS:88; Fig. 300; Pl. IX*a,* top centre). Finally there is the very small specimen 2GS:245 (Pl. IX*a,* bottom centre; red ware; di. of head 0.9 cm.; only fragmentary). [In 1981 a complete small cone of this type was found, L. 4.3; Di. of head 1.1 cm.; 2G36:186 (J.N.P.)]. Other exceptions are two buff-coloured and slipped cones (e.g. 3GS:4; Fig. 301; Pl. IX*a,* top left). A few pieces have traces of black paint (in Uruk black, white and red coloured specimens occur), and/or a hollow depression in the head (e.g. 2GS:170; Fig. 302; Pl. IX*a,* bottom right).

The surface distribution of cones is shown in Figs. 295-6; cf. comments in Chapter 4.

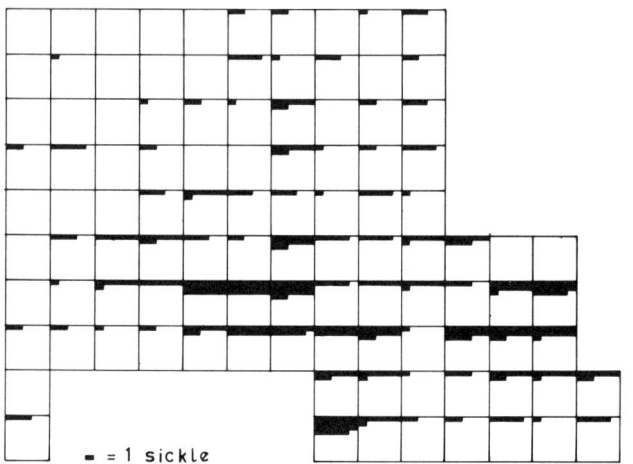

Fig. 303. Clay sickles distribution — Surface.

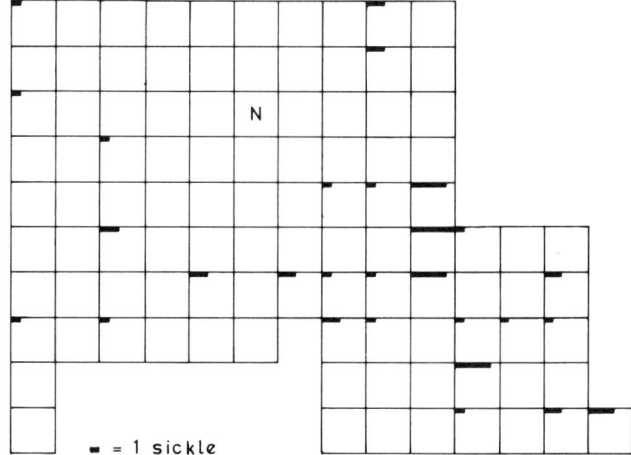

Fig. 304. Clay sickles distribution — Sub surface.

5.2 *Clay sickles* (Jesper Eidem)   Plate IX*b*

The surface and sub-surface distribution is shown in Figs. 303-4; see comments in Chapter 4 (p. 52). Clay sickles are found on the surface of many southern Mesopotamian sites (Adams & Nissen 1972, p. 208), and apart from the painted specimens found during the 'Ubaid period (cf. Hall & Woolley 1927, p. 48 and Pl. XV,4), there seems to be very little difference between them at all. Adams & Nissen suggested an increase in size—from about 15 cm. length of the blade in the 'Ubaid period—for the later periods, and this seems to fit with the material from the West Mound. Although no complete sickles were found, the great number of fragments confirms a general uniformity in size, shape and colour. With very few exceptions they are all made of highly fired clay and of a greenish colour. A reconstruction from fragments of five different pieces points to a blade length of about 20 cm. (Fig. 313).

Two lumps of three sickle fragments fused together were found on the West Mound (2GS:23 and 114), showing that the sickles were certainly locally produced. A similar fused group was also found on the NW Mound. A comparison with the sickles from Tell 'Uqair showed no noticeable differences.[1] A special problem is presented by the shape of the sickles: they all have one flat and one curving surface, and granted that the curving surface would be face-up, they were probably made for use in the left hand (cf. Adams & Nissen 1972, p. 208). Unfortunately we have no pictures of people actually using sickles, but it would seem highly impractical to hold it with the left hand. More important, the wearing of the blade points to use with the right hand.

Illustrated sickle fragments

Fig. 305	5016	2G20 Sub-surface	Fig. 309	5078	2G54 Surface
306	5076	2G44 Surface	310	5071	2G64 Surface
307	5123	2G47 Sub-surface	311	5109	2G66 Sub-surface
308	5044	2G52 Sub-surface	312	5005	2G70 Sub-surface
313	Composite reconstruction from fragments from batches 5037, 5071 and 5063.				

[1] I would like to thank Mr. Michael Müller-Karpe for permission to study the surface material from the 1978 season at Tell 'Uqair.

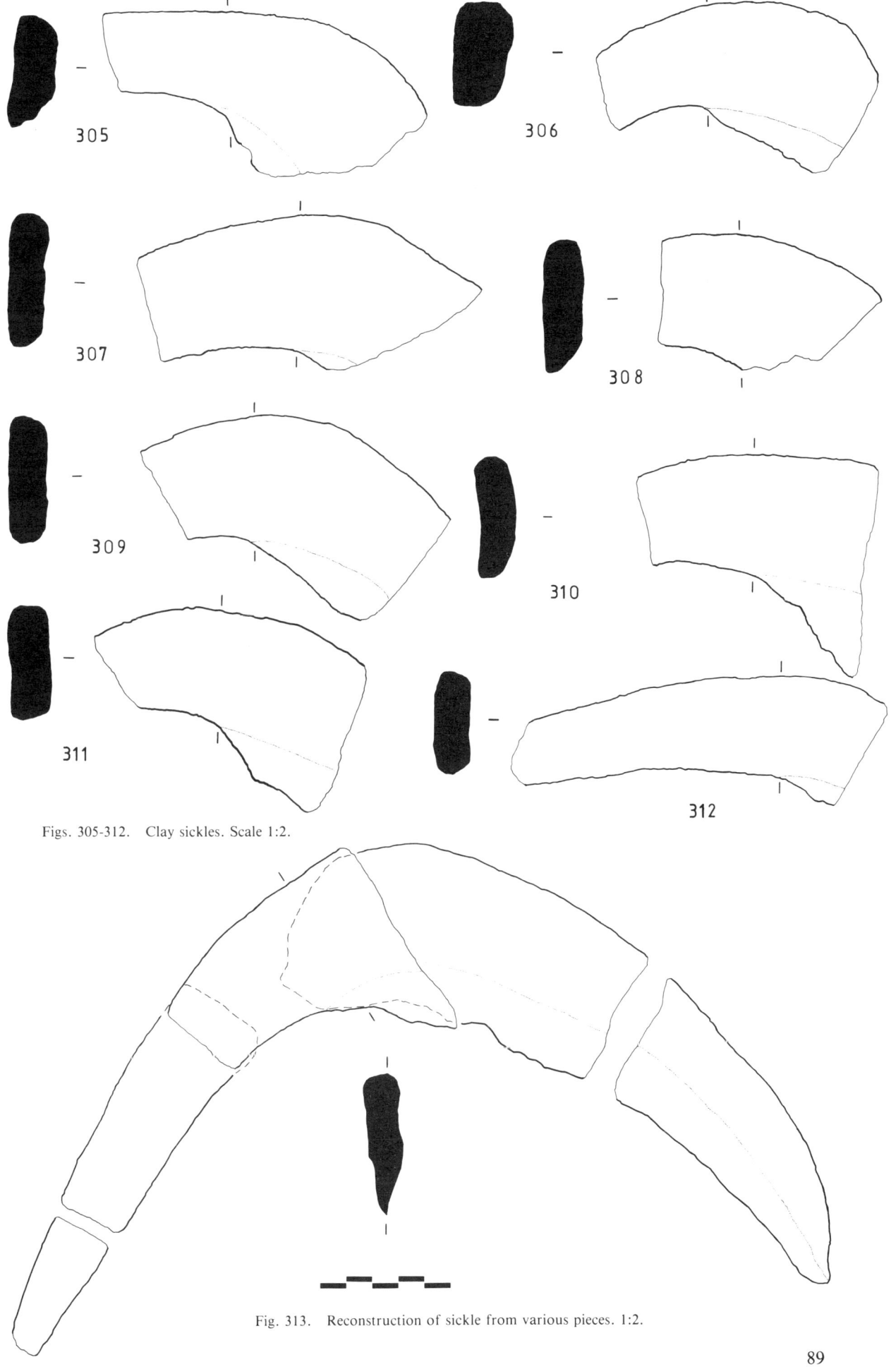

Figs. 305-312. Clay sickles. Scale 1:2.

Fig. 313. Reconstruction of sickle from various pieces. 1:2.

5.3 Miscellaneous clay items (J. N. Postgate)

2GS:15   5021   2G61 Surface   Fig. 314   Plate X*a*
Animal figurine. Sun-dried(?) clay. Forepart only preserved; horns broken off; forefeet joined together and hardly separately indicated.
H. 5.3; W. (extant) 3.3 cm.

2GS:45   5020   2G00 Sub-surface
"Wheel". Reddish clay; slightly over half preserved. Flat disc with central perforation; one face almost flat, the other, though lost, must have been more convex.
Di. 8.8; Di. of perf. 1.0; Th. (max. extant) 2.4 cm.

2GS:64 = AbS 1447   5033   2G21 Surface   Plate X*b*
Seal impression. Irregularly shaped lump, with probable string-marks on reverse; on obverse, rolling of a cylinder seal showing a frieze of walking quadrupeds.
4.6 x 5.3 cm.

2GS:66   5034   2G11 Sub-surface   Fig. 315
Terracotta ring. Slightly less than a quarter of a ring-shaped object in hard-fired olive-green clay. It has a flat base (W. ca. 5 cm.), and is built in two tiers, the second tier being narrower but higher; Fig. 315 shows a cross-section.
H. 6.5; Max. di. (est.) 15 cm.; inner di. (min.) ca. 4 cm.

2GS:82   5037   2G62 Surface
Terracotta ring. About one-third preserved; yellow, hard-fired clay. Type of ring commonly identified as a net-sinker, on the basis of a find in the Temple Oval at Khafajah (Delougaz 1940, 55-6).

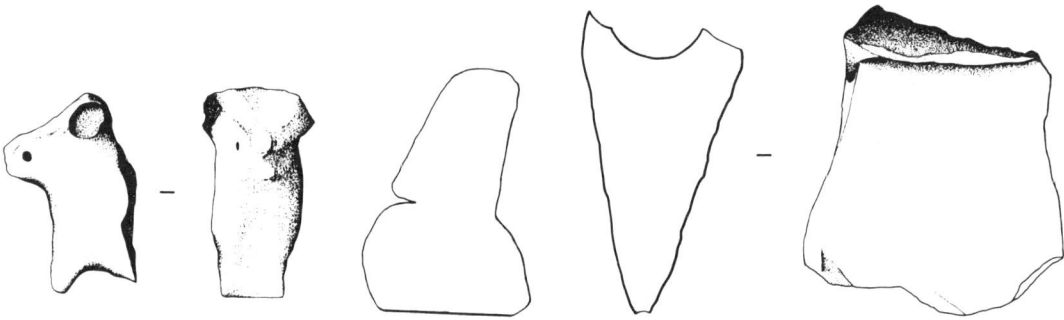

Fig. 314. 2GS:15.   Fig. 315. 2GS:66.   Fig. 315a. 2GS:134.

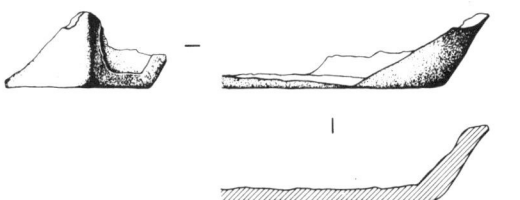 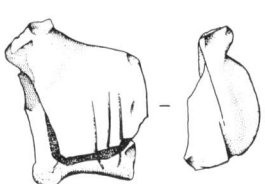

Fig. 316. 2GS:226.   Fig. 318. 2GS:273.

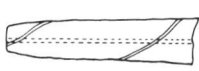 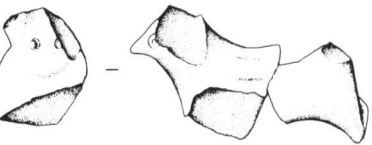

Fig. 317. 2GS:249.   Fig. 319. 2GS:287.

Miscellaneous clay items. Scale 1:2.

2GS:134   5091   2G65 Sub-surface   Fig. 315a
  Baked clay axe-head. Edge of blade broken, and only half of shaft-hole surviving; the upper and lower edges of the blade splay out from the shaft-hole.
     L. (max. ext.) 7.7; H. (at shaft-hole) 5.5 cm.

2GS:156   5105   2G23 or 33, cut
  Fragments of clay sealing. Flat base, approximately conical shape, but no seal impression on obverse. Traces of ends of string on base of obverse; reverse surface broken.
     H. 4.1; W. 5.8 x 4.3 cm.

2GS:205   5109   2G66 Sub-surface
  Spool-shaped object. Little more than half preserved; reddish clay with whitish slip. Rather coarsely made, but could be the spool-shaped lug from a jar.
     W. 4.3; H. 3.4-3.7; Th. 3.6 cm.

2GS:226   = AbS 1477   5123   2G47 Sub-surface   Fig. 316
  Model boat. One end only; fine buff fabric, grit temper, greenish surface.
     L. (ext.) 7.4; W. (max.) 4.5; H. (at prow) 2.0 cm.

2GS:249   = AbS 2093   5151   2G49 Sub-surface   Fig. 317
  Clay bead. About half preserved; fine green/buff clay, grit temper; burnished along its length giving angular facets. A spiralling groove runs round it, completing one turn in 4.2 cm.
     L. (ext.) 5.3; Di. (max.) 1.4; Di. of perf. 0.1 cm.
  In 1981 two further examples of this type of bead were found on the West Mound in Uruk levels, and are also included in AbS 2093.
  Such beads are known from Fara and Jamdat Nasr, and imitate others made from the core of a large shell, attested at Warka (see Mackay 1931, Pl. LXXI.17-18 and LXXIV.2595-7 [in the Ashmolean: 1926.421-2 (GN 2597*-8)]; Fara: F 922 from Jamdat Nasr level in DE 38/39; Warka: Heinrich 1936, Taf. 31 with p. 41; shell beads also at Kish, Watelin 1934, Pl. XIX.4). I am very grateful to Drs. Harriet Martin and P. R. S. Moorey for these references. (See also de Genouillac 1934, Tome 1, Pl. 34, 3c).

2GS:255   = AbS 1557   5161   2G77 Sub-surface   Plate Xc
  Human figurine; worn, head only surviving. One ear missing, back of head hollowed out, with impression of ancient finger-print.
     H. 2.3; W. 1.7; Th. 1.5 cm.

2GS:273   5161   2G77 Sub-surface   Fig. 318
  Animal figurine. In two joining pieces; leg and side preserved. On the back, three incised lines.
     H. 4.0; L. (ext.) 3.2 cm.

2GS:287   5181   2G98 Sub-surface   Fig. 319
  Animal figurine. In two joining pieces; part of body and head preserved.
     H. 3.5; L. 5.9 cm.

3GS:22   5907   3G81 Sub-surface
  Pottery discs. Two discs coarsely made from rubbed-down sherds; not perforated.
     Dis. 3.0 and 2.5 cm.

(*unnumbered*) It seems worth illustrating here as a matter of curiosity a small group of unbaked clay figurines collected by R. D. Biggs from the surface of the West Mound in 1976, where they had been left by the shepherd-boy who had been making them. The group (Plate X*d*) includes plates, dishes and a coffee-pot (top left), a bed(?) (top right), and pieces of animals (dog, sheep, goat(?); bottom).

5.4 *Stones*

Since all stone is necessarily imported, we tried to retain even unworked pieces for study. Certain broad categories emerged, and three are dealt with separately below: stone bowls (Chapter 5.5), ground and polished stone tools (Chapter 5.6) and flaked stone (i.e. flints, Chapter 5.7). Most of the remainder, although we have listed them above under their provenance in Chapter 3, have not been granted separate treatment, being shapeless lumps. For a cylinder seal see Chapter 5.8.

The distribution of stone artefacts on the surface has been plotted, as with sherds and clay sickles and cones (Figs. 319-20). It is noteworthy that both the tools and the stone vessels tend to occur in groups, doubtless reflecting the places where certain types of deposit are at the surface. Note also that sub-surface finds are more numerous than those on the surface.

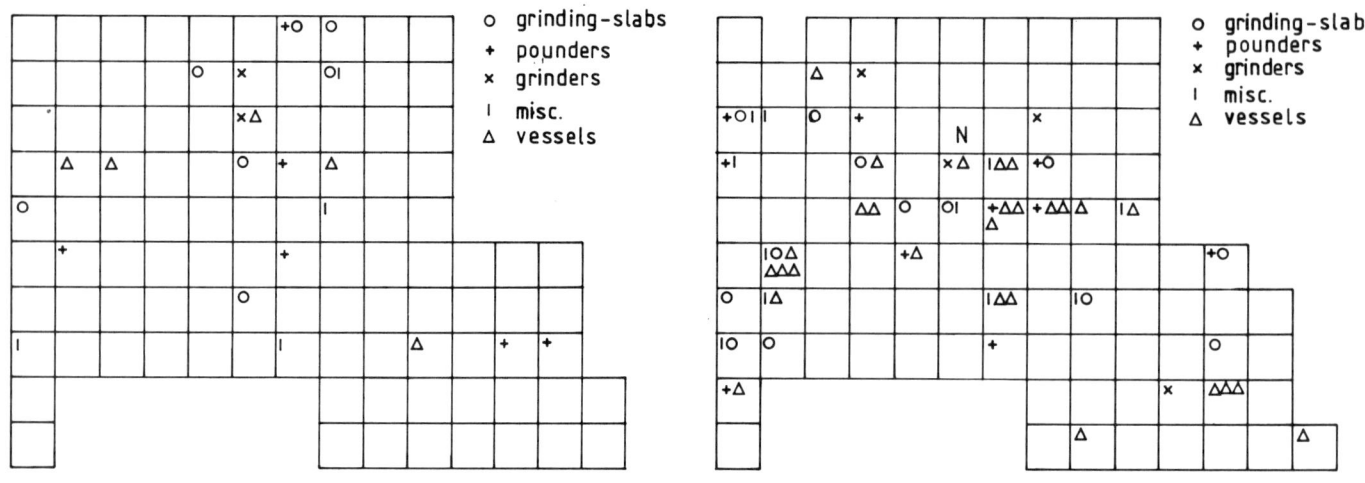

Fig. 320. Distribution of stones—Surface.

Fig. 321. Distribution of stones—Sub-surface.

5.5 *Stone vessels* (J. N. Postgate)

It has been observed before that stone vessels occur less frequently as the Early Dynastic period advances, and this may account for the surprising number of complete, or at least reconstructible, stone vessels found on the West Mound. On the other hand, the evidence for ancient repairs (e.g. 2GS:162, 163) proves that even at the beginning of the Early Dynastic stone bowls were prized possessions.

Materials A selection of stone vessel sherds from Abu Salabikh was submitted for examination to the Mineralogy and Petrology Department of the University of Cambridge, and kindly examined for me by Dr. I. D. Muir. The great majority of the sherds came from limestones of varying kinds, and the only exception was provided by two fragments of chlorite. The range of materials on the West Mound, though presumably earlier than the bulk of the material from the rest of the site, was little different. Most of the sherds below were thought to be limestone, but the identifications need confirmation from a specialist. However, we do have a vessel in a soft bituminous stone (3GS:19), and one or two fragments of greenish stone which may well be chlorite (e.g. 2GS:54 and 96). More precise identifications must await a more detailed investigation of the stone vessels for the site as a whole. Of the limestones, one may pick out as distinctive to the layman a fine translucent sherd (2GS:87), pinkish stone (2GS:248), and a yellower type which takes a high polish and is used for fine, thin-walled bowls (2GS:77 and 169). Most of the remainder are of dull whitish or greyish stones, although one heavy base is in a light grey stone with rather attractive white banding (2GS:159).

Shapes The majority of stone vessels are simple circular bowls, usually more or less steeply conical with plain rims and flat bases. A slight out-turning of the rim or groove below it on the exterior is sometimes present (e.g. 2GS:87 and 3GS:44). A flat rim which is rather unusual is found on 2GS:229 and 145; these lack their bases, but it seems possible that they come from rather shallow, thick-walled dishes. Other shapes include the rectangular trough (2GS:158; cf. 2GS:183), a piriform jar (3GS:17), a miniature jar (2GS:280), and the elegant black funnel (2GS:164).

2GS:2   5001   2G80 Surface   Fig. 322
Fragment; pink limestone. Two worked surfaces, very thick wall; perhaps from a heavy bowl or more likely a mortar.

2GS:54   5023   2G61 Sub-surface   Fig. 323
Sherd from base of bowl; speckled greenish stone.
5.9 x 1.5 cm.; Th. of wall 1.0 cm.

2GS:56   5027   2G51 Sub-surface   Fig. 324
Rim sherd from bowl; dull yellowish limestone.
4.2 x 3.4 cm.; Th. at break 0.9 cm.

2GS:57   5027   2G51 Sub-surface   Fig. 325
Base sherd; dull yellowish limestone.
4.9 x 4.3 cm.; Th. of wall 1.0 cm.

2GS:58 5027 2G51 Sub-surface
Body sherd from wall of a heavy stone vessel; marbly limestone.
9.5 x 4.0 cm.; Th. of wall 3.0-3.7 cm.

2GS:67 5036 2G31 Surface Fig. 326
Base sherd; dull yellowish limestone. Nearly vertical wall, perhaps from a low-sided dish, large and thick.
H. (ext.) 5.5; Di. of base ca. 24 cm.; Th. of wall at break 1.5 cm.

2GS:77 5046 2G32 Surface Fig. 327
Rim sherd; fine yellowish limestone, well polished inside.
6.2 x 5.5 cm.; Th. at break 0.8; Rim di. ca. 14 cm.

2GS:87 5062 2G43 Sub-surface Fig. 328
Rim sherd; translucent white limestone. Rim rounded outwards; well smoothed inside.
5.2 x 4.5 cm.; Th. at break 0.8 cm.; Rim not estimable.

2GS:89 5051 2G12 Sub-surface Fig. 329
Large rim sherd and small body sherd from large bowl; dull yellowish limestone.
H. (ext.) 6.7; Rim di. ca. 40 cm.; Th. at break 1.8 cm. Body sherd: 4.8 x 3.2; Max. Th. 2.1; possibly from close to base.

2GS:96 5059 2G33 Sub-surface Fig. 330
Rim sherd from plain bowl; speckled greenish stone.
8.8 x 5.5 cm.; Th. at break 0.9 cm.

2GS:119 5062 2G43 Sub-surface Fig. 331
Rim sherd; dull yellowish stone. Bowl. Possible traces of red paint on interior surface.
7.8 x 5.2 cm.; Th. at break 1.6 cm.; Rim di. not estimable.

2GS:126 5096 2G25 Surface
Body sherd; dull yellowish limestone. Outer surface much worn, inner surface smoothed, so presumably a bowl. Similar to 2GS:67.
7.5 x 4.3 cm.; Th. 1.8 cm.

2GS:145 5098 2G35 Sub-surface
Rim sherd(?); dull yellowish limestone. If part of the rim survives, it is a flat rim 1.0 cm. wide to a low-sided vessel, but it is not certain that it is any more than a smooth break.
H. (ext.) 2.2 cm.; W. 5.3 cm.

2GS:149 5079 2G54 Sub-surface
Body sherd; pinkish limestone with micaceous inclusions. The sherd is well finished both sides, and also convex each side, which makes it difficult to place in a normal vessel; possibly not a vessel at all.
6.0 x 3.7 cm.; Th. (max.) 1.1 cm.

2GS:158 5109 2G66 Sub-surface Fig. 332
Sherd from side of trough; dull yellowish limestone. Preserved piece is entirely straight-sided for a length of 15.2 cm., and the regularly curving profile is probably preserved down to base.
H. ca. 6.5 cm.; W. ca. 12 cm.; Th. at base 1.2 cm.

2GS:159 5109 2G66 Sub-surface Fig. 333
Base sherd; light grey stone with white banding. Flat base, either from bowl or jar.
H. (ext.) 3.2; Di. of base ca. 7 cm.; Th. at break 1.2 cm.

2GS:162 = AbS 1468 5113 2G46 Sub-surface Fig. 334 Plate XI*a*
Profile of stone bowl; white limestone. Large shallow stone bowl with straight sides and a slightly rounded base. Five mend holes along the edges broken in antiquity. Found close to 2GS:163 and 164.
Rim di. 28.0; Base di. 4.4; H. 8.0 cm.

2GS:163 = AbS 1467 5113 2G46 Sub-surface Fig. 335 Plate XI*b*
Half a stone bowl; greenish-white limestone. Large shallow bowl, with slightly rounded sides and a flat base. Six mend holes preserved, three along each broken edge. Found close to 2GS:162 and 164.
Rim di. 27.0; Base di. 12.0; H. 6.6 cm.

2GS:164 = AbS 1466 5113 2G46 Sub-surface Fig. 336 Plate XI*c*
Funnel; fine-grained black stone (limestone ?). Base, and parts of rim and body missing. In the absence of the base it is impossible to be certain that this was actually a funnel rather than a vessel designed to hold liquids, but comparison with contemporary pottery funnels strongly suggests it (cf. *Iraq* 40 [1978] 87:6). Found just south of 2GS:162 and 163, in fill above the black bricks of the thin northernmost enclosure wall.

2GS:169   5115   2G36 Sub-surface   Fig. 337
   Profile of bowl; fine yellowish limestone with slight rust-coloured banding.
      Rim di. ca. 16 cm.; Base di. 4.8; H. 6.6 cm.

2GS:183   5115   2G36 Sub-surface
   Body sherd; dull yellowish limestone. Perhaps from long side of an oval vessel or trough.
      L. 8.3; W. 3.8; Th. 0.8 cm.

2GS:223   5124   2G37 Surface
   Possibly a rim sherd; very coarse dull yellowish limestone from a thick bowl.
      5.1 x 5.0 cm.; Th. at break 2.4 cm.

2GS:229   5123   2G47 Sub-surface   Fig. 338
   Rim sherd; dull greyish limestone. Small bowl with curving sides and a distinctive flat rim.
      H. (ext.) 3.0; Rim di. ca. 9 cm.; Th. at break 0.9 cm.

2GS:240   5123   2G47 Sub-surface
   Body sherd; heavy bowl or jar in yellowish marbly limestone.
      5.8 x 5.5 cm.; Th. 0.8-1.5 cm.

2GS:247   5151   2G49 Sub-surface   Fig. 339
   Rim sherd; black stone.
      10.9 x 3.3 cm.

2GS:248   5149   2G48 Sub-surface   Fig. 340
   Rim sherd; pink limestone. Plain rim, rather thick wall. From Room 45 (see plan).
      H. (ext.) 6.1; L. of sherd 5.8; Th. at break 1.1 cm.

2GS:263   5168   2G79 Surface   Fig. 341
   Body sherd, carinated. Shape of vessel not clear.
      6.3 x 4.0 cm.

2GS:280   = AbS 1758   5181   2G98 Sub-surface   Fig. 293   Plate VIIe
   Miniature jar; marbly limestone. Slightly out-turned rim leading directly into rounded shoulder and base. Found with miniature pottery jar, 2GS:281.
      Rim di. 3.6; Max. di. 5.1; H. 5.8 cm.

2GS:290   5027   2G51 Sub-surface   Fig. 342
   Rim sherd; dull yellow-grey limestone. Roughly incised frond pattern on exterior.
      Rim di. ca. 10 cm.; Sherd 5.0 x 3.2; Th. at break 0.9 cm.

3GS:17   5907   3G81 Sub-surface
   Lower part of jar. White limestone, very badly corroded, so that vessel cannot be restored or drawn. Pointed ovoid base and body; definite shoulder carination, with remains of a horizontally pierced lug; 2 deliberate holes pierced by base. Found close to 3GS:18 and 19.
      H. (max. ext.) ca. 14 cm.; W. of sherd ca. 12 cm.

3GS:18   = AbS 1821   5907   3G81 Sub-surface   Fig. 343   Plate XId
   Bowl, virtually complete. Fine yellowish limestone, with rust-coloured markings. Plain rim, with slight rounding to about 0.8 cm. below rim on exterior. Side curves regularly to base, which is flattened though still slightly convex.
      Rim di. 21.2; Base di. ca. 5 cm.; H. 7.9-8.1 cm.

3GS:19   = AbS 1822   5907   3G81 Sub-surface   Fig. 344   Plate XIe
   Bowl, several sherds missing. Soft, bituminous black stone which has cracked and warped. Slight rounding below rim on exterior. Side curves regularly to scarcely perceptible though still slightly flattened base. Found with 3GS:17 and 18.
      Rim di. 19.0; Base di. ca. 3.2; H. ca. 8.5 cm.

3GS:44   5935   3G93 Sub-surface   Fig. 345
   Rim sherd. Fine pink and yellowish limestone. A rather shallow bowl with distinctly out-turned rim.
      Rim di. ca. 22 cm.; Sherd 7.9 x 6.6; Th. at break 0.9 cm.

5.6 *The ground and polished stone industry* (Jesper Eidem)   Plate XIIa

Most of the stones from the West Mound can be classified into tool-types. All stones were collected, and only a little less than a third are natural pebbles or fragments too small for identification. These are not included in the catalogue.

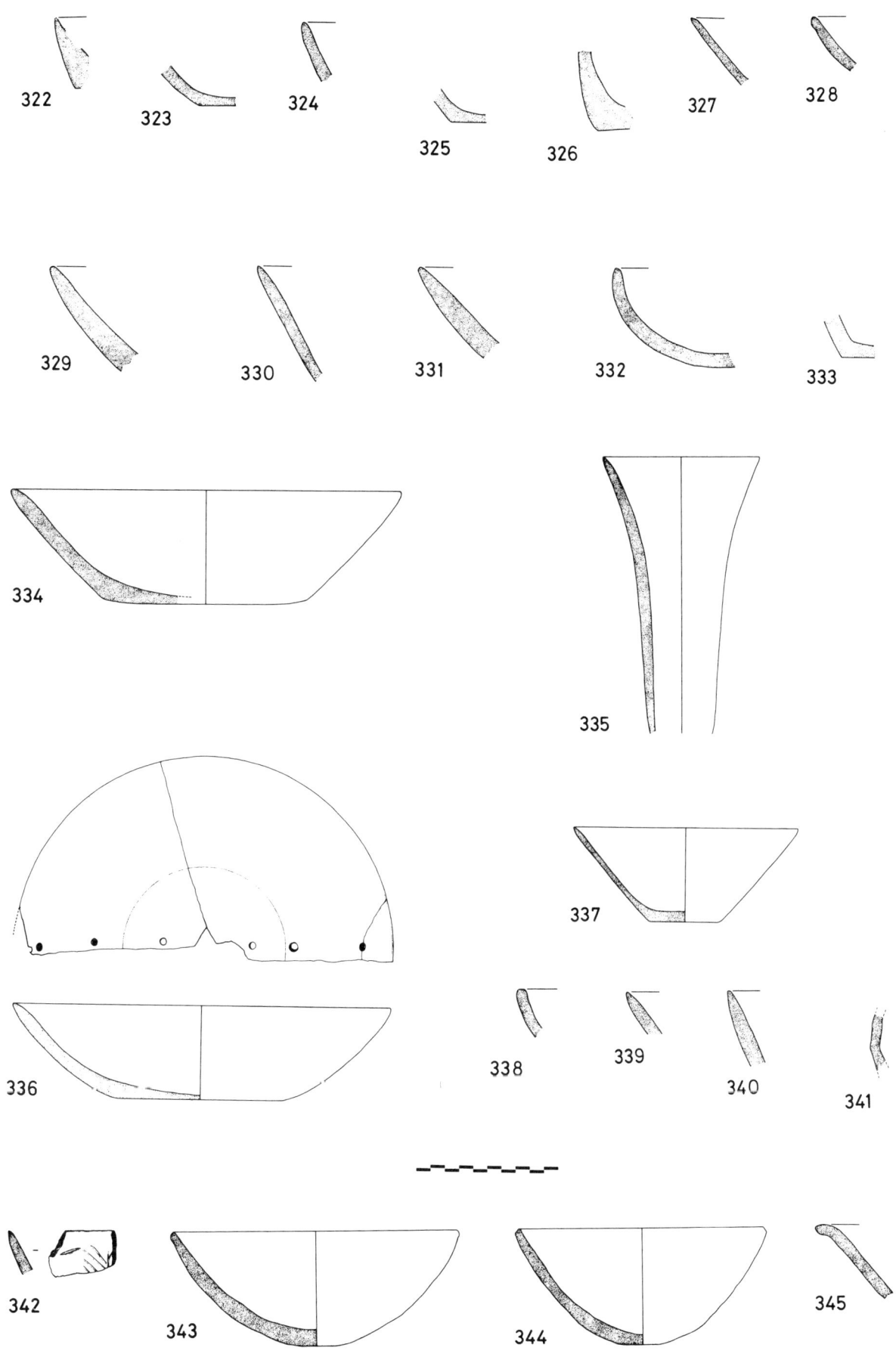

Stone vessels. Scale 1:4. See pp. 92-4.

Pounders Mostly crude, round stones, but some are oblong and highly polished (e.g. 2GS:28 and 2GS:238). Often of a dark grey, black or red, rather hard stone. All show signs of use except one specimen (2GS:182). A single example of a combined pounder and smoother was found (3GS:34).

Grinders and grinding slabs These occurred frequently. The majority are of a buffish or white limestone or black pumice. All grinders have traces of use. Only fragments of slabs were found, but all have the usual plano-convex shape.

Cubes Small, round stones with flattened polished sides. These occur in early levels on many Mesopotamian sites, and are often interpreted as weights. But the specimens from the West Mound have clear traces of wear on the flattened surface, suggesting a use as specialized pestles.

Smoothers Stones with one flat, heavily polished surface, usually of a hard purplish-red stone.

Pierced stones Ring-shaped stones, polished and with a central, biconical piercing. Both size and material vary. They are traditionally interpreted as weights. One conical-shaped specimen (2GS:42) is unique within this group.

NB. Brackets ( ) round a measurement mean that it is broken, and not the full original dimension. See also p. 20.

2GS:7 5004 2G80 Sub-surface
Fragmentary pestle; green stone.
(10.8 x 6.1 x 2.6) cm.

2GS:8 5005 2G70 Sub-surface
Fragment of grinding-slab; black pumice.
(13.5 x 7.5) x 3.1 cm.

2GS:18 5008 2G40 Surface
Two fragments of grinding-slabs; black pumice.
(15.7 x 7.8) x 3.7 cm. and (7.5 x 5.3) x 2.8 cm.

2GS:25 5002 2G70 Surface
Fragment of smoother; red stone.
(4.3 x 7.9) x 2.6 cm.

2GS:27 5016 2G20 Sub-surface
Fragment of grinding-slab; black pumice.
(6.6 x 6.7) x 2.5 cm.

2GS:28 5016 2G20 Sub-surface Plate XIIa
Pounder; dark grey stone.
15.5 x 7.1 x 4.7 cm.

2GS:29 5014 2G30 Sub-surface
Pounder; black stone.
5.3 x 5.5 x 5.4 cm.

2GS:30 5014 2G30 Sub-surface
Smoother; red stone.
6.6 x 6.4 x 3.7 cm.

2GS:31 5016 2G20 Sub-surface Plate XIIa
Cube-shaped stone; possibly small pestle; white limestone.
4.4 x 4.3 x 3.5 cm.

2GS:33 5006 2G60 Sub-surface
Fragment of grinding-slab; black pumice.
(9.7) x (6.5) x 2 cm.

2GS:39 5024 2G71 Sub-surface
Fragment of grinding-slab; black pumice.
(8.6) x (6.4) x 2.4 cm.

2GS:40 5027 2G51 Sub-surface
Fragment of grinding-slab; black pumice.
(7.4) x (8.8) x 4.4 cm.

2GS:42 5027 2G51 Sub-surface Plate XII*a*
Conical stone with central, biconical piercing; marbly limestone, about half preserved.
Di. 10 cm.; Th. 7.1 cm.; Di. of perf. 4.0-1.9 cm.

2GS:47 5026 2G51 Surface
Fragment of pounder; dark grey marbly limestone.
(5.2) x 6.1 x 3.9 cm.

2GS:60 5030 2G21 Sub-surface Plate XII*a*
Ring-shaped stone with central biconical piercing; black pumice; about half preserved.
Di. 7.9; Th. 3.7; Di. of perf. 3.3-1.9 cm.

2GS:71 5048 2G22 Sub-surface
Fragment of grinding-slab; black pumice.
(11.5) x (6.2) x 4.0 cm.

2GS:90 5056 2G13 Sub-surface
Fragment of grinder; white marbly limestone.
(7.8) x (6.5) x 5.5 cm.

2GS:95 5059 2G33 Sub-surface
Fragment of grinding-slab; black pumice.
(10.7) x (3.0) x 2.4 cm.

2GS:125 5096 2G25 Surface
Grinder; pinkish granular stone.
7.0 x 5.5 x 4.0 cm.

2GS:128 5097 2G35 Surface
Fragment of grinding slab; buffish limestone.
(10.5) x (7.0) x 4.0 cm.

2GS:132 5077 2G44 Sub-surface
Two fragments of grinding-slabs; black pumice.
(15.9) x (5.5) x 2.1 cm. and (11.4 x 9.0) x 1.3 cm.

2GS:135 5079 2G54 Sub-surface
Fragment of pounder; grey stone.
8.3 x 8.0 x (4.4) cm.

2GS:138 5084 2G14 Surface
Fragment of grinding-slab; black pumice.

2GS:144 5098 2G35 Sub-surface
Fragment of grinder; buffish limestone.
8.2 x (7.4) x 6.3 cm.

2GS:148 5090 2G65 Surface
Two fragments of grinding-slabs; buffish limestone.
(15.2) x (11.6) x 5.1 cm. and (7.6) x (6.4) x 3.0 cm.

2GS:168 5115 2G36 Sub-surface
Ring-shaped stone with central biconical piercing; white limestone; about half preserved.
Di. 13.0; Th. 4.5; Di. of perf. 3.7-2.3 cm.

2GS:171 5113 2G46 Sub-surface Plate XII*a*
Pounder, rounded; white stone.
7.9 x 8.9 x 7.1 cm.

2GS:181 5101 2G15 Surface Plate XII*a*
Grinder; white stone.
8.5 x 8.3 x 3.8 cm.

2GS:182 5110 2G56 Surface
Pounder, unused; greenish stone.
7.4 x 7.2 x 4.8 cm.

2GS:186 5115 2G36 Surface
Fragment of pounder; red stone.
7.1 x 3.4 x 1.0 cm.

2GS:196 5106 2G76 Surface
Ring-shaped stone with central biconical piercing; about half preserved.
Di. 8.0; Th. 3.8; Di. of perf. 2.8-0.9 cm.

2GS:199 5095 2G45 Sub-surface Plate XIIa
Fragment of grinding-slab; black pumice.
(10.1) x (6.8) x 2.5 cm.

2GS:200 5120 2G06 Surface
Fragment of grinding-slab; white porous stone.
(14.0 x 11.4) x 4.1 cm.

2GS:204 5095 2G45 Sub-surface
Ring-shaped stone with central biconical piercing; white limestone; about half preserved.
Di. 13.4; Th. 5.6; Di. of perf. 4.7-2.6 cm.

2GS:208 5120 2G06 Surface
Fragment of pounder; grey stone.
10.1 x (8.5) x (5.3) cm.

2GS:209 5109 2G66 Sub-surface
Fragment of smoother; white marbly limestone.
8.8 x 7.4 x (4.0) cm.

2GS:222 5125 2G37 Sub-surface
Fragment of pounder; white marbly limestone.
6.6 x 6.5 x (3.4) cm.

2GS:225 5125 2G37 Sub-surface Plate XIIa
Fragment of grinding-slab; black pumice.
(11.4 x 8.8) x 1.7 cm.

2GS:230 5130 2G07 Surface
Fragment of grinding-slab; black pumice.
(10.2) x (5.8) x 3.1 cm.

2GS:231 5127 2G27 Sub-surface Plate XIIa
Grinder; buffish limestone.
6.9 x 6.2 x 6.3 cm.

2GS:233 5130 2G07 Surface
Fragment of grinding-slab; coarse whitish stone.
(8.3) x (6.6) x 3.7 cm.

2GS:235 5128 2G17 Surface
Fragment of grinding-slab; black pumice.
(6.5) x (6.3) x 1.8 cm.

2GS:236 5128 2G17 Surface
Cube-shaped stone; possibly small pestle; white limestone.
5.4 x 5.4 x 4.2 cm.

2GS:237 5131 2G07 Sub-surface
Pounder; black stone.
(10.0) x 7.5 x 3.4 cm.

2GS:238 5123 2G47 Sub-surface
Pounder; black stone.
13.8 x 7.1 x 5.0 cm.

2GS:251   5151   2G49 Sub-surface
   Ring-shaped stone with central biconical piercing; buffish limestone; flat one side, rounded the other; about half preserved.
   Di. 14.0 cm.; Th. 4.1 cm.; Di. of perf. 3.4-1.6 cm.

2GS:271   5163   2G68 Sub-surface
   Fragment of grinding-slab; buffish limestone.
   (5.2) x (4.7) x 2.2 cm.

2GS:272   5163   2G68 Sub-surface
   Ring-shaped stone with central biconical piercing; buffish limestone; about half preserved.
   Di. 9.5; Th. 4.6; Di. of perf. 3.8-1.5 cm.

2GS:292   5107   2G76 Sub-surface
   Pounder; grey-brown flint-like stone. Narrows towards one end along one axis, but becomes broader along the other, like a stone celt; end chipped.
   5.2 x (7.0) x 4.2 cm.

3GS:15   5904   3G80 Sub-surface
   A. Fragment of grinder; buffish limestone.
      (7.5) x (6.3) x (3.6) cm.
   B. Fragment of grinding-slab; buffish limestone.
      (6.0) x (5.9) x 4.0 cm.

3GS:28   5913   3G70 Sub-surface   Plate XIIa
   Cube-shaped stone, possibly small pestle; reddish, fine-grained stone.
   5.0 x 5.1 x 5.2 cm.

3GS:32   5922   3G72 Surface
   Pounder(?); one or two faces worn; sandy reddish stone.
   (7.5) x (7.0) x 3.5 cm.

3GS:34   5919   3G51 Sub-surface
   Combined pounder and smoother; dark grey stone.
   10.0 x 8.0 x 7.0 cm.

3GS:35   5919   3G51 Sub-surface
   Fragment of grinding-slab; greyish granite.
   (13.0 x 9.0) x 5.0 cm.

3GS:37   5915   3G71 Sub-surface
   Fragment of grinding-slab; black pumice.
   (8.7) x (9.0) x 5.8 cm.

3GS:40   5911   3G61 Sub-surface   Plate XIIa
   Smoother; broken; purplish-red stone.
   (10.0) x 5.1 x 3.9 cm.

3GS:43   5914   3G71 Surface
   Rounded end of pebble, perhaps used as tool; stone fine-grained, discoloured.
   (5.8) x 6.2 x 2.1 cm.

5.7 *The flaked stone industry* (Joan Crowfoot Payne)

Materials A fine banded brown flint is used, but coarser stones, grey-green, banded dark and light grey, and pink are equally common. A single piece of obsidian was found in this operation (2GS:244).

Primary flaking There are a few prismatic blade cores, with plain striking platform and chisel end. The backs of the cores are flat or slightly convex, covered with cortex or roughly flaked transversely. Narrow parallel-sided blades are removed round the front of the core, despurring of the core making a neat butt. Core-tablets are removed to renew the striking platform when necessary.

Secondary flaking Sections of blades are used to make sickle-blades, none complete; the ends of the blade sections may be snapped, or squared by direct retouch; the edges are lustrous, and coarsely denticulated by either direct or inverse retouch.

Conclusions There are very few specimens in all. However, some differences between this industry and that of the Early Dynastic III levels of Abu Salabikh (see J. C. Payne, *Iraq* 42, 105 ff.) appear to exist: these are the use of various coarser stones as well as fine brown flint, and the use of either direct or inverse retouch to denticulate the sickle-blades. Early Dynastic III sickle-blades are completely standardized, with coarse denticulation invariably made by direct retouch.

Note to catalogue: All flints from one provenance were usually assigned the same number; hence some of the numbers in the ensuing catalogue comprise several different pieces.

2GS:5   5002   2G70 Surface   Fig. 346   Plate XII*b*
   Sickle-blade fragment, brown flint. One edge lustrous and denticulated by inverse retouch, the other denticulated by direct retouch.
      3.3 x 1.4 cm.
   Sickle-blade fragment, grey banded stone. One edge denticulated by direct retouch.
      1.7 x 1.6 cm.

2GS:6   5003   2G90 Sub-surface
   Flake, light brown banded flint. Edges abraded.
      5.2 x 3.1 cm.
   Pebble (and joining chip), grey-green stone. Some small flakes removed.
      8.3 x 5.4 cm.

2GS:14   5005   2G70 Sub-surface   Fig. 347
   Chunk, banded brown flint.

2GS:20   5008   2G40 Surface
   Blade fragment, banded grey-brown flint. Edges abraded.

2GS:32   5007   2G50 Surface
   Blade fragment, grey stone.

2GS:52   5021   2G61 Surface
   Three chunks: banded brown flint; calcined flint; grey stone.

2GS:55   5029   2G31 Sub-surface
   Flake fragment, calcined flint.

2GS:61   5030   2G21 Sub-surface
   Blade fragment, light brown flint. Edges abraded.

2GS:75   5043   2G42 Sub-surface
   Core-trimming flake fragment (?), coarse banded grey stone.
   Flake, calcined flint.
      4.0 x 2.2 cm.

2GS:83   5037   2G62 Surface
   Blade fragment, coarse grey stone. Edges abraded.
   Flake fragment, banded brown flint.
   Chunk, calcined flint.

2GS:108   5063   2G53 Surface
   Chunk, brown banded flint.

2GS:116   5065   2G63 Surface   Fig. 348   Plate XII*b*
   Sickle-blade fragment, banded brown flint. Both edges lustrous and denticulated by direct retouch.
      3.0 x 1.4 cm.
   Blade fragment, grey-brown flint.

2GS:120   5071   2G64 Surface
   Blade fragment, banded brown flint. Edges abraded.
   Two flakes, coarse grey stone.
      a. 3.2 x 2.1 cm. b. 2.7 x 2.0 cm.
   Flake, dark grey flint.
      2.3 x 2.1 cm.

2GS:124   5096   2G25 Surface
   Flake, coarse grey stone.
      5.0 x 3.3 cm.

2GS:133   5077   2G44 Sub-surface
Flake fragment, light brown banded flint. Edges abraded.

2GS:136   5089   2G75 Sub-surface
Core, coarse deep pink stone. Prismatic blade core, D-shaped plain striking platform, chisel end. Flat back partly covered cortex, partly transversely flaked, with short crest at one side.
6.1 x 4.3 x 2.7 cm.

2GS:142   5077   2G44 Sub-surface   Fig. 349   Plate XII*b*
Sickle blade fragment, light brown banded flint. Lustre and denticulation made by direct retouch along one edge.
2.8 x 1.5 cm.

2GS:151   5079   2G54 Sub-surface
Blade fragment, light brown banded flint. Edges abraded. Traces of bitumen over upper surface.

2GS:152   5093   2G55 Sub-surface
Flake fragment, brown flint.

2GS:160   5105   2G23 or 33 cut   Fig. 350   Plate XII*b*
End scraper, light brown flint. On blade, steep direct retouch and wear round end only. Side edges abraded. Traces of bitumen over both ends.
7.4 x 1.3 cm.

2GS:191   5113   2G46 Sub-surface
Blade, light brown flint. Edges abraded.
8.5 x 2.0 cm.

2GS:192   5114   2G36 Surface
Blade, banded brown flint. Edges abraded.
6.6 x 2.3 cm.

2GS:195   5112   2G46 Surface
Fragment of calcined flint.

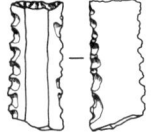
Fig. 346—2GS:5.

Fig. 347—2GS:14.

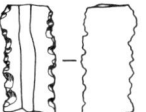
Fig. 348—2GS:116.

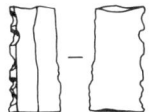
Fig. 349—2GS:142.

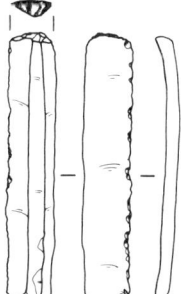
Fig. 350—2GS:160.

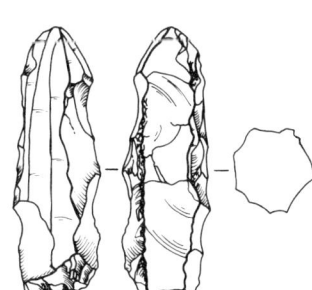
Fig. 351—2GS:279.

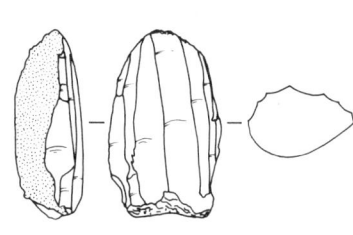
Fig. 352—3GS:31.

Selected flints. Scale 1:2. See pp. 99-103.

2GS:203 5095 2G45 Sub-surface
  Flake fragment, brown flint.

2GS:214 5127 2G27 Sub-surface
  Blade, brown flint. Edges abraded.
    7.3 x 1.6 cm.

2GS:220 5059 2G33 Sub-surface Plate XII*b*
  Sickle-blade fragment, calcined flint. One edge denticulated by direct retouch.
    2.7 x 1.4 cm.
  Sickle-blade, light brown banded flint. ? Unfinished, ends snapped, one partly retouched. One edge denticulated by inverse retouch.
    3.0 x 2.2 cm.

2GS:224 5129 2G17 Surface
  Chunk, brown flint.

2GS:239 5123 2G47 Sub-surface
  Blade fragment, banded brown flint. Edges abraded.

2GS:244 5145 2G18 Sub-surface
  Blade fragment, coarse brown stone.
  Blade fragment, obsidian.
    2.0 x 0.7 cm.

2GS:257 5171 2G89 Sub-surface
  Blade, banded brown flint, patinated white. Edges abraded.
    8.1 x 1.5 cm.

2GS:259 5156 2G57 Surface
  Blade fragment, patinated flint. Edges abraded.

2GS:262 5155 2G59 Sub-surface
  Chunk, banded brown flint.

2GS:269 5174 2G88 Surface
  Blade fragment, coarse grey stone. Edges abraded.

2GS:274 5168 2G79 Surface
  Core, coarse grey stone. Roughly prismatic. Back partly covered cortex, part roughly flaked. Chisel end.
    6.5 x 5.0 x 3.0 cm.

2GS:276 5171 2G89 Sub-surface
  Fragment, banded brown flint, calcined.

2GS:279 5181 2G98 Sub-surface Fig. 351
  Core, coarse grey stone. Prismatic. Narrow back with two crests made by flaking from both sides. Rounded end.
    7.0 x 2.1 x 1.9 cm.
  Blade fragment, calcined flint; chunk, banded brown flint.

3GS:6 5901 3G90 Sub-surface
  Blade fragment, patinated flint.
  Blade fragment, calcined flint.
  Flake, banded brown flint.
    4.3 x 2.3 cm.

3GS:10 5905 3G80 Sub-surface
  Blade fragment, calcined flint. Edges abraded.

3GS:14 5904 3G80 Surface
  Blade fragment, coarse grey stone. Edges abraded.
  Blade fragment, calcined flint.

3GS:23 5912 3G70 Surface
  Blade fragment, grey stone.
  Blade fragment, grey stone. Edges abraded.
  Blade fragment, patinated flint, calcined.
  Flake, banded brown flint.
    3.4 x 3.3 cm.

3GS:25   5912   3G70 Surface

Core, patinated brown flint. Conical, oval cross-section. Back partly covered by cortex, part roughly flaked. Pointed end.
     5.5 x 4.3 x 3.0 cm.

Blade fragment, calcined flint.

3GS:30   5928   3G52 Surface

Flake, coarse grey stone.
     3.9 x 2.7 cm.

Chunk, brown flint.

3GS:31   5922   3G72 Surface   Fig. 352

Core, calcined flint. Prismatic blade core, oval striking platform, plain, chisel end. Convex back covered by cortex.
     4.7 x 2.8 x 1.8 cm.

Flake, coarse grey stone. Edges abraded.
     3.9 x 2.3 cm.

3GS:33   5910   3G61 Surface

Core-tablet fragment, coarse grey stone. Truncated blade scars round part of edge. Struck from ridge between scars.
     3.2 x 2.8 cm.

Flake, coarse grey stone. Edges abraded.
     5.6 x 3.1 cm.

Fragment calcined flint.

3GS:39   5911   3G61 Sub-surface

Core fragment, banded brown flint. Striking platform lost. Roughly oval cross-section, chisel end. Roughly flaked across back, one crest at side of back.
     4.3 x 3.6 x 2.6 cm.

3GS:42   5909   3G60 Sub-surface

Chunk, banded brown flint.

5.8 *Miscellaneous items*

Cylinder seal

2GS:94   = AbS 1446   5060   2G23 Sub-surface   Plate X*e*

Flecked dark green stone; bored from each end. Frieze of "goats" (with pairs of vertical short horns), with geometric filling motifs between them. Classic "Brocade Style" of the type best known from the Diyala region (see Frankfort 1955, Pl. 23 Nos. 235-7). For the find-spot by the N face of the N wall of Room 14 see plan.
     H. 3.1; Di. 0.9 cm.

Metal Apart from one bowl (2GS:102) which is probably of recent date, the metal finds consist of a few very corroded fragments of copper. Among these are fragments of a pin(?) (2GS:11), a possible bead (2GS:22), the head of a nail (2GS:69), and two pieces of copper slag (2GS:122).

2GS:3   5001   2G80 Surface

Two fragments of a copper pin or ring; curving, tapering towards one end.
     a. L. 1.7; Di. 0.5 cm.
     b. L. 0.8; Di. 0.4 cm.

2GS:11   5005   2G70 Sub-surface

Two fragments of a pin(?); one shapeless lump.
     L. 2.5; Di 0.8 cm.

2GS:17   5008   2G40 Surface

Shaped fragment from unidentified object.
     W. 1.5 cm.

2GS:21   5010   2G50 Sub-surface

Shapeless flat lump of copper.
     L. 1.1 cm.

2GS:22   5011   2G40 Sub-surface

Spherical lump of copper; bead?
     Di. 0.7 cm.

2GS:69 5044 2G52 Sub-surface
Copper nail(?); part of shaft and roughly rounded head.
L. 2.1; Max. di. 1.2 cm.

2GS:102 = AbS 1460 5081 2G34 Sub-surface Fig. 353
Copper or bronze bowl. Low sides, rounded base with added vertical ring foot (part missing); bent in places. Found inverted, just below surface in no recognizable architectural context (see plan for exact position).
Rim di. 14.6; Base di. (max.) 8.5; H. 4.8 cm.

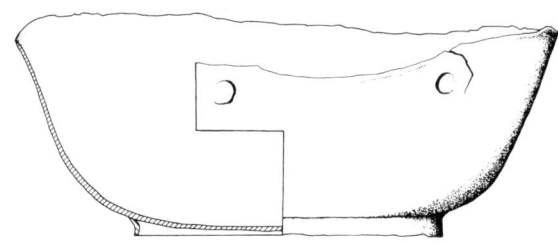

Fig. 353. Copper bowl, 2GS:102. Scale 1:2.

2GS:122 5095 2G45 Sub-surface
Two fragments of copper slag(?). The term slag is used loosely for a waste product with no recognizable form and should not be taken to imply definite evidence for smelting.

Glass A single piece of recent origin; a few glazed sherds were also found but these have not been separately recorded.

2GS:16 5006 2G60 Sub-surface
Fragment from base of a green glass bottle.
3.4 x 2.0 cm.

Bitumen
2GS:43 5027 2G51 Sub-surface
Fragments only.

2GS:166 5105 2G24 stratigraphic cut
Two fragments of bitumen with domed obverse and string impressions on reverse (6.2 x 4.5 and 4.3 x 3.3 cm.); one fragment, flatter, with reed impressions (7.2 x 4.1 cm.).

Shells Little was recovered, and all pieces came from bivalves, probably all *Unio tigridis*. They varied in length from 1.9 to 7.5 cm. The standard of recovery for shell and bone was probably less complete than for other classes of material.

2GS:9	5005	2G70 Sub-surface
2GS:10	5006	2G60 Sub-surface
2GS:13	5005	2G70 Sub-surface
2GS:246	5145	2G18 Sub-surface
2GS:260	5171	2G89 Sub-surface
3GS:2	5907	3G81 Sub-surface
3GS:5	5901	3G90 Sub-surface
3GS:7	5903	3G91 Sub-surface

Bone See note on shell above; as with the shells, all bone came from sub-surface batches and one would not normally expect to find recoverable organic materials on the surface of so salty a site.

2GS:167	5105	2G24 stratigraphic cut
2GS:198	5095	2G45 Sub-surface
2GS:277	5171	2G89 Sub-surface

BIBLIOGRAPHY AND BIBLIOGRAPHICAL ABBREVIATIONS

Note: for simplicity articles in our journal *Iraq* are usually quoted by *Iraq* volume number and page reference only; most other works are cited by the Harvard system as indicated below:

Adams 1981	R. McC. Adams, *Heartland of Cities* (Chicago).
Adams & Nissen 1972	R. McC. Adams & H. J. Nissen, *The Uruk Countryside* (Chicago).
Curtis 1982	J. Curtis (ed.), *Fifty Years of Mesopotamian Discovery* (London).
Delougaz 1933	P. Delougaz, "Plano-convex bricks and the methods of their employment", *Studies in Ancient Oriental Civilization,* 7 (Chicago), 1-38.
Delougaz 1940	id., *The Temple Oval at Khafājah* (Chicago, Oriental Institute Publications, Vol. 53).
Delougaz 1952	id., *Pottery from the Diyala Region* (Chicago, Oriental Institute Publications, Vol. 63).
Eridu	F. Safar, M. A. Mustafa, S. Lloyd et al., [Final report on Iraq Government excavations at Eridu], in press.
Frankfort 1955	H. A. Frankfort, *Stratified Cylinder Seals from the Diyala Region* (Chicago, Oriental Institute Publications, Vol. 72).
de Genouillac 1934	H. de Genouillac, *Fouilles de Telloh, I, Époques présargoniques* (Paris).
Gibson 1981	McG. Gibson (ed.), *Uch Tepe I: Tell Razuk, Tell Ahmed al-Mughir, Tell Ajamat* (Chicago & Copenhagen; State Organization of Antiquities and Heritage, Baghdad: Hamrin Report No. 10).
Hall & Woolley 1927	H. R. Hall & C. L. Woolley, *Al-'Ubaid* (Oxford, Ur Excavations Vol. 1).
Haller 1932	A. von Haller, "Die Keramik der archaischen Schichten von Uruk", in A. Nöldeke et al., *Vierter vorläufiger Bericht über die . . . in Uruk unternommenen Ausgrabungen* (Berlin, Preuss. Akad. d. Wissenschaften, Phil.-Hist. Kl., Nr. 6) 31-47.
Hansen 1965	D. P. Hansen, "The relative chronology of Mesopotamia, Part II. The pottery sequence at Nippur from the Middle Uruk to the end of the Old Babylonian period (3400-1600 B.C.)", in R. W. Ehrich (ed.), *Chronologies in Old World Archaeology* (Chicago).
Heinrich 1936	E. Heinrich, *Kleinfunde aus den archaischen Tempelschichten in Uruk* (Leipzig, Ausgrabungen der Deutschen Forschungsgemeinschaft in Uruk-Warka, 1).
Invernizzi 1980	A. Invernizzi, "Excavations in the Yelkhi Area (Hamrin Project, Iraq)", *Mesopotamia* 15 (Florence), 19-49.
Le Breton 1957	L. Le Breton, "The early period at Susa, Mesopotamian relations", *Iraq* 19, 79-124.
Le Brun 1971	A. Le Brun, "Recherches stratigraphiques à l'Acropole de Suse (1969-1971)", *Cahiers de la Délégation Archéologique Française en Iran* 1 (Paris), 163-216.
Le Brun 1978	id., "Le niveau 17B de l'Acropole de Suse (campagne de 1972)", *Cahiers de la D.A.F. en Iran* 9, 57-154.
Le Brun 1980	id., "Les "écuelles grossières": état de la question", in M.-Th. Barrelet (ed.), *L'archéologie de l'Iraq, Perspectives et limites de l'interprétation anthropologique des documents* (Paris, C.N.R.S., Actes du Colloque International No. 580), 59-70.

Mackay 1931	E. Mackay, *Report on Excavations at Jemdet Nasr, Iraq* (Chicago, Field Museum of Natural History, Anthropology Memoirs Vol. I No. 3).
Margueron n.d.	J. Cl. Margueron (ed.), *Le Moyen Euphrate* . . . (Actes du Colloque de Strasbourg 10-12 mars 1977).
Matson 1966	F. R. Matson (ed.), *Ceramics and Man* (Viking Fund Publications in Anthropology 41).
McCown, Haines & Biggs 1978	D. E. McCown, R. C. Haines & R. D. Biggs, *Nippur, II, The North Temple and Sounding E* (Chicago, Oriental Institute Publications, Vol. 97).
Moon 1981	J. A. Moon, "Some new Early Dynastic pottery from Abu Salabikh", *Iraq* 43, 47-75.
Nissen 1970	H. J. Nissen, "Grabung in den Quadraten K/L XII in Uruk-Warka", *Baghdader Mitteilungen* 5, 101-191.
Redman & Watson 1970	C. L. Redman & P. J. Watson, "Systematic, intensive surface collection", *American Antiquity* 35, 279-91.
Steve & Gasche 1971	M. J. Steve & H. Gasche, *L'Acropole de Suse* (Paris, Mémoires de la Mission archéologique de Perse: Mission de Susiane, Tome 46).
Sürenhagen 1975	D. Sürenhagen, *Keramikproduktion in Ḥabūba Kabira-Süd* (Berlin, Acta praehistorica et archaeologica 5/6).
Watelin 1934	L. Ch. Watelin, *Excavations at Kish, IV* (Paris).
Wright 1969	H. T. Wright, *The administration of production in an early Mesopotamian town* (Ann Arbor, Museum of Anthropology, University of Michigan, Anthropological Papers No. 38).
Wright 1980	H. T. Wright, N. Miller & R. Redding, "Time and process in an Uruk rural center", in M.-Th. Barrelet (ed.), *L'archéologie de l'Iraq, Perspectives et limites de l'interprétation anthropologique des documents* (Paris, C.N.R.S., Actes du Colloque International No. 580).
Wright 1981	H. T. Wright (ed.), *An early town on the Deh Luran plain: Excavations at Tepe Farukhabad* (Ann Arbor, Museum of Anthropology, University of Michigan, Memoirs No. 13).

LIST OF ABS NUMBERS

AbS 1446	= 2GS:94	= IM 80933	see Ch. 5.8
1447	2GS:64	IM 80934	Ch. 5.3
1453	2GS:70	IM 80939	Ch. 4.4
1460	2GS:102	IM 80948	Ch. 5.8
1461	2GS:85	IM 80945	Ch. 4.4
1463	2GS:93	IM for study	Ch. 4.4
1466	2GS:164	IM for study	Ch. 5.5
1467	2GS:163	IM for study	Ch. 5.5
1468	2GS:162	IM for study	Ch. 5.5
1470	2GS:190	IM 80954	Ch. 4.4
1474	2GS:104 +	IM for study	Ch. 4.4
1475	2GS:103	IM 80957	Ch. 4.4
1477	2GS:226	IM 80955	Ch. 5.3
1480	2GS:84	IM 80960	Ch. 4.4
1481	2GS:172	IM 80961	Ch. 4.4
1483	2GS:216	IM 80963	Ch. 4.4
1484	2GS:219	IM 80958	Ch. 4.4
1557	2GS:255	IM 84182	Ch. 5.3
1757	2GS:281	IM for study	Ch. 4.4
1758	2GS:280	IM 84164	Ch. 5.5
1795	2GS:284	IM for study	Ch. 4.4
1821	3GS:18	IM 84152	Ch. 5.5
1822	3GS:19	IM 84158	Ch. 5.5

CONCORDANCE OF BATCH NUMBERS

5000	2G90 Surface	5059	2G33 Sub-surface
5001	2G80 Surface	5060	2G23 Sub-surface
5002	2G70 Surface	5061	2G43 Surface
5003	2G90 Sub-surface	5062	2G43 Sub-surface
5004	2G80 Sub-surface	5063	2G53 Surface
5005	2G70 Sub-surface	5064	2G53 Sub-surface
5006	2G60 Sub-surface	5065	2G63 Surface
5007	2G50 Surface	5066	2G63 Sub-surface
5008	2G40 Surface	5067	2G23 Sub-surface pottery group
5009	2G90 Sub-surface, NE cut	5068	2G73 Surface
5010	2G50 Sub-surface	5069	2G73 Sub-surface
5011	2G40 Sub-surface	5070	2G12 Sub-surface (drain area)
5012	2G80 Sub-surface, from cut	5071	2G64 Surface
5013	2G30 Surface	5072	2G64 Sub-surface
5014	2G30 Sub-surface	5073	2G74 Surface
5015	2G20 Surface	5074	2G74 Sub-surface
5016	2G20 Sub-surface	5075	2G03 Sub-surface, group in S
5017	2G10 Surface	5076	2G44 Surface
5018	2G10 Sub-surface	5077	2G44 Sub-surface
5019	2G00 Surface	5078	2G54 Surface
5020	2G00 Sub-surface	5079	2G54 Sub-surface
5021	2G61 Surface	5080	2G34 Surface
5022	2G71 Surface	5081	2G34 Sub-surface
5023	2G61 Sub-surface	5082	2G24 Surface
5024	2G71 Sub-surface	5083	2G24 Sub-surface
5025	2G41 Surface	5084	2G14 Surface
5026	2G51 Surface	5085	2G14 Sub-surface
5027	2G51 Sub-surface	5086	2G04 Surface
5028	2G41 Sub-surface	5087	2G04 Sub-surface
5029	2G31 Sub-surface	5088	2G75 Surface
5030	2G21 Sub-surface	5089	2G75 Sub-surface
5031	2G11 Surface	5090	2G65 Surface
5032	2G01 Surface	5091	2G65 Sub-surface
5033	2G21 Surface	5092	2G55 Surface
5034	2G11 Sub-surface	5093	2G55 Sub-surface
5035	2G01 Sub-surface	5094	2G45 Surface
5036	2G31 Surface	5095	2G45 Sub-surface
5037	2G62 Surface	5096	2G25 Surface
5038	2G72 Surface	5097	2G35 Surface
5039	2G62 Sub-surface	5098	2G35 Sub-surface
5040	2G72 Sub-surface	5099	2G25 Sub-surface
5041	2G52 Surface	5100	2G15 Surface
5042	2G42 Surface	5101	2G15 Sub-surface
5043	2G42 Sub-surface	5102	2G05 Surface
5044	2G52 Sub-surface	5103	2G05 Sub-surface
5045	2G22 Surface	5104	2G12, drain, sub-surface
5046	2G32 Surface	5105	2G23, pottery in cut
5047	2G32 Sub-surface	5106	2G76 Surface
5048	2G22 Sub-surface	5107	2G76 Sub-surface
5049	2G12 Surface	5108	2G66 Surface
5050	2G02 Surface	5109	2G66 Sub-surface
5051	2G12 Sub-surface	5110	2G56 Surface
5052	2G02 Sub-surface	5111	2G56 Sub-surface
5053	2G03 Surface	5112	2G46 Surface
5054	2G13 Surface	5113	2G46 Sub-surface
5055	2G03 Sub-surface	5114	2G36 Surface
5056	2G13 Sub-surface	5115	2G36 Sub-surface
5057	2G23 Surface	5116	2G26 Surface
5058	2G33 Surface	5117	2G26 Sub-surface

5118	2G16 Surface	5169	2G79 Sub-surface
5119	2G16 Sub-surface	5170	2G89 Surface
5120	2G06 Surface	5171	2G89 Sub-surface
5121	2G06 Sub-surface	5172	2G99 Surface
5122	2G47 Surface	5173	2G99 Sub-surface
5123	2G47 Sub-surface	5174	2G88 Surface
5124	2G37 Surface	5175	2G88 Sub-surface
5125	2G37 Sub-surface	5176	2G87 Surface
5126	2G27 Surface	5177	2G87 Sub-surface
5127	2G27 Sub-surface	5178	2G97 Surface
5128	2G17 Sub-surface	5179	2G97 Sub-surface
5129	2G17 Surface	5180	2G98 Surface
5130	2G07 Surface	5181	2G98 Sub-surface
5131	2G07 Sub-surface	5182	2G48/58/49/59 Sub-surface
5132	2G09 Surface	5183	2G58 Sub-surface, 2nd scrape
5133	2G09 Sub-surface	5900	3G90 Surface
5134	2G19 Surface	5901	3G90 Sub-surface
5135	2G19 Sub-surface	5902	3G91 Surface
5136	2G29 Surface	5903	3G91 Sub-surface
5137	2G29 Sub-surface	5904	3G80 Surface
5138	2G39 Surface	5905	3G80 Sub-surface
5139	2G39 Sub-surface	5906	3G81 Surface
5140	2G38 Surface	5907	3G81 Sub-surface
5141	2G38 Sub-surface	5908	3G60 Surface
5142	2G28 Surface	5909	3G60 Sub-surface
5143	2G28 Sub-surface	5910	3G61 Surface
5144	2G18 Surface	5911	3G61 Sub-surface
5145	2G18 Sub-surface	5912	3G70 Surface
5146	2G08 Surface	5913	3G70 Sub-surface
5147	2G08 Sub-surface	5914	3G71 Surface
5148	2G48 Surface	5915	3G71 Sub-surface
5149	2G48 Sub-surface	5916	3G50 Surface
5150	2G49 Surface	5917	3G50 Sub-surface
5151	2G49 Sub-surface	5918	3G51 Surface
5152	2G58 Surface	5919	3G51 Sub-surface
5153	2G58 Sub-surface	5920	3G62 Surface
5154	2G59 Surface	5921	3G62 Sub-surface
5155	2G59 Sub-surface	5922	3G72 Surface
5156	2G57 Surface	5923	3G72 Sub-surface
5157	2G57 Sub-surface	5924	3G82 Surface
5158	2G67 Surface	5925	3G82 Sub-surface
5159	2G67 Sub-surface	5926	3G92 Surface
5160	2G77 Surface	5927	3G92 Sub-surface
5161	2G77 Sub-surface	5928	3G52 Surface
5162	2G68 Surface	5929	3G52 Sub-surface
5163	2G68 Sub-surface	5930	3G73 Surface
5164	2G78 Surface	5931	3G73 Sub-surface
5165	2G78 Sub-surface	5932	3G83 Surface
5166	2G69 Surface	5933	3G83 Sub-surface
5167	2G69 Sub-surface	5934	3G93 Surface
5168	2G79 Surface	5935	3G93 Sub-surface

DETAILED DESCRIPTIONS OF PLATES

Plate I*a*	View of the West Mound from Area A, before surface clearance (Autumn, 1975). In the narrow gap between the two mounds can be seen a strip of low scrub with goats grazing.
Plate I*b*	Looking N over 2G47-07 after clearance: the 10 m. squares are strung out (the 2 m. pole lies along the border between 2G37 and 27), the markers indicate points to be planned. For a picture of the clearance process in colour, see Curtis 1982, Plate 3*c* (opp. p. 62), in area of 2G51.
Plate II*a*	2G54 and 53 viewed from E after clearance. Yellow-brick enclosure wall clearly visible on right of picture as a lighter band; two shallow cuts made up to its S face are on line of black-brick wall. On left, lower part of bipod. This picture overlaps with *Iraq* 40 (1978) Pl. XIII*b*.
Plate II*b*	ED I jars in Room 8 (2G03) viewed from N. Foreground: 2GS:104; behind: 2GS:101; against W side of 2GS:104 is body of 2GS:93.
Plate II*c*	Outflow of drain in 2G12, viewed from S. On left: final tubular segment; on right: perforated outflow piece (2GS:219); in mouth of tubular piece: sherds of a conical bowl (2GS:218).
Plate III*a*	Drain in 2G12, viewed from SE, showing its full length after clearance (cf. Plate II*c*). Upper side of further segments has been eroded by exposure close to surface.
Plate III*b*	FI 77/02 after surface scraping in 2G07, viewed from SE (see pp. 16-7, with Fig. 6). Narrower white lobes at each end are made by wood-ash accumulated in the entrance channels to the two fuel-chambers.
Plate III*c*	FI 77/11: *in situ* remnants of an inverted jar-top used as a hearth, in 2G31 (2GS:99).
Plate III*d*	FI 77/12: *in situ* inverted jar-top used as hearth in 2G33 (2GS:189).
Plate IV*a*	Selected mass-produced sherds. *Left to right:* bevelled-rim bowls—large conical bowls—tall cups (wider)—tall cups (narrower)—solid-footed goblets proper.
Plate IV*b*	Selected decorated sherds. *Left (from top):* Fig. 122—batch 5912 (not drawn)—Fig. 120—batch 5904 (not drawn)—Fig. 118—Fig. 123. *Left centre:* batch 5925 (not drawn)—Fig. 129—Fig. 128—batch 5913 (not drawn). *Right centre:* Fig. 125—Fig. 114—Fig. 127—Fig. 117. *Right:* Fig. 113—Fig. 112—Fig. 126—batch 5912 (not drawn)—Fig. 111.
Plate V*a*	Sherds with painted decoration. *Top left:* 2GS:213 (Fig. 231). *Bottom left:* batch 5921 (not drawn). *Top right:* Fig. 99. *Bottom right:* Fig. 110.
Plate V*b*	Miscellaneous body sherds from ED squares, including examples of various decorative techniques, ribs, handles and spouts. Note diagonal reserved slip (*top right*), horizontal reserved slip, fragments of fenestrated hollow stands.
Plate VI*a*	Selected sherds of larger vessels, from ED squares. Note perforated ribbed sherds (*top left* (Fig. 279), and *bottom left* (Fig. 278)), bowl with applied socket and rib (*top centre*, Fig. 171); sherd of funnel (*next on right*, Fig. 277) and heavy jar shoulder with applied U-shaped cable (Fig. 257).
Plate VI*b*	Miscellaneous handles. *Left (from top):* strap-handle to jar rim (Fig. 92)—everted rim with impressed decoration (Fig. 97)—rope handle fragment (Fig. 96). *Centre:* strap with incised lines (Fig. 94)—impressed decoration at junction with rim (Fig. 93). *Right:* tab-handle at rim (Fig. 98)—lug with horizontal perforation (Fig. 99).
Plates VII-VIII	(see captions on Plate)
Plate IX*a*	Miscellaneous baked clay wall-cones. *Left (from top):* 3GS:4 (Fig. 301)—2GS:289 (Fig. 298)—3GS:24 (Fig. 299). *Centre:* 2GS:88 (Fig. 300); 2GS:245 (not drawn). *Right:* 3GS:47 (Fig. 297)—2GS:227 (not drawn)—2GS:170 (Fig. 302).
Plate IX*b*	Miscellaneous clay sickle fragments. *Left:* 2GS:12 (batch 5005). *Centre (from top):* 2GS:117 (5071)—2GS:131 (5078)—2GS:241 (5123; red ware!). *Right:* 2GS:69? (5036?)—2GS:131 (5078).
Plates X-XI	(see captions on Plate)
Plate XII*a*	Selected ground stone tools. *Left (from top):* stone rings (2GS:42—2GS:60). *Left centre:* stone cubes (3GS:28—2GS:31). *Right centre:* spherical rubbers (2GS:231—2GS:181). *Right:* hammer-stone (2GS:171), pestles (2GS:28—3GS:40).
Plate XII*b*	Flint blades. *Left (from top):* 2GS:220—2GS:5. *Centre:* 2GS:142 (Fig. 349)—2GS:220—2GS:160 (Fig. 350). *Right:* 2GS:116 (Fig. 348)—2GS:5 (Fig. 346).

PLATE I

a. West Mound seen from Area A.

b. Squares 2G07-47 during clearance.

PLATE II

a. Stretch of enclosure wall after clearance.

b. Group of pots in Room 8.

c. Drain-end in 2G12.

PLATE III

a. Drain in 2G12 from SE.

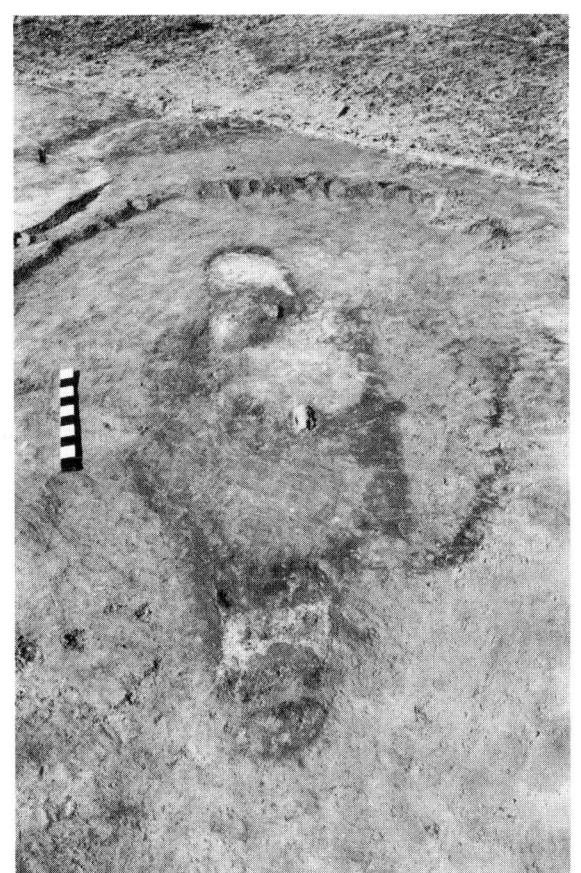

b. Double oven in 2G07.

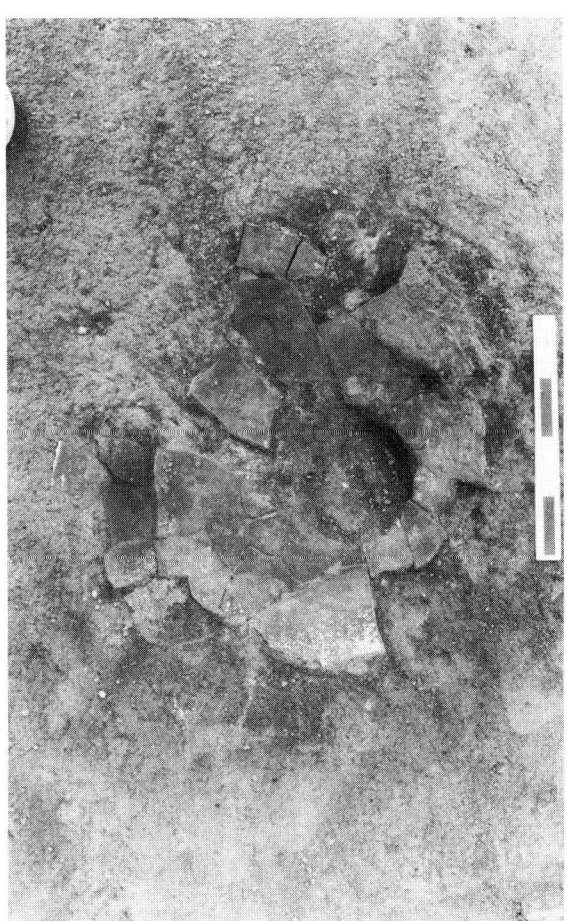

c. Jar-hearth, 2G31.

d. Jar-hearth, 2G33.

PLATE IV

a. Mass-produced pottery types.

b. Decorated sherds from "Uruk" squares.

PLATE V

a. Painted sherds.

b. Miscellaneous sherds from ED squares.

PLATE VI

a. Sherds of coarse vessels from ED squares.

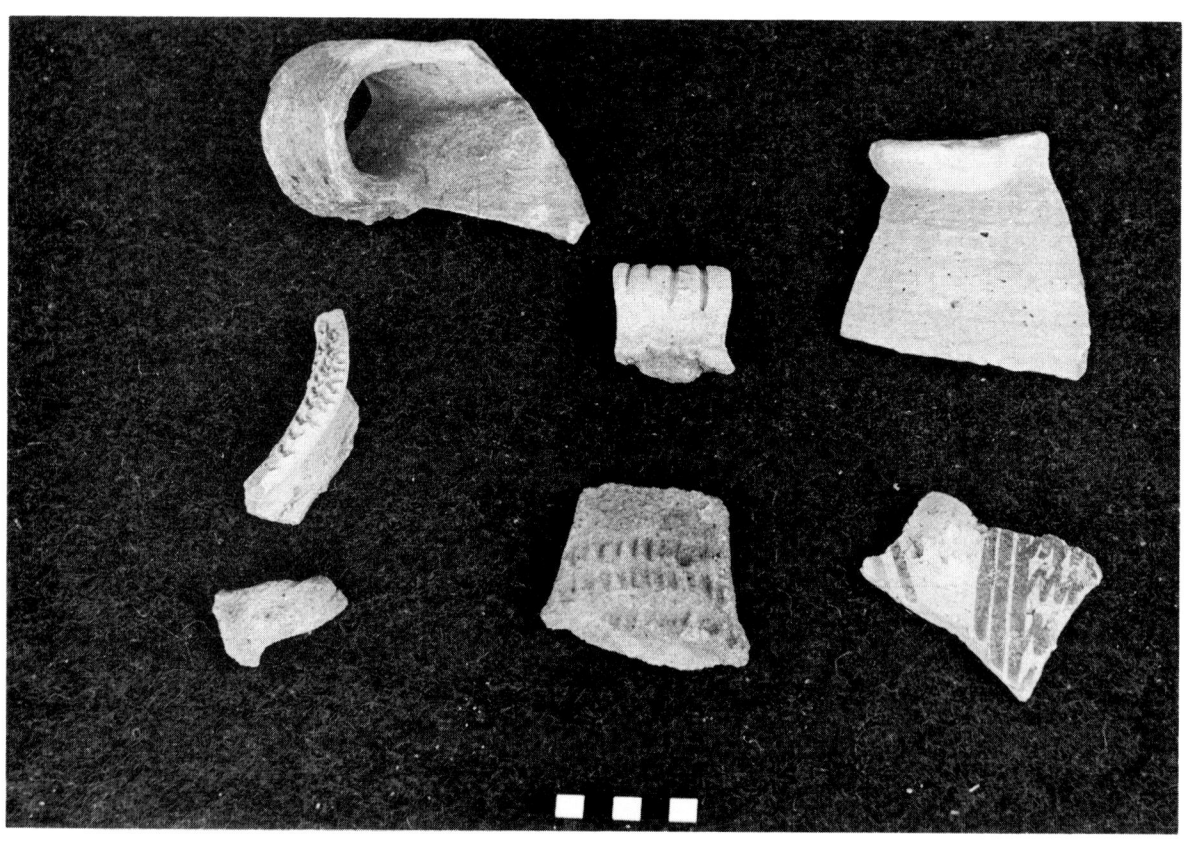

b. Miscellaneous handles.

PLATE VII

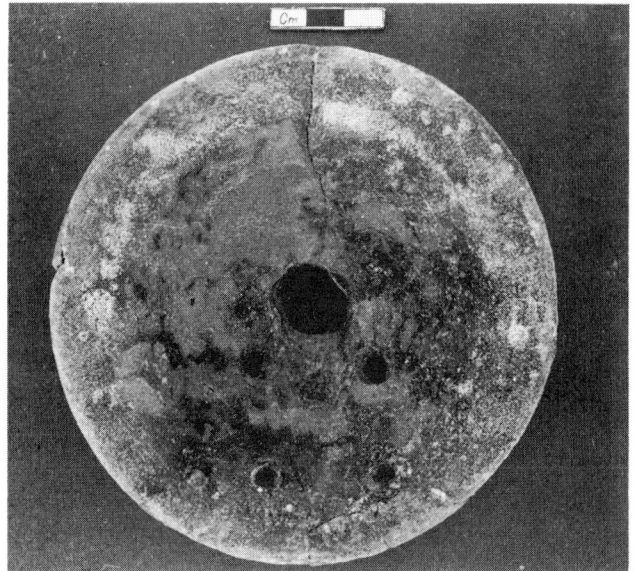

a. Perforated ladle (2GS:70).

b. Lid or net-float (2GS:85).

c. Ring-shaped vessel (2GS:216).

d. Incised jar-sherd (2GS:284).

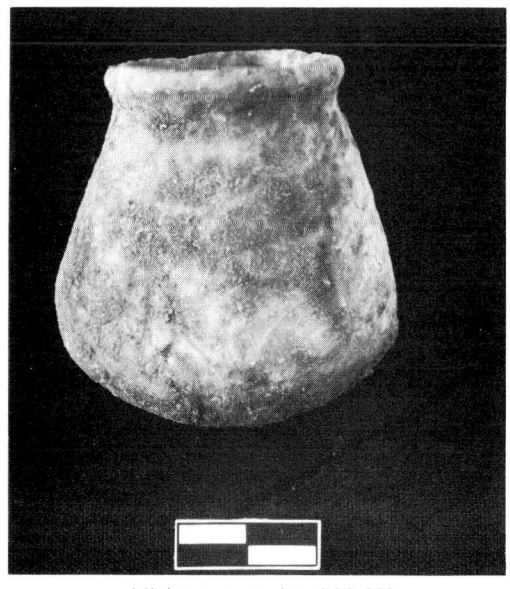

e. Miniature stone jar (2GS:280).

f. Miniature pottery jar (2GS:281).

PLATE VIII

a. Jar with rope decoration (2GS:101; see Pl. IIb).

b. Cut-ware jar (2GS:104; see Pl. IIb).

c. Miniature jar sherd with inscription (2GS:190).

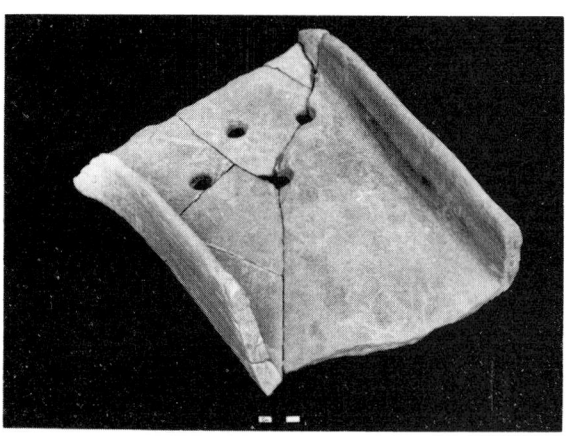

d. Pottery drain outflow (2GS:219; see Pl. IIc).

PLATE IX

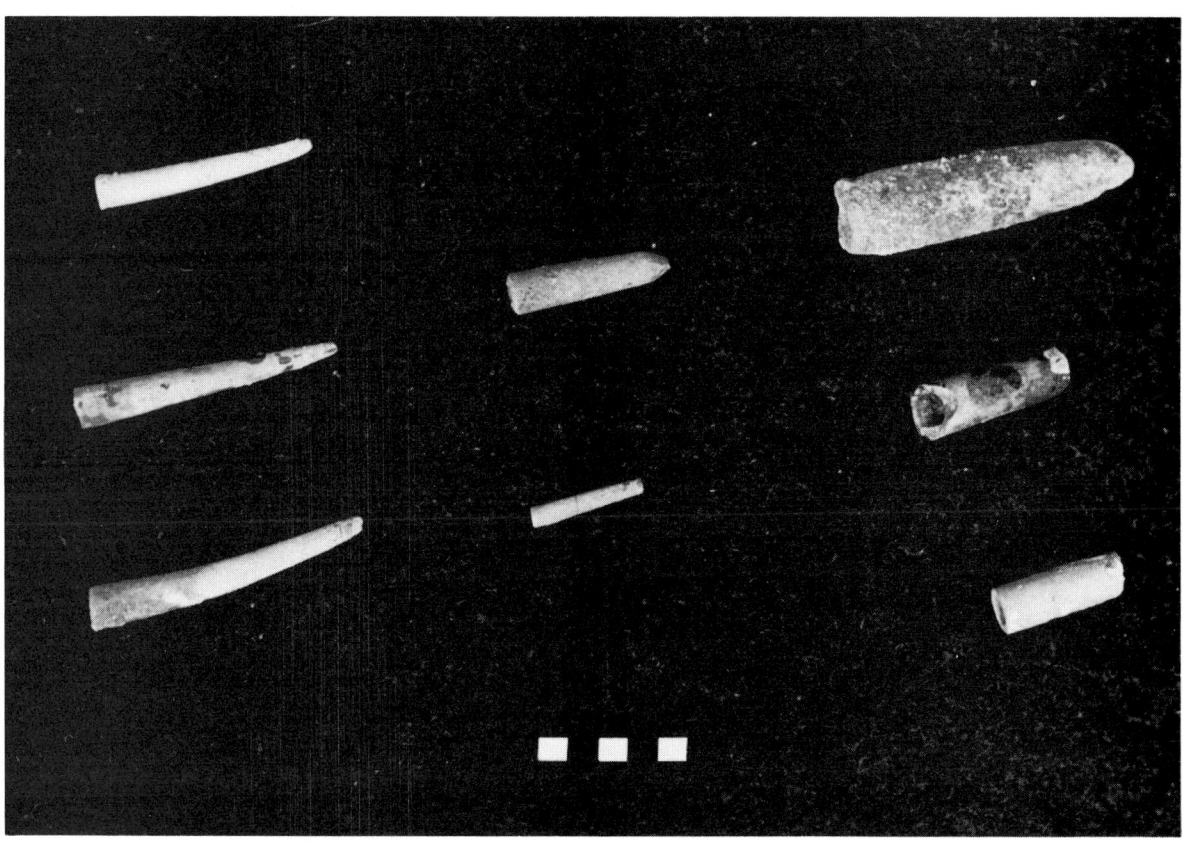

a. Selected clay wall cones.

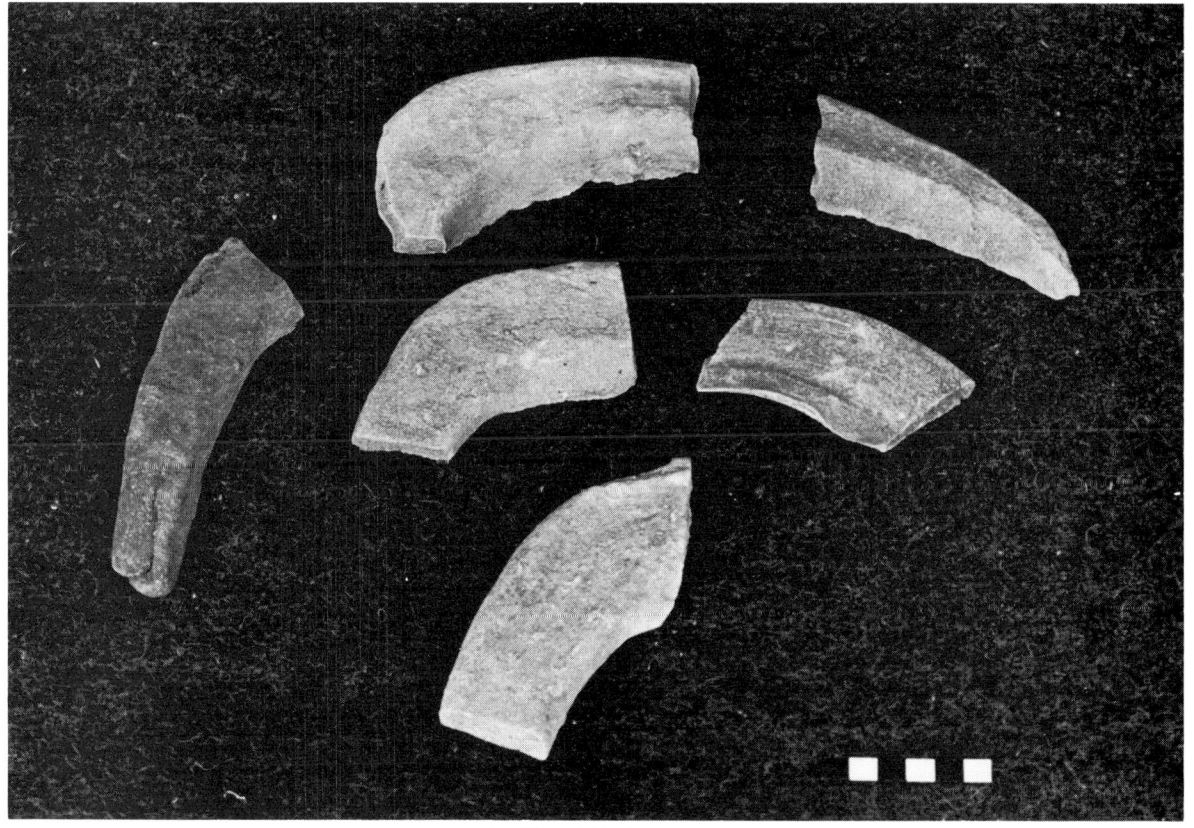

b. Clay sickle fragments.

PLATE X

a. Animal figurine (2GS:15).

b. Clay sealing (2GS:64).

c. Human figurine (2GS:255).

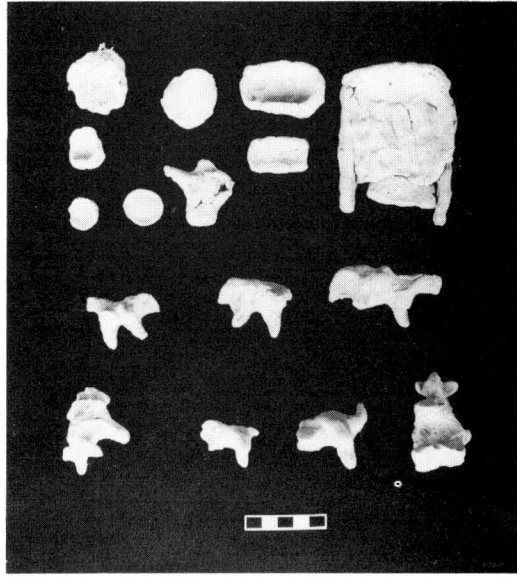

d. Modern figurines from West Mound surface.

e. ED I cylinder seal and rolling (2GS:94).

PLATE XI

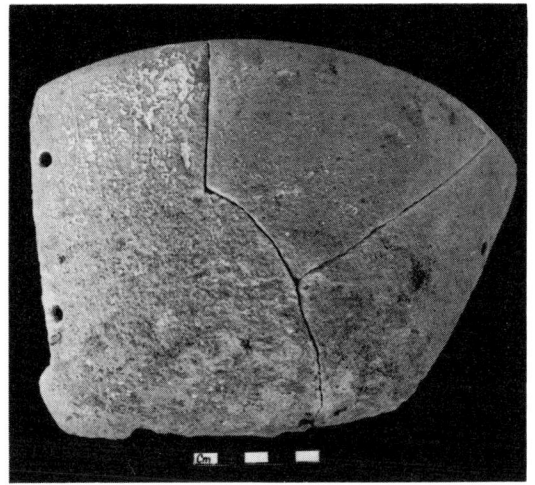

a. Stone bowl with mend-holes (2GS:162).

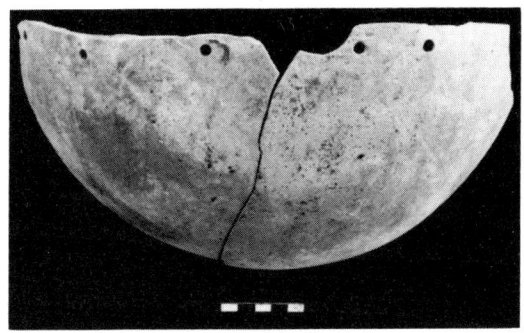

b. Stone bowl with mend-holes (2GS:163).

c. Black stone rhyton (2GS:164).

d. Limestone bowl (3GS:18).

e. Bituminous stone bowl (3GS:19).

PLATE XII

a. Miscellaneous stone tools.

b. Selected flint blades.

PLATE IX

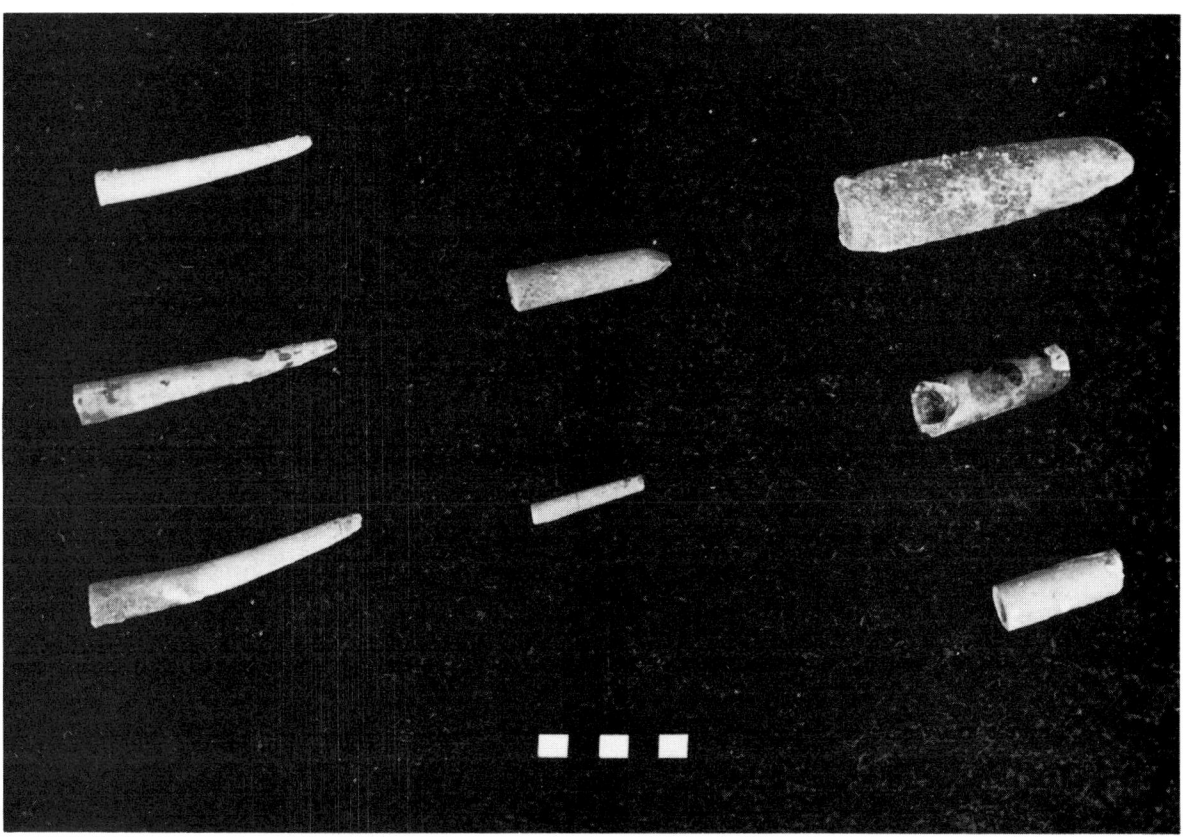

a. Selected clay wall cones.

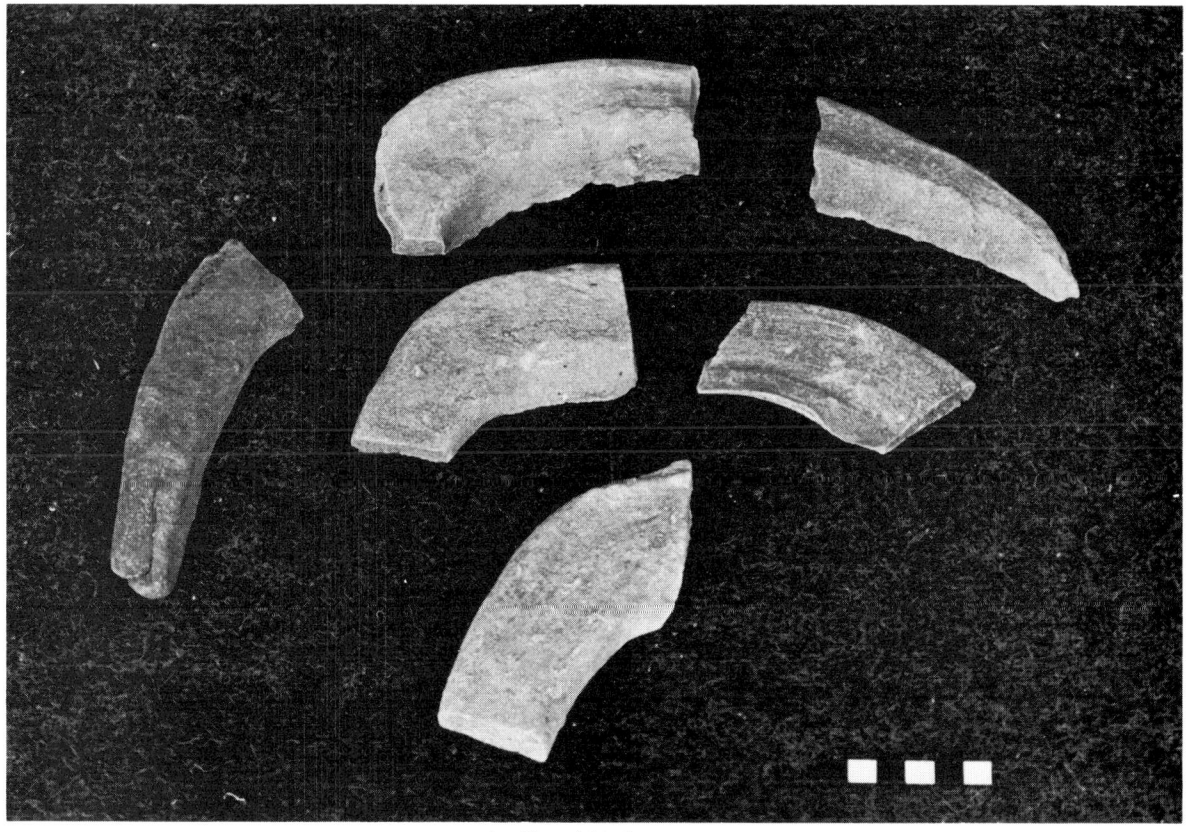

b. Clay sickle fragments.

PLATE X

a. Animal figurine (2GS:15).

b. Clay sealing (2GS:64).

c. Human figurine (2GS:255).

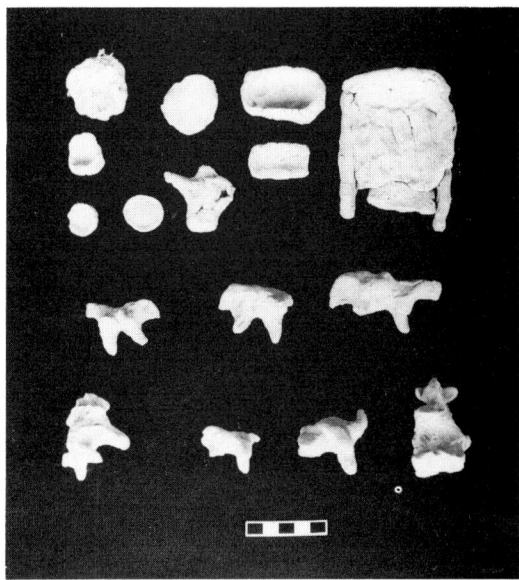

d. Modern figurines from West Mound surface.

e. ED I cylinder seal and rolling (2GS:94).

Fig. 354: Plan of features after clearance of West Mound surface, 1977-78. Scale 1:1000.

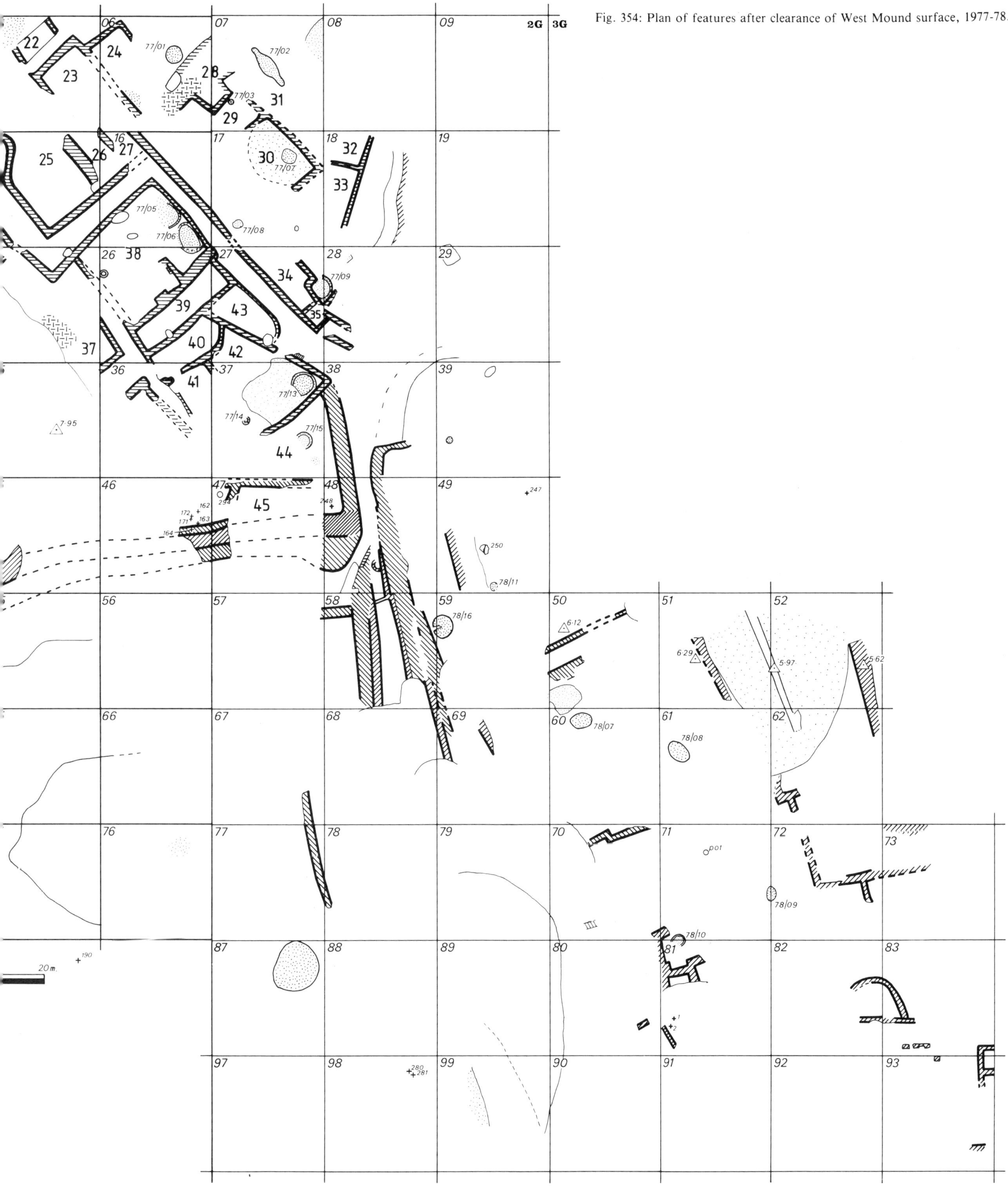

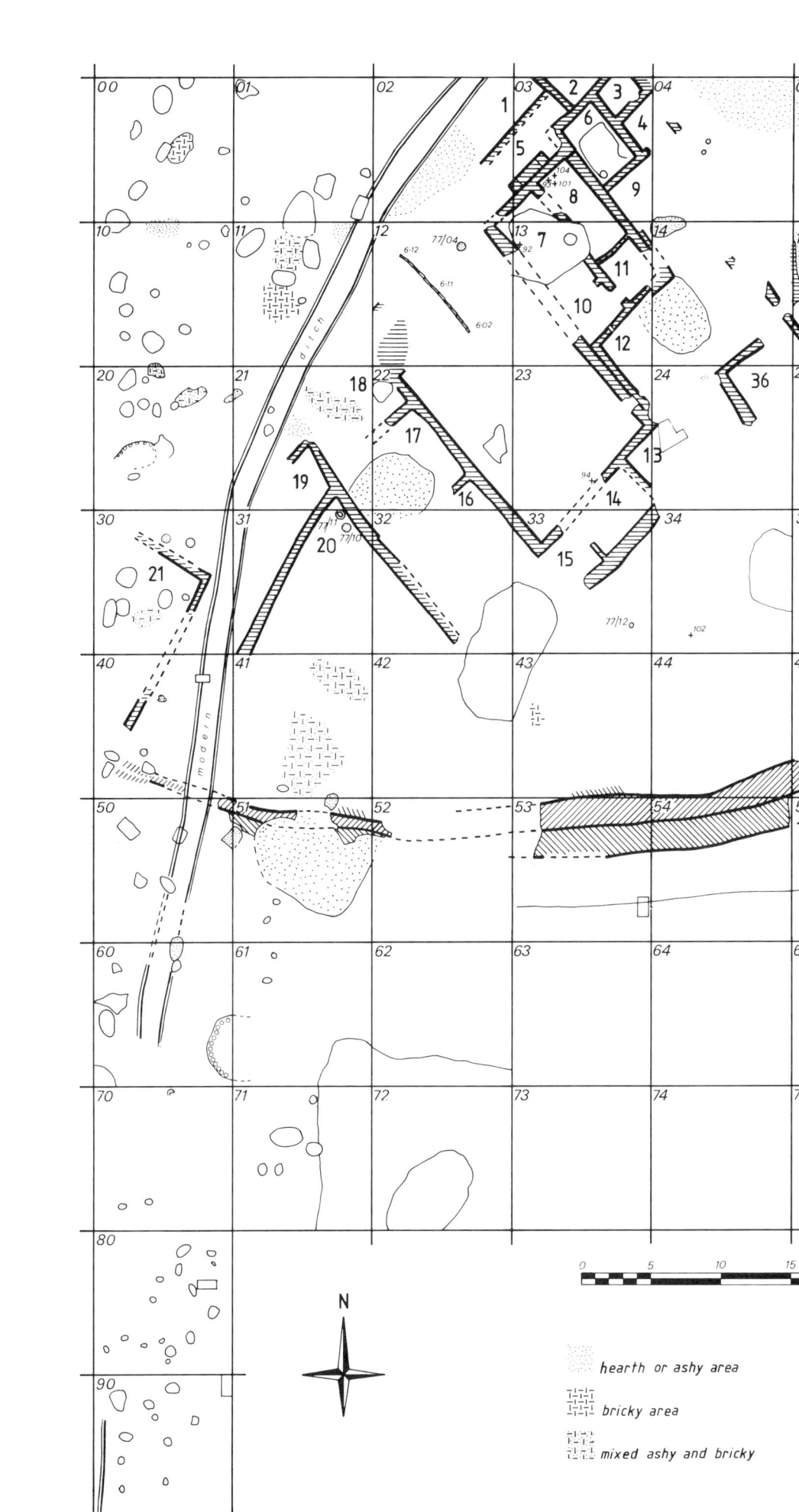